D1233723

ATION

Herbs for Every Garden

Herbs for Every Garden

NEW, REVISED EDITION

By Gertrude B. Foster

Fellow of the Royal Horticultural Society,
Member of the Herb Society of America,
Editor of *The Herb Grower Magazine*

A SUNRISE BOOK
E. P. DUTTON & CO., INC.

Outerbridge & Lazard, a subsidiary of E. P. Dutton & Co., Inc.

"Our Fathers of Old" from *Rewards and Fairies* by Rudyard Kipling.
Reprinted by permission of Mrs. George Bambridge, Doubleday & Company, Inc., A. P. Watt & Son and The Macmillan Co. Ltd.

Line drawings by Elizabeth B. Hull

To my husband, Philip,
my first publisher, best printer, perfect spouse

Acknowledgments

A book sometimes grows like a plant. Through twenty years this one has been more or less dormant while I was editing first a monthly and then a quarterly magazine. The book and the publication were rooted in a garden of over 200 kinds of herbs which was moved three times during that period.

The original idea was encouraged by Miss Elizabeth Hall, Associate Curator of Education at the New York Botanical Garden. F. F. Rockwell, former editor of *The New York Times* Garden Section and of *The Home Garden Magazine,* checked the manuscript in its early stages. Mrs. Frances R. Williams, Honorary Corresponding Secretary of the Herb Society of America, read it and made helpful corrections. Helen M. Fox, President-at-large of the Herb Society of America, has helped from the beginning—as friend, artist, great woman gardener and excellent author.

Many wonderful people promoted the growth of the manuscript: the late Lewis Gannett, a very dear friend and close neighbor; Dr. Arthur H. Graves, of the Brooklyn Botanic Garden and Professor W. C. Muenscher, of Cornell University.

Others who have inspired me by their own work are Dr. Edgar Anderson, Curator of Useful Plants at the Missouri Botanical Garden; Dr. George H. M. Lawrence, Director of the Hunt Botanical Library; also Anne Ophelia Dowden, with whom I discussed herbs while she was doing exquisite water colors of the plants for another book; the late Rosetta Clarkson and her husband, Ralph, who gave me Gerard's *Herball* along with other treasures of rare horticultural books; and Isabella Gaylord, culinary editor and author of *Cooking with an Accent,* The Herb Grower's Cookbook.

Special thanks are due to Elizabeth B. Hull, whose line drawings, executed from plants in the garden, help to illustrate this book.

NOTE FOR THE REVISED EDITION

To an author the opportunity to revise a book is a bit like having a chance to send a child back for eyes of a different color. In re-reading the text, surprisingly, there is not a great deal that I would change, not that it lacks imperfections but rather because the means to iron them all out had better come in another book.

Within the realities of space allowed for rewriting after five editions, I find that not much new has happened in our herb garden or to our methods of cultivating and harvesting it. Since I cannot catalog all of the more than three hundred herbs growing there, I find that a change of emphasis, to point out their value to other plants, particularly vegetables, is required.

Herbs are the original, unperfected species of many plant families—not hybridized, not enlarged and revised. Herein lies the key to their fascination as well as their vigor. They have survived since before the biblical declaration in Genesis 1:29, where the Lord said, "Behold, I have given you every herb bearing seed, which is upon the face of the earth, and every tree, in which is the fruits of a tree yielding seed; to you it shall be for meat."

This has been interpreted by cooks and gardeners of all ages in different ways. Some of them take it to mean that a "dinner of herbs" should take the place of one beefed up with animal products. Such an extreme does not appeal to me, but in times of soaring food prices, herbs have proven invaluable in making alternatives to meat, and the cheaper cuts of meat, palatable.

All of us would live better "where love is" as the rest of the line in the Bible reads. A love of herbs is increased by sharing them with others. The letters from hundreds of readers in this country and abroad indicate that *Herbs for Every Garden* has done that, to my great satisfaction.

Gertrude B. Foster
Falls Village, Connecticut

Contents

Illustrations

Herbs for Every Garden

CHAPTER I

Something for Everyone

Not long ago a family of three visited our herb garden. The husband had taken a course in gourmet cooking: he wished to see chervil and shallots growing so that he could start them in his own garden. The wife had a list of plants which grew in a Hungarian garden belonging to her mother: she wished to know how to grow chamomile, rue and rosemary.

The couple had come to the garden primarily for their thirteen-year-old daughter who was planning a project for her Science Fair. But as her mother and father listened to my description of the uses of the fragrant plants she wandered away. The new collie puppy she had brought for a day's outing in the country had priority for the moment. She paid attention, though, when she heard me say that chamomile tea used after a shampoo highlighted blonde hair.

And once I had her interest, I made sure that the junior miss realized that garlic is of importance to the health of dogs—that if she concealed garlic cloves in her pet's fresh meat she would help to prevent it from having worms.

I tried to make the family's trip home pleasanter by giving the wife a bouquet of rose, peppermint and nutmeg scented geraniums: a bunch of sweet herbs placed on the back window shelf of a car adds enjoyment to a long ride. I should have added a bunch of mint to scatter on the car floor to make it seem cooler after its long wait in the hot sun: strewing herbs has given way to floor waxes in our homes, but the use of herbs might well be renewed for traveling.

THE HUMANITIES OF HORTICULTURE

"Anything green that grew out of the mould
Was an excellent herb to our fathers of old."

Kipling did not live to see the day when even the "mould" held treasures of healing in the form of antibiotics derived from the soil. In his day people were still dependent upon botanical drugs extracted from the herbs mentioned in the poem:

"Eyebright, Orris and Elecampane.
Basil, Rocket, Valerian, Rue,
(Almost singing themselves they run)
Vervain, Dittany, Call-me-to-you—
Cowslip, Melilot, Rose of the Sun."

There is more to the plants in Kipling's lyrical study of "Our Fathers Of Old" than pretty names. They are bits of living history. Some provide drugs so potent that they are dispensed only by physicians in order to avoid disaster.

"Wonderful little, when all is said,
Wonderful little our fathers knew,
Half of their remedies cured you dead—
Most of their teaching was quite untrue—"

Strangely it is the poisonous herbs which remain in our materia medicas. Though literature has accounts of death from tea of foxglove leaves, the dried leaf of foxglove provides digitalis, the valuable heart medicine. Beautiful *Colchicum autumnale*, autumn crocus, as it is commonly known, which throws up lovely chalices of lavender in the fall, has bulbs that are poisonous. Yet, it is from these bulbs that an ancient gout remedy, still in good repute, is derived.

There is much to learn from a garden of herbs.

"Wonderful tales had our fathers of old—
Wonderful tales of the herbs and the stars—

> The sun was Lord of the Marigold,
>   Basil and Rocket belonged to Mars."

A garden of herbs or even a few plants on a kitchen window-sill bring a tale to us in their perfume: a tale of the women who tossed about for weeks in sailing ships on their way to a New World. In their trunks were little packets of seeds and roots, the herbs they would need: fennel to soothe a baby's colic or tansy to keep ants out of the cupboard. Most of our wild flowers along the roadsides are descendants of herbs brought by the early settlers. Touching them in the garden, as you weed rows of sweet marjoram and thyme, you feel, with Kipling, an atavistic thrill of pleasure. You can understand the plea of the men who recognized their dependence upon plants in his words:

> "Then, be good to us, stars above!
>   Then, be good to us, herbs below!
> We are afflicted by what we can prove;
>   We are distracted by what we know—
>   So—ah so!
>   Down from your heaven or up from your mould,
>   Send us the hearts of our fathers of old!"

TIME FOR A DEFINITION

Now for the question of just what is an herb (whether it is pronounced with the "h" as in England, or without it as is commonly done here). By dictionary definition it is "a plant whose stem does not become woody and persistent." Also it may be a plant "when valued for its medicinal purpose, flavor or scent." But the first statement would not only eliminate the spices which come from tropical trees, such as cinnamon, nutmeg and even pepper, but it would also rule out rosemary and bay. Better to call them double-purpose plants for each one has at least two uses: for scent and for flavor, or for healing and for interest.

A GARDEN OF HERBS

A garden of herbs is the composite of all the pleasant rewards of horticulture. From it may be garnered diverse satisfactions. There is the pleasing effect of oddly patterned foliage, some evergreen, in many shades of gray and green. On the hottest summer day, especially in a drought, the gray-leaved artemisias seem to temper the heat. It is impossible to work with herbs without brushing against the plants and thus releasing the volatile oils. Just breathing the sweet aromas is a stimulating experience. And the seasoning magic and in some cases the high vitamin and mineral content of herbs are extra dividends not found in most ornamental plants.

One of the joys of growing herbs is that there is no need to wait for a particular time to harvest. You can have the tender sprigs of annuals in salad as soon as you begin thinning the rows. Herb gardens hold their beauty through the season. There are no between flowering doldrums. The foliage is as colorful and in-

Rock garden with herbs (Philip W. Foster)

Sweet Woodruff, *Asperula odorata* (Philip W. Foster)

teresting as the blossoms and sometimes more so. Long after a killing frost, the emerald green parsley, bronzed summer savory, gray lavender, blue-green rue and silvery wormwoods delight the eye.

It is not absolutely necessary to have a whole garden set aside for the cultivation of herbs. Many of the sturdy herb perennials such as lavender, lemon balm and hyssop can be planted with flowers of the perennial border. Annual sweet basil, especially the purple-leaved form, enhances the bright colors of annual flowers by contrasting tones of foliage. Germander, winter savory and thymes make pungent mats in a rock garden. Dill, sweet fennel, parsley, chives and sweet marjoram mingle well with vegetables and help to deter insects. Sweet woodruff as a ground cover under flowering crabapple trees showers the pointed leaves of its spreading clumps with white stars of bloom in May.

But each kind of herb has different requirements. These are taken up under the listing of genera and species.

A small sunny corner near the kitchen door makes a convenient place for a tiny herb garden. It is easy to reach out and snip a few savory sprigs as they are needed in cooking. If more space can be devoted to the charming and useful plants, a square or rectangle bordered with hyssop, germander or gray santolina and marked with flagstone paths interplanted with creeping thyme makes a restful fragrant spot on a hot summer day. A low stone wall or evergreen hedge placed around the herb garden seems to hold the sweet scents within bounds.

FOOD FOR THE GOURMET

The herbs you grow will allow you to embark on the adventure of gourmet dining if you use them well. Their presence should be detectable only by a savory aroma and provocative tang. They should never greet the palate with an obvious stage whisper. Too many well-seasoned dishes at one meal confuse the taste with competition. A spicy tomato juice cocktail will sharpen the appetite for a rare roast beef made superb by just a sprinkling of fresh thyme. Place the thyme upon the upperside of the meat before cooking but scrape it off before serving. But if the *pièce de résistance* is a shoulder of lamb, made pungent with herbs and tender by marinating first in vinegar, it should be preceded by a simple clear soup.

Strong herbs such as tarragon, lovage, sage and rosemary produce a gastronomic cacophony when they are used together. On the other hand, savory, basil or parsley may be combined with one of the heavier herbs such as lovage. And chervil, chives and sweet marjoram are good mixers. Actually there are as many combinations of flavor possible with herbs as there are individual tastes. But become acquainted with the characteristics of each one before you mix them. Try reading recipes for foreign dishes to get new ideas for your herbs. Coriander, for example, is used for hot breads, pastries and cookies in our cuisine, but Egyptians and other Middle Easterners add the green leaves to salads and meat dishes; you can modify the pronounced pungency of fresh coriander by mincing it for adding to a meat loaf.

Shallots give a definitely Parisian character to any dish where they are appropriate. The use of chervil instead of parsley as a garnish is distinctly French. The Germans frequently add savory, which they call "bohnenkraut," to green beans, as the name meaning "bean herb" suggests. The Greeks use oregano and probably gave it to Italian cooking; spaghetti sauce would be unrecognizable without a combination of oregano and sweet basil. Tomato paste is frequently packed with a leaf of "basilico" in each can.

Use fresh herbs wherever possible, for the rich savor of the essential oils is somewhat lost in drying. You can freeze leaf herbs such as chervil and tarragon to have the truest possible winter substitute for fresh herbs.

Individual bouquets of culinary herbs offered in small paper cups provide the makings of a toss-your-own salad luncheon. Put sweet basil, chervil, garlic chives, sweet marjoram and small blades of French sorrel in each cup for your guests. Then all you need are large bowls of crisp lettuce, a platter of red and yellow cherry tomatoes, a glass dish of sliced cucumbers dusted with salt and cracked pepper, rings of sweet purple onions and a cruet stand of oil, vinegar, salt, pepper and paprika, plus individual salad bowls. Several pairs of small scissors which can be shared by the guests for snipping the herbs into their salads, and an un-inhibited attitude, will go a long way towards making serve-yourself salads fun.

Several terms appear in all good cookbooks to signify the means of adding herbs to foods:

Fines Herbes means herbs chopped or cut fine and added directly to the dish. The blend usually includes chervil and chives with a touch of tarragon, thyme, sweet basil or sweet marjoram. Another way of explaining the mixture is to say that it consists of one member of the onion family, one of the parsley family, and one of the mint family. The minced herbs are added during the last few minutes of cooking or sprinkled on an omelette just before folding. Thus the bits of fresh greenery serve as a garnish and seasoning for the finished product.

Ravigote is a mixture of tarragon, chervil, chives and burnet.

It may be tossed with the greens of a salad or steeped in the dressing.

Bouquet garni, or herb bouquet, means sprigs of fresh herbs tied in a bunch before they are immersed in a soup or stew. They may be left in during the cooking process or removed as soon as the desired flavor is attained. Only the aroma and taste of the herbs linger in the finished dish. A bay leaf, thyme, and parsley or chervil are traditional in the herb bouquet, but other combinations of herbs may be used to enhance hot or cold foods. (To make an *herb bouquet* with dried herbs, tie a tablespoonful of the leaves in a square of cheese cloth to make a bag to be dunked by its string.)

Court Bouillon is a fish stock seasoned with an herb bouquet and a dash of tarragon vinegar. The savory liquid may be used in making the sauce to serve with the fish.

Herb butter is made by creaming butter or margarine with fresh or dried herbs. The butter should stand for several hours before it is used for sandwiches, vegetables, or fish.

Marinade is a sauce of wine or wine vinegar, herbs, salt and pepper, in which to steep meats before cooking. The herb flavor penetrates the flesh, and the wine or vinegar tenderizes it. Tough, strong or gamey meats basted with a marinade before and during roasting become as tender and tasty as the choicest cuts. Barbecue sauce is similar.

HERBS FOR DIETS

Using herbs well is important to health as well as to harmony in the household. A friend who had a garden of culinary herbs for two years and never made much use of it, phoned me one day to say that without herbs she couldn't face cooking for her husband who had discovered he had diabetes. He was limited to a fat-free, wine-free diet, and fresh herbs supplied the piquancy which would be lacking otherwise.

It is very important for people on diets to enjoy their food, and if the cook and/or wife feels that she has several strings to her bow, even after salt, garlic and oil have been stricken from the ingredients list, the chances are that neither the dieter nor the cook will be disconcerted. Mild herbs are permitted on ulcer diets, though pepper and spices are not. Sweet basil, sweet marjoram, chervil and savory can take the place of salt and pepper for seasoning vegetables. The amount of sodium which they will add to the salt-free diet has been carefully measured by Doctors C. A. Elvehjem and C. H. Burns of the University of Wisconsin. With the exception of allspice, whole mace, celery seed, dehydrated celery and parsley flakes, more than fifty readily available herbs and spices tested below 0.1% sodium.

In our herb garden is a tombstone of blue slate on which is inscribed:

"In memory of Mrs. Thankful Hogeboom
Who died Jan. 29, 1785 in the 78th year of her life."

It was turned up at the site of a house excavation not far from our property and given to us because our home was built by some of the first Dutch settlers around that time. I wish she could tell me just how she used the plants which I am growing. Instead, I have to gather bits and pieces of information from the "herbals" of the period, written by English doctors of the 17th and 18th century to describe plants and their "Vertues." From some of these treasures in our library I have compiled a list of herbs which might have served the Colonial lady as medicine, cosmetics and household aids. Some of them can serve the same purpose today, others must have given comfort to those who felt they must be doing something for a cold or other minor ailment while waiting for it to pass. Mrs. Thankful Hogeboom could choose from the following plants to treat the minor ills of the family or use some of them to preserve her own and her daughters' beauty:

For the hair
Rosemary rinse was thought to preserve the color and curl in brown or black hair.
Chamomile tea as a rinse to bring up the highlights of blonde hair.

Fumitory leaves applied to plucked eyebrows to prevent the
   regrowth of hair.
Parsley seed was rubbed on the head for three or four months
   to discourage baldness.
Hyssop leaves steeped in oil to relieve itching of the scalp.

For the complexion
Fruit of strawberries rubbed on the face to remove freckles
   and sunburn.

For the eyes
Clary sage seed was inserted to remove foreign bodies.
Fennel tea was believed to strengthen the sight.
Rue leaves steeped in water for an eye wash.

For the teeth
Fennel stalks were chewed for toothache.
Sage in wine as a mouthwash.

For a sweet breath
Lavender water as a mouthwash.
Parsley leaves chewed to remove odors of garlic and onion. (A
   most useful remedy.)
Coriander seeds, candied to make "comfits," to freshen the
   mouth.

For the feet
Pennyroyal, sage, rosemary and angelica mixed with four
   ounces of juniper berries and boiled to make a foot bath.

To get thin
Fennel eaten daily.
Summer savory used as a seasoning.

To promote sleep
Anise seed steeped in warm milk.
Catnip tea taken at bedtime.
Dill in syrup to soothe fretful infants.
Lady's mantle to calm hysterics in women. (Taken as a tea.)

To cheer the spirits
Tea made of the dried leaves of lemon balm.
Borage flowers floating in a wine cup.
Sweet woodruff infused in Rhine wine.
Lavender flowers sniffed to calm the nerves.
Elecampane roots eaten candied to cause mirth.

For a cold
Rosemary tea to clear the head.
Sage in wine or made into tea for a gargle for sore throat.

FRAGRANCE FOR YOUR HOME

You can make unusual table arrangements with either fresh or dried herb flowers, or even with just the foliage. For example, fill a low bowl full of purple and green basil; add variegated sage to pick up the mahogany tone of the purple basil, and silvery wormwood to repeat the markings of silver on the sage leaves. If you set the bowl before an open window, the summer breeze will stir the leaves and the scent will fill the room. In winter, put in the center of rose, peppermint and nutmeg geranium leaves a spike of bright red pineapple sage blossoms. The leaves will last a week without fading and the pineapple sage may root in the vase. Some striking effects have been created with purple heads of chives or with better smelling alliums such as garlic chives, *Allium tuberosum,* whose blossoms smell of tuberoses.

Many of the herbs which cut well for bouquets also dry satisfactorily. The art of dried arrangements has grown with the interest in modern furniture and architecture. Herbs fit in well because they are functional, serving more than one purpose. They help to keep the water sweet in the vase as well as adding color and fragrance to the arrangement.

It is true that many of the culinary and medicinal herbs have small blossoms in pastel shades, but there are also vivid exceptions. Pleurisy root or butterfly-weed, *Asclepias tuberosa*—used originally as a medicine for coughs by American Indians—is the most exciting. It is easily grown from fresh seed sown in the fall. Though it takes three years to reach blooming size this is the only way to obtain the flowers for bouquets. Butterfly-weed is on the conservationists' lists because it has been rooted out of much of its native habitat. Once you get it started in the garden it will self-sow sufficiently to permit picking for fresh or dried arrangements. First year plants may be transplanted but after that the deep tap root presents great difficulty, and disturbing it usually results in the demise of the plant. The orange blossoms are made to seem more vivid by the addition of blue delphinium to the bouquet.

Small loaves of French bread make unusual holders for arrangements of fresh herbs. Remove the middle of the loaf and line the cavity with aluminum foil. Then insert a piece of porous florists' foam which has been soaked well and drained. Then you are ready for your design: try the blossoms of chives, sprigs of basil—possibly purple basil for added color—sprigs of curly parsley, little knotted buds of sweet marjoram and, here and there, a feathery yellow head of dill to complete the picture. Even people who have never noticed herbs before exclaim over such an arrangement. You can make eggplant, squash, or other fat vegetables the base, as long as you use them right away.

DRIED BOUQUETS

Drying flowers and herbs in three dimensions occupied Mrs. Frances R. Williams of Winchester, Massachusetts, for many years. She used layers of borax as a dehydrating material. This is an ancient method which is time-tested: the flowers are picked as soon as they open and placed on a half-inch layer of borax; then more borax is sifted over them, and carefully filled in under each head until the flower is entirely covered; the box is left open at room temperature for three weeks. The newer silica gel can also be used as a medium: the flowers are treated similarly, but the container is closed so that the material will not take up moisture from the air. And I have found that the less expensive material used for cat litter works just as well, though it tends to deodorize flowers like lavender when first taken out of it. But the scent comes back. For large heads of wild flowers or tall herbs where silica gel or even borax would be very costly, the litter serves the purpose.

Mrs. Williams made miniature bouquets of tiny blossoms and scented herb leaves to decorate gift boxes from her dried ma-

Dried arrangement of herbs

terials. They were as good to look at as to open for their contents.

A larger arrangement of Silver King wormwood, teasel heads, yarrow Coronation Gold, ambrosia, seed pods, woad seed heads and tansy was worked out for the author by Edna King of Suffield, Connecticut. It kept its beauty all winter because all the material was dried before placing in the container.

Herbs are especially appropriate for use in churches: in olden times the sweet-scented leaves were strewn in the aisles of churches to raise a grateful incense to the Lord. Where the Romans crowned the victors at athletic games with chaplets, the Christians later adorned statues of the Virgin Mary with wreaths of herbs and flowers.

Parsley, surprisingly enough, was revered by the Greeks in the belief that Hercules chose it for his garlands. A crown of dried parsley served for the winners of the Isthmian games, and the green herb was used for the champions of the Nemean games. We have perpetuated only the Olympian games but the Greeks had several such contests. At banquets in Greek homes guests were often decorated with crowns of parsley, partly with the idea that the herb insured tranquility and good appetite and partly to please the gods. Laurel or bay, as we call it, was used in the same fashion. Caesar is said to have been very proud to have had the right to wear a crown of *Laurus nobilis*. It covered his bald head, which in those days was considered something of a disfigurement.

Parsley never came into the church as a garland, as far as I have read, but it was supposed to be planted on Good Friday, perhaps to give it time to "go to the Devil nine times and back" before it germinates. When it came up spottily in the garden, the Devil was said to have taken his tithe of the seed. Laurel was used to deck Christian churches, especially at Christmas. In 19th century Greece it was still spread upon the aisles of churches on certain holy days. The Greeks cut the aromatic evergreen branches as we would gather hemlock greens, for true laurel grows into a fair-sized tree along the Mediterranean.

Once a year I cut my twenty-year-old bay plant to take some foliage to our church. The shrub, now five feet tall, was nursed through cold winters in my house and then in a deep cold frame. The first Sunday in Advent I have the privilege of putting herbs on the altar, and our rector always mentions the delight of smelling the pungent bay as he stands near the pewter vases holding the herbs. The warmth of the candles releases the scents of the fresh herbs. When dried material is used, such as wormwood for its sad symbolism or candelabra-like heads of teasel, it is necessary to place the vases below the candles lest the latter burn down and ignite them. If you combine some green herbs, such as rosemary and bay, with the dried materials and put them in containers partially filled with water, you will give fragrance to a dried arrangement.

Advent wreaths have become popular again in churches and homes. They are usually composed of rosemary, sage, thyme and other gray and green herbs quite different from the evergreen boughs used at Christmas. The season is a penitential one in the church calendar, and the bitter herbs, such as rue and thorny teasel, are especially fitting. Candle holders with tapers to be lighted each Sunday before Christmas Eve are interwoven with herbs for Advent ceremonies.

Herb wreaths may be of any size from tiny circles designed to surround a candle to large ones which can be hung on the front door. I still treasure a miniature wreath sent to me by the late Helen Noyes Webster, who helped to revive interest in herbs in New England through her garden and her book. The sweetness of the rosemary remains although the little circlet is now twenty years old.

A closely woven wreath comprised of winter savory, rosemary, golden thyme and a few dried blossoms of oregano makes a useful gift for an imaginative cook. Bits may be plucked out for cooking without disturbing the effect of the wreath.

To make an herb wreath, take small sprays of foliage and twist a fine wire or green thread, such as carpet thread, around each bunch. Then lap the bunches over each other with more thread

Kitchen wreath of herbs (Philip W. Foster)

or wire, so that they will hold on a firm background such as a bent wire coat hanger. You can use styrofoam circles for a wreath that is to be purely ornamental, but you cannot snip off pieces from a kitchen wreath if the stems have been merely stuck into a base: you will spoil the arrangement. Whorls of sweet woodruff leaves add the sweetness of new-mown hay to a garland of herbs. It is one of the herbs which is more fragrant when dried than when green.

CHAPTER II

Of the Earth, Earthy

To say that herbs need poor soil is not strictly true; they can't be planted in the sub-soil left from digging the house foundation or under large trees where nothing else grows. But it is true that a number of them will survive almost anything but soggy ground and withstand drought better than most plants. They will make a good showing under conditions which would prove inimical to most horticultural specimens. Herbs are accustomed to struggling for existence in rocky, dry soil typical of the Mediterranean garigue. This is a "rock heath" area which contains plants which are often covered with woolly gray hairs or glandular leaves rich in aromatic oils. From it have come most of our culinary herbs, especially those of the mint family such as thymes, marjorams and savories.

The one absolute necessity for growing healthy herbs is good drainage. Every garden plant except those which are truly aquatic or marsh plants needs proper drainage. Herbs are no exception. There are instances of edible herbs which grow in low spots with their roots standing in water: sweet flag, *Acorus calamus*, with its nutflavored roots and basal stems, which can be eaten in salad or candied as a sweet-meat, as was done in the Colonial era; water-cress is another but neither would be easy to fit into a garden plan. Really poor drainage can be improved by removing the top soil and putting in a layer of cracked stone when the beds are dug.

Herbs are versatile. If you think yourself a total failure at developing a green thumb, just try rubbing it by handling mints in five natural flavors—pineapple, orange, peppermint, apple and spearmint—guaranteed to grow even in partial shade. Sweet woodruff, angelica, and chervil actually like a northern exposure, such as in the shade of the house. For the most part, however, herbs can be said to need full sun.

The supposition that herbs are more fragrant and thrifty in poor soil may have come from observation of them in their native lands. It is true that the sunshine, warmth, and misty weather along the Mediterranean shores are so beneficial to rosemary that its "fragrance can be smelled at sea" when the land breeze reaches boats. No one has published a soil analysis of Mt. Hymettus where wild thyme gives its inimitable flavor to the famous honey of literature. Possibly some trace elements that are unmeasurable are washed down upon these plants from the mountain slopes during the winter rains. Plants do pick up minerals from the soil and this selection does affect their flavor. Canadian visitors to our garden maintained that any borage they had tried to grow had none of the cucumber taste recorded in books. To them the juice of the leaves had a fishy taste. Yet, when they chewed young leaves of the plants in our garden in northwestern Connecticut, they admitted that there was a cool, cucumber tang.

Herb gardeners discover that certain species do well some years and others another, according to the amount of rainfall and the hours of sunshine or the location of the plant in the garden. Fortunately, under the worst conditions of continued drought the gray-leaved artemisias with their dense hairs which conserve moisture are quite undismayed. Lavenders seem more intense in their perfume. There is little damage to thymes which sometimes rot in wet weather.

Planting annuals and perennials in separate sections of the garden aids in the proper preparation of the soil. In a formal garden, there is little chance for herbs to go to seed as they must be clipped to keep the design clear. Yet, in a less formal planting the volunteer seedlings (those that have self-sown) of annuals

Rosemary, *Rosmarinus officinalis*, in garden (Philip W. Foster)

and biennials may be transplanted out of the paths and returned to the proper location.

Small beds of individual herbs are more easily cared for than a mixed border. They may be rotated in position from year to year without upsetting the garden plan. Where alliums such as shallots, garlic chives or rocambole have been grown for two or more years, some member of the mint family should be set the next season. In the case of onions or any of their family, a replenishing of the soil with bonemeal and dried sheep manure would be essential before planting another herb family there.

Commercial fertilizers are strong and may burn the roots of shallow-based plants. Therefore, we play it safe by using bonemeal, dried sheep manure (which is free of weed seeds) and compost as food for herbs: they will not scorch the plants' roots.

In choosing a site for the herb plantings, the first consideration should be that it has sun for at least half the day. Freedom from tree roots is important, too. The shade of overhead branches is not as detrimental as the absorption of moisture by the tree's roots which spread to the outer extremity of the leafy umbrella. If the location you have chosen has thick sod or tall weeds, your task is easy: the French landlord at our first home used to say that it takes good soil to grow weeds. What we call weeds are frequently the herbs our ancestors brought to this country for medicinal purposes. Some came from seed which clung to the wool of sheep or was mixed with grains of cereals. The old Anglo-Saxon "weod" which may have become our word "weed" was derived from the Dutch and Belgian words for "woad"; an ancient dye plant of the mustard family.

Where little grows upon your chosen location, you may have to do some double-digging to ready the soil for annuals and perennials. If the top soil is six inches or more deep, remove the sod or weed growth and spade the ground when it is dry enough not to cake when you squeeze a fistful in your hand. If you strike hardpan or clay at the first forkful, dig a trench two spades deep and remove the top soil, laying it aside for filling in later. Then remove the lower layer, or subsoil, to the depth of a spade and replace it with turned-over sod, compost, and if the ground is heavy, a mixture of soil and sand. Loosening the hardpan with a sharp spade, crowbar or pick is beneficial for the plants with long roots such as sweet cicely. Place the top soil from the next trench, opened in the same way, on the one you have filled with loose material to make humus. Then you will have a finished bed instead of a huge pile of top soil at the end of your digging. The effort of this process is extremely worth while and will be repaid over the years: hardy perennial herbs such as sage will thrive in a double-dug border or bed for more than five years.

But if you feel that the labor involved is too much for an experimental planting of herbs, just spade and rake the bed smooth and then sow your seeds or set out plants. You will probably

Raised beds of herbs (Philip W. Foster)

want to rearrange the pattern after a year or two, anyway, and lifting and dividing those perennials with heavily intertwined roots, such as tarragon, will preserve fertility in the soil.

If the garden has to be planted in a low spot, raised beds will afford drainage and facilitate making a design which when looked down upon from the house is beautiful in winter and summer. If you plant single kinds of perennials in separate small beds, you can lift out all the plants at one time and remake the bed with fertilizer and compost without upsetting the flowering schedule of other herbs. Late fall is a good time to add nutrients to herb beds especially if you have well-rotted compost to spread over them. It will serve as a safe covering for plants which put

out creeping stems to make next year's growth and the snow and
rain will wash its valuable plant food into the soil. Plants which
you want to increase by layering—allowing to root where the
stems touch the earth and then cutting off in the spring to make
new plants—especially benefit by a fall-covering of compost.

To make raised beds in sandy soil which needs no improvement beyond the addition of compost to increase the humus content, all you need to do is stake out the rectangle, diamond or
circle which will be the outer perimeter. Then mark off the paths,
using string to show you where the beds come in relation to them.
Take the soil from the paths and heap it into the beds to give
them a slight elevation. Some sort of edging will be necessary to
hold the earth in place. You can use redwood siding, cedar logs,
or metal strips four to eight inches deep. If you want grass paths,
the beds will have to be dug after the border material is in place.
We have used logs in one garden, asbestos shingles cut in half
and set side by side, and finally asbestos board sawed into 6 inch
strips with a special blade on the power saw. The last has been
the most satisfactory.

Our paths have been plain earth because limestone chips are
very expensive even though several lime quarries are within half
a mile of our home. Pea stone or blue stone are fine if they are
rolled firm to prevent catching in one's shoes. Sawdust paths are
soft to walk upon and quite permanently weed free, yet permit
seedlings of the herbs in the beds to spring up and be transplanted easily. They, too, need a barrier to keep the material
from getting into the garden bed. A layer of stones put under
the top soil, which must be removed to do it, helps to improve
drainage as well as give the beds more height.

The soil reaction—the acidity—will determine the growth of
the plants. If the soil is too acid, many herbs will not be able to
make use of the nutrients available. It is possible to send soil
samples to your county agricultural agent or state experiment
station for analysis. Ask for the mailing kit which will hold a
number of soil samples taken from different parts of the garden.
Sweet herbs are said to like a "sweet soil." This means one which

has a place on the pH scale somewhere between 7, or neutral, to 7.6—8.2. A low reading below 5.3 or 5.4 will call for the addition of ground limestone before planting. Dr. Louis Pyenson, author of *Keep Your Garden Healthy*, states that it takes three pounds of ground limestone per 100 square feet to bring sandy soil up one pH; a silt loam requires about 6 pounds per 100 square feet; and a clay loam about 8 pounds per 100 square feet.

Bonemeal as a fertilizer reduces soil acidity as do hardwood ashes while cottonseed meal and complete soluble fertilizers may tend to increase acidity. Pine trees and oak woods are usually considered acid-tolerating and acid-producing. If your herb garden must be located near such trees add ground limestone to the soil and top dress the plants with it. That means digging it in close to their roots during the growing season. Some herb gardeners crumble egg shells around the roots of the plants for natural soil sweetening but in the country this might attract skunks to the garden.

TO MULCH OR NOT TO MULCH

The advisability of mulching herb beds depends upon the material available to you. Some peat mosses increase acidity; all absorb moisture from the soil. Grass clippings, plain straw, or hay are not pretty and bring weeds. Buckwheat hulls will rot in a wet season and cause some of the semi-evergreen herbs to rot also. Cocoa hulls mildew if they are not free of all cocoa butter and oils. Leaves and clean straw put through a chopper do make attractive mulching materials. Sawdust is satisfactory if it is put over compost so that it will not draw nitrogen from the soil in the process of breaking down into humus.

The only mulching I do is for winter cover to keep plants *cold*. I find salt hay makes the perfect light, airy and easy-to-apply winter cover. But, it is not a weed suppressing mulch for the same reason: the wiry hay permits plants to grow up through it and it does not rot down to smother weeds. As a matter of fact, it decays so little that it is possible to stack it and use it again the following fall. Pine needles and clippings from the Christmas tree are also serviceable for winter mulching. They are laid over the plants after the ground has frozen. This keeps it from thawing too soon in the spring with the resultant heaving of shallow-rooted plants out of the earth. Pine needles can be picked up in the woods anytime the ground is free of snow. They make an easy-to-handle, light and clean mulch. If you remove them in the spring, there is no acidifying of the soil either. They can be placed around azaleas or mountain laurel bushes which need less alkaline soil than do herbs.

To get a good cover with pine needles you need to cut back the taller perennials which will die down to the ground anyway. Persistent foliage such as that of gray and green santolina should be covered to keep snow off the tops as well as to prevent them from windburn. Salt hay is better for this purpose as less is needed to cover plants more than six inches in height. But if pine needles are all you have, combine them with branches of spruce or balsam to make a mound over the plants. Even the sun, in winter, can be damaging to evergreen plants such as box, creeping thyme and chamomile.

The difference between winter and summer mulch should be understood. Peat moss, buckwheat hulls and other weed-smothering materials are not suitable for winter mulch. They are put on the garden to cover the ground between plants, keep down weeds and help to conserve the moisture in the soil. Salt hay, clean straw and pine needles are used to cover plants which might otherwise suffer from winter winds and sun. They need to lie lightly on gray santolina and shrubby English lavender. The rain and melting snow must be able to penetrate the mulch yet the material should help to keep the ground frozen. Winter mulch is put on after the ground freezes to prevent mice and rabbits from using the blanket as housing for the cold season. Do not remove it until the maple trees begin to bloom. Earlier uncovering will cause the evergreen creeping thymes and chamomile to lose their leaves which are somewhat tender from the protection.

If your plants must be irrigated by overhead sprinkling, you should use a mulch. Thomas Kendall, owner of Snow-Line Farm in Yucaipa, California, spreads chopped straw around the plants which have been dressed first with several inches of compost. Mr. Kendall puts sawdust in the paths between the raised beds of herbs. If you wish to use sawdust as a mulch it is advisable to place a layer of two or three inches of organic compost under it so that it will not rob the plants of nutriments in the process of its own decomposition. Mr. Kendall combines this with granite dust and ground limestone to feed the plants at the same time he mulches them. In addition he sprinkles them every two weeks with liquid seaweed fertilizer during the growing season. An engineer who has studied the needs of food plants over a period of forty years, he has worked out a combination which produces magnificent, healthy herbs of good flavor. Constant sprinkling of sandy soil causes the plant food to leach out. But if the water filters down through a layer of compost, it brings nourishment with it; the surface quality of proper aeration is preserved by the loose material spread upon the soil.

I never thought that a pile of the friable, black humus we call compost could be a thing of beauty until I visited Snow-Line Farm. Mr. Kendall makes 20 tons of compost a year to use on three acres of herb crops. With a tractor and scoop he manages the process without turning the pile at all. All the weeds taken from the herb rows and around the landscape plantings of the property are heaped up throughout the spring and early summer. Then barnyard manure is brought in and the layer "cake" is constructed: first he puts down six inches of weeds and other materials gathered in the cleaning up; then two inches of manure; followed by another six inches of weeds, dirt and clippings of surplus herbs.

The whole pile is brought to a height of at least three feet. This produces the heating necessary to break down the fibers of the plant material, kill seeds of weeds and reduce the whole to compost. Mr. Kendall's method of soil improvement is based upon the teachings of Sir Albert Howard, but his results are the work of an artist. The compost pile is held in place perfectly by bales of straw. (Spoiled hay could be used just as well, as long as it was baled first.) As the heap settles during its daily watering, it can be used to decompose kitchen vegetable wastes which are buried within the fermenting mass. When it is time to use the compost, a few bales are removed from one end, so that the humus can be forked easily into a barrow.

If you use the same method in a small scale garden, you will have a handsome, odor-free rectangle of black, nutritious earth within the tawny bounds of hay or straw bales. Quite a different sight from the untidy heap of green with weeds that most of us sport for a compost pile. I feel that the value of adding herbs to the compost is becoming increasingly evident. Nettles, which are said to be activators of fermentation, contain iron. Other herbs thought to be especially endowed with minerals which can be incorporated into the compost are the dandelion which absorbs between two and three times as much iron from the soil as other weeds; salad burnet with its rich magnesium content; sheep's sorrel which takes up phosphorus; chicory, goosegrass and bulbous buttercup which accumulate potassium. Horsetail shares with ribwort and bush vetch a capacity for storing cobalt. Thistles contain copper as trace elements. So instead of destroying weeds, why not practice a little barnyard magic and return them to the soil in the form of compost?

Compost makes the best fertilizer for herbs. It can be dug in around them during the summer and heaped over the low-growing spreading varieties in the fall to keep the rooted stems from heaving. If you are lucky enough to have a source of the material before you start herb gardening, be sure to work a generous amount into the top six inches of the soil, especially if it is sandy. Compost, ground limestone and bonemeal are our main source of fertilizers for over 200 species of herbs. When ants became a problem during a very dry series of summers, ground rock phosphate was sprinkled around the plants under which they had taken up residence. This quickly dispatched them and added a safe, non-burning fertilizer at the same time.

CHAPTER III

Start Some from Seed — Annuals and Biennials

Because of the increased interest in herb gardening, more plant nurseries are offering culinary herbs in the spring. But since this is still a rather specialized field of horticulture, the prices are generally higher than for flowers and vegetables. Then, too, many dealers do not stock annuals, because they are difficult to transplant and ship unless taken very young. So if you want to acquire a good collection of herbs with a minimum of expense, start some from seed. If they thrive and become thrifty specimens, how much greater is the satisfaction in watching their development than if half or full-grown plants are purchased and set out for immediate effect. How much less, too, is the monetary loss if they do not prosper.

Note, though, that there are a few important herbs of which the seed is unobtainable. French tarragon and horse-radish do not set seed capable of germinating. Also, mints seldom come true to variety from seed. And lavender and rosemary grow so slowly that it is hardly worthwhile starting them from seed if you want an effect the first year. Nevertheless, the majority of easy-to-grow, culinary and fragrant herbs can be started from seed. And some—such as annuals and biennials which are described in the following pages—can be propagated *only* in this fashion.

PLANTING SEEDS

Whenever called upon to give directions for sowing seed of a particular herb, I think of the experience a friend had with fox-glove. For years she had tried to start it from seed. She had planted carefully; covered the row with wet burlap to keep it moist until germination started. But despite her ministrations she had little success. One spring day as she was walking through her garden, she discovered a half-empty packet of seed in her pocket. She threw it away under some shrubs and the seed scattered as it fell. About two weeks later she was astonished to find a thick carpet of foxglove seedlings under the bushes. In the same way that nature so lavishly distributes seeds over the earth, my friend had hit accidently upon the best method for sowing foxglove. From that time on she was never without generous patches of the biennial thimble-shaped flowers which seeded themselves happily for many years.

Although all seeds cannot be broadcast or merely dropped on the prepared ground, more seed is wasted by being buried too deeply than by washing out in heavy rains. If you are sure that the surface of your garden is rich in humus and will not dry out before germination occurs, you can leave seeds uncovered. But it is safer to make a slight depression or furrow in which to sprinkle them. This will keep them in neat, easily marked rows and prevent the evaporation of moisture when you cover them with a layer of soil.

There is such a diversity in the size of the various kinds of herb seeds that the best rule for how deep to plant them is the old rule of thumb: cover them to a depth of at least twice but not more than four times the width of the seed. For example, coriander averages $\frac{1}{8}$ inch in diameter, while sweet marjoram is only $\frac{1}{40}$ of an inch wide. The closest to an average size is sweet basil, which is $\frac{1}{20}$ inch in diameter, and so we can use that as an example. The maximum of four times its diameter of $\frac{1}{20}$ of an inch would be $\frac{1}{5}$ of an inch. You don't have to use a ruler to measure the depth of each furrow as it is made but do use some measure for the first sowing. You will be astonished to see how close to the surface the seed should be planted, particularly in the spring. Mid-summer plantings may be deeper to reach the lower level of moisture in the soil.

A SEED BED OR SEMINARY

Though biennials can be planted in the spring, they are often started in late summer to give the roots enough time to grow before plants run to flower and seed the following year. Plant them in a seed bed which can be shaded against the hot sun either by shrubs and trees or by one of the new plastic mesh materials used in nurseries. In summer a seed bed is easier to manage than a flat. Soak the seed bed—or "seminary" as it was called by the 17th century garden writer, John Evelyn—before sowing biennial seeds, letting it dry enough to cultivate before planting. Then follow the advice of the learned Mr. Evelyn, for it is as sound today as it was when he first wrote it. Of seedlings he says:

> "Whatsoever you now Sow or Plant of this sort, water not over hastily, nor with too great a Stream, for it hardens the Ground, without penetrating; rather endeavour to imitate the natural shower; but spare not Watering if necessary."

In time of drought put wet burlap over the soil or shredded sphagnum moss which covers the seeds. Lay the burlap in strips over individual rows. After the first week the seeds of different herbs will sprout successively. You will need to raise the burlap covers often to make sure that seedlings are not being flattened as they begin to sprout. You may thin or transplant when they have four true leaves or leave biennials until the fall rains make it easy to set them in their future garden sites.

FALL-SOWING

Sowing seeds of hardy annuals and biennials in the late fall saves precious time in the spring and usually produces a sturdier

stand of plants. The trick in planting at the end of the season is
to wait until after the last warm spell, known as Indian Summer,
is over. Then seeds may be safely planted in a seed bed or coldframe. The action of frost and snow will soften the seed coats
which protect the tiny live plants inside each grain, but not
enough for them to push forth until the ground warms in the
spring. Insulate the seminary from an early thaw by covering it
with chopped straw, salt hay or pine boughs after the ground
freezes. Winter covering is to keep the ground frozen and prevent
thawing which opens cracks and exposes the seeds to the air.
But do not put it on while the earth is still warm or mice or chip-
munks may tunnel through the seed bed. Be prepared to uncover
the seminary early in the spring.

HERBS TO GROW FROM SEED

Ambrosia (*Chenopodium botrys*) is also called Jerusalem oak,
feather geranium and oak-leaf geranium, although it is not in
either family.

Height. 18 inches

Leaf and blossoms. The young leaves of ambrosia look like
miniature oak leaves but are soon hidden in two-foot feathery
sprays of yellowish-green, minute, wind-fertilized blossoms without petals. The deeply-veined leaves, which are reddish before
they turn light green, and the grooved stems and green blossoms
are covered with a sticky substance—the plant is intensely fragrant—derived from glandular hairs which release the essential
oils when touched or crushed. The blossoms begin to appear early
in July when the plants are a few inches tall, but do not cut them
until the arching plumes of open-forking cymes of sessile flowers
develop.

Culture. Ambrosia grows easily from seed sown in a well-
drained, sunny place. The fine granules may be sprinkled on top
of well-prepared soil in the spring. Though it self-sows year after
year, it is not a weedy pest. If plants are cut for fresh or dried
bouquets, there will be little chance of scattered seed. But the

surplus seedlings are easy to extirpate, especially in the spring when the ruddy young leaves appear.

Habitat. An annual native to Europe, Asia and North Africa, ambrosia has become naturalized in some parts of North America. Another annual of the same family (*Chenopodiaceae*), which is also called ambrosia but lacks its sweet scent, is *C. ambrosioides,* American wormseed, used in Mexico and in the Southwest as a worm medicine or vermifuge. A strong tea made from the whole plant is used also to swab floors and porches to deter insects and worm larvae in tropical America. *C. capitatum,* called strawberry blite, has a reputation in Europe as being a source of food coloring because of the red, berry-like seed bunches on the stems. Though botanists give its habitat as Europe, the plant occurs in the wild in light soil and newly cleared land from Quebec to Alaska. In the fiftieth state it is eaten boiled as a source of greens in the spring.

Uses. A flower-arranger's friend, ambrosia develops graceful curves as the weight of the blossoms bends some stems to the ground. In a vase, the fresh herb keeps the water sweet even when combined with zinnias. The golden plumes of maturing plants are a nice foil for bright fall flowers and will dry to a tawny shade without any special attention, if hung up in a bunch for use in dried arrangements.

Comment. As Dioscorides, the first century Greek herbalist, remarked, of ambrosia: "all of it of a wonderful sweet scent, wherefore it is also laid amongst cloths." It is the sort of rare, old-fashioned annual which is not listed in most seed catalogs. When you have at last secured a start from seed or young plants which can be transplanted easily, you may find that a neighbor has been weeding it out of her garden for years.

Angelica (*Angelica archangelica*)

Height. 6 to 10 feet in flower

Leaf, blossom and stem. The compound leaves are cut into three sections except where the end one is joined. There may be five to nine leaflets on the stalk. The slightly toothed edges of the leaves have a golden cast. When the two-inch round, succulent hollow main stem develops, the clasping leaf stalks branch out at two or three foot intervals, directly opposite each other.

As angelica is a biennial which sometimes takes three years to come into bloom, the basal clumps are only two to three feet tall. The stems are smooth, hollow, round and slightly ribbed. The color of *A. archangelica* is bright green whereas the wild angelica, *A. atropurpurea,* has reddish stems. Both leaves and flower buds appear to be wrapped in layers of yellowish-green, striped tissue, tucked in at the blunt tips like a pair of rolled up socks. After the umbels (blossoms which radiate out from a central axis) unfold to spread out tiny white blossoms, they are followed by ribbed green seeds which turn brown as they ripen. A plant which has been allowed to go to seed may be transformed by a hoar frost on a fall morning into a glistening model for the royal scepter. It truly suggests some angelic form.

Culture. Angelica should be started from fresh seed. The fruits lose their vitality very quickly in storage but they may be kept in a freezer to preserve some of it. They should be sown as soon as ripe or allowed to fall about the old plants. After the seedlings develop two strap-like first leaves (cotyledons), they produce a pair of broad, true leaves. Later more finely divided leaves emerge as the thick stems develop. If angelica seedlings are potted in this stage it is possible to grow them as tub plants but strict attention must be paid to their requirement for ample water. Angelica seed sown in mid-summer will continue to make root growth through most of the winter. The herb requires loamy soil, rich in humus, and a location that receives shade during the heat of the day. Mature plants should stand three feet apart. Transplanting is difficult except when angelica is in the seedling stage.

Habitat. *A. archangelica* is native to Lapland and northern Europe. The New England species *A. atropurpurea* occurs in wet meadows as far south as northern Connecticut. Another native species, *A. lucida,* called seacoast angelica or wild celery, has a wide range from Alaska to the Arctic coast and yet it has been found in the southern states. William Bartram describes it as "nondo," in his "Travels of William Bartram," 1791, a journal of a trip through the wilderness of North and South Carolina, Georgia and Florida.

Uses. Candied angelica stems are valued by confectioners for decorating cakes. Its succulent stalks can be cooked with rhubarb to reduce the need for sugar and complement the flavor. Angelica has been considered a cure for indigestion through the ages and described as "cordial" and "stomachic" by the old herbalists. It is one of the chief flavorings of gin and Chartreuse but a 19th century doctor remarked that if the candied stems are taken in quantity they will cause a disgust for alcoholic liquors: it was even said that angelica helped to dispel lust in young persons. Campers might wish to try the notion that the aroma of angelica, which smells very like that of gin, will drive away serpents and other venomous beasts, if the herb is burned upon "quick coles." Scandinavians wrap fish in the leaves to preserve it from flies and help to keep it cool on a camping trip. The Aleutians eat the stems of *A. lucida* instead of celery. The wild angelica of New England was used as a substitute for garden angelica by the Shakers who really started the patent medicine and seed catalog businesses in the 18th century in this area. The roots were used medicinally, the stems and extracted oil for flavoring.

Candied Angelica

Cut young stalks of angelica in four inch lengths. Wash, peel off the thin outer skin and soak overnight in cold water to which 1 tablespoon salt and 1 tablespoon white vinegar have been added. Drain, cover with water and parboil until the stems become quite green. Make a sugar syrup of 1 cup water to 2 cups granulated sugar. When boiling add a few drops of green coloring. Put in drained angelica stems. Cook stems slowly in boiling syrup until they become translucent. Place in a sterilized glass jar and cover with syrup to exclude air; then seal.

Comment. It is a good idea to start out with at least three plants of angelica even if you have to buy them as potted plants. You will want one to mature so that you can save the ripe seeds after it blossoms the second or third year. Another should be cut

for candying shortly before the flower buds open. Some writers
declare that this will keep the root perennial if done early
enough in the summer of its blossoming but I have not had success with it. You might try it on the third plant because angelica
is worth a good deal of trouble to keep going in the garden. Also
there is safety in numbers, I have found, when a woodchuck
decides that he needs the aromatic herb to flavor his vegetarian
diet. If you have several to work with you have a better chance
of perpetuating the species by planting the seed or letting it self-
sow. Watch for aphids on the ripening seeds; they can do much
damage to the crop. If the plant is not to be used for food again,
an all-purpose garden spray will protect the seed heads from insects. I prefer a pyrethrum-derived insecticide not only because it
is "herbal" but for its safety to warm-blooded animals. Also it does
not leave a residue that may prove toxic to birds.

Anise (*Pimpinella anisum*)

Height. 18 inches

Leaf, blossoms and fruit. Anise has two very different leaf
patterns: at the base are bright green, round, toothed leaves
about three-fourths of an inch long; on the flowering stems are
finely cut leaflets. It is an annual with lacy blossoms of pure white
in delicate umbels. The seeds are grooved, gray, roundly ovate
with one side flattened. They, like most of the carrot family,
hang from thin stems in pairs.

Culture. A native of the Mediterranean lands from Greece to
Egypt, anise is difficult to grow in New England. Some gardeners
say to sow it while the ground is cool, early in the spring; others
claim it likes warm weather. Both are correct in one respect.
Anise does germinate better in cool ground but it needs warm
sun to bring the plants to maturity with a good head of seed.
Sow in shallow drills where the plants are to remain. Young
plants can stand quite close, as the stems are weak and require
hilling up (mounding the soil slightly around the bases) when
they are young. If the plants become top-heavy with flowers and
seeds, they may need to be held up by a loop of string on either
side attached to stakes at the ends of the row.

Habitat. Greece to Egypt is given by Hortus II as the range for the single species.

Uses. Oil of anise is more and more substituted for licorice extract in the manufacture of candy. Licorice is a much larger plant, with more harvestable root than anise could possibly produce seed, and so it seems strange that one should be substituted for the other. But there are many strange stories which could be told of the spice and drug trade. In the parlance of the trade, oil of "anise" may refer to the distilled essence of star-anise (*Illicium anisatum*), a small tree of the Far East. The chemical composition of the oil from the annual herb and that from the tropical tree are very similar and the flavor is almost identical. As it takes 50 pounds of anise seed to produce one pound of anise oil, it is no wonder that the manufacturers of liqueurs, such as anisette, would seek a more productive source.

Anise seeds steeped in hot milk make a soothing bedtime drink that has been said to promote sleep. Many people recognize anise by association with Christmas cookies flavored with the seeds.

Anise Cookies

¾ cup sugar	2 eggs
1½ c. flour	½ teaspoon anise seed

Beat eggs until thick and lemon-colored. Add sugar, continue beating, add sifted flour and anise seed which has been ground with a pestle in a mortar. Drop from a spoon or put through a cookie press on a greased cookie sheet. Let stand overnight. Bake in a slow oven, 20 to 30 minutes, until firm but not brown. Store in a tin box for several days before using.

Comment. If your space is limited, leave anise off your list of herbs for the culinary garden as it takes four months to ripen. Seldom is it possible to get mature plants in New England before a freeze.

To dry anise and other seed herbs, allow the seeds to ripen on the plants. Test before cutting to see if they will leave the umbels with a gentle tug. Then cut the stems and wash the seeds in a strainer with hot water to remove insects. Spread them on a dry towel or large brown paper bag split open and spread flat, after they have been drained of moisture. Set the spread out seeds on an elevated rack, in the sun, to dry. Keep them off the ground because the sweet flavor of anise is attractive to ants. (Oil of anise is used to track honey bees to their hives in the old country practice of "bee-lining.") Take the seeds in at night and return to the sun by day. In four or five days they will be ready for bottling. Warning: if seeds are picked too green and stored without being thoroughly dry, they will mold. Try to crush a few with a pestle before storing to make sure that they are crisp.

Basil, Sweet (*Ocimum basilicum*)

Height. 2 feet

Leaf and blossom. Annual basil is one of the handsomest herbs in all its diverse varieties from the large lettuce-leaf type, with wrinkled and shining leaves, sometimes three inches wide, to the diminutive purple bush basil with leaves not more than one-half inch in size. The typical sweet basil is a neat little bush with ovate, smooth, bright-green leaves, about one and one-half inches long. The margins are slightly toothed. Small white flowers are almost hidden by the conspicuous green calices shaped like medieval headdresses. But the arrangement of green and white whorls of blossoms and sepals in dense layers on the stiffly erect, branching stems makes the flowering herb resemble a many-sided candelabrum. The surface of the leaves and stems are dotted with tiny oil glands which release a clove-like pungency if the plants are moved by hand or by a breeze. The first blossoms open in July, but the basils do not reach their full beauty until late summer.

Culture. Basil is easily grown from seed planted directly in the garden. The herb may be started indoors in flats at the same time as peppers and tomatoes and set out when the ground is warm. It will not germinate in cold ground. Basil resembles sweet pepper in appearance and growing requirements. It succumbs to the first frost but may be potted before that to bring into the house. For this purpose a second sowing in late June is usually made to give small plants for winter window boxes. Slips will root in water. Sometimes basil cut for bouquets will last so long that the sprigs have grown roots in the vase. It is an herb which needs ample water during its growth but the seeds should not be planted in wet ground unless some dry sand is sprinkled over them. This is because they contain a gelatin that upon contact with water surrounds the hard black seeds and floats them out of the furrow. If they remain uncovered they dry out and cannot sprout. This is one reason for the old idea that basil should be sown with cursing and stomping.

Seed of basil is available among the herbs in vegetable seed catalogs. Frequently the "basilico" in the packet marked sweet basil is the lettuce-leaf form. There are great possibilities for hybridizing in a planting of several varieties of basil. When we sold herb seed, we selected the best and most typical bush basil and from it developed one that had purple leaves but was only six inches tall; a cross with purple basil. In partial shade, sometimes, the purple forms become streaked with green. The variety Dark Opal is uniformly purple in leaf and stem but the older type of purple basil was often partly green, showing its mixed origin. Seed of basil will remain viable for fifteen years, we discovered, if it is kept in a freezer.

Basil is a good herb for the impatient gardener. It germinates in four to five days in warm earth. You can transplant it when it is in bloom without setting it back too much. Usually the blossoms are superfluous for your purpose of bringing the seasoning herb indoors or closer to the house by potting it for the terrace. The first flower buds should be pinched out to encourage branching. If several cuttings are desired for drying, make the first one as soon as two or three blossoms emerge.

Habitat. Species of basil are tropical in origin. Some appear in South America, India and Africa, but they are most often found in cultivation as the herb has been carried around the world by man. Wild basils are not as flavorful as the culinary garden types. One with camphor-scented leaves, *O. kilimand-scharicum*, is perennial. It grows in Kenya and thus is named for the famous mountain. Natives consider it important as a tea for colds and fevers.

Lemon basil was introduced to this country in the 1940's from Thailand. It forms a dainty, more lax plant, with widely spaced leaves, not as shiny as those of sweet basil. Sacred basil, *O. sanctum*, is similar, more stiffly erect, and possessed of a strange pungency in all parts of leaves, flower heads and stems. It is grown for use in temples in India and probably originated there. It is the only basil to self-sow in New England gardens if the season is long enough for it to set seed.

Uses. Italian tomato paste is usually packed with a leaf of basil in each can. The plant has a special affinity for tomato dishes, salads and pea soup. The dried herb does not remain as green as does parsley, but it has a good pungency.

In bouquets the basils are especially beautiful because of their glossy foliage. The Mediterranean custom of placing a pot of growing basil on the windowsill to keep unscreened windows free of flies can be adapted to terraces or barbecue tables in our country. Even when just laid over tomatoes in a bowl, basil sprigs deter fruit flies.

Pesto — or Basil Sauce

Place 1 cup olive oil in a blender. Cut in ¼ cup of fresh basil sprigs and ¼ cup parsley tops. Turn on blender for one minute. Add more leaves, blending for one minute at a time until ¾ cup more of basil and parsley have been used. Add 4 cloves of garlic and ½ cup pine nuts or walnuts and blend again. Store in the refrigerator in a covered jar. Use on vegetables, spaghetti or fish dishes.

It is often said that herbs enhance everything but dessert. However, sweet basil is one herb which can be used to give a subtle but indefinable flavor to pound cake.

Mary Lou's Basil Pound Cake

½ lb. butter	pinch of salt
2 c. sugar	½ teaspoon dry basil, ground fine
4 whole eggs	2 c. plus 1 tablespoon flour

Cream butter and sugar. Beat eggs and blend with creamed mixture. Sift in salt, basil and sifted flour, beating well. Put in a small loaf pan which has been greased and bake 1½ hours at 350° F. Keeps well if wrapped in aluminum foil.

Comment. Sweet basil is so popular in Italian cookery that we tend to think of it as one of the modern herbs. Actually, it is mentioned by Theophrastus, 300 B.C.:

"Basil has a succession of flowers, the lower part of the plant flowering first, and then, when that bloom is over, the upper part."

This gives a clue as to how to handle the plants. Cut them three or four inches from the tops as the first buds appear. Then the whole plants will become bushy and produce more leaves than flowers. As with most herbs, the amount of foliage is greatest just before the blossoms develop. The essential oils are stronger then too.

You can clip the plants when they first come into bloom and then have a second or third cutting later. The small sprigs gathered from the first cutting may be laid in wax paper sandwich bags, which may be stapled together, and placed in a freezer container for storage in the deep freeze. The amount of herb needed for one dish may be removed in one envelope without disturbing the rest. It is not necessary to blanch herbs before freezing. You can cut them up while still frozen to add to cooked food or use as a garnish.

At the end of the season, before frost, I harvest the plants I am not saving for seed by cutting them off at the root. I tie the stems together in loose bunches, dip them carefully in water to remove any mud and hang them up to drain. Basil bruises easily and the leaves will turn almost black in drying if they are not handled very carefully. It is possible to wash down the plants in the row just before cutting if you don't wish to wash them after they are harvested.

When the leaves are free of droplets, I place the bunches in large brown paper bags with the mouth of the bag closed with a string about the stem ends. The bags are hung in an airy pantry to dry. A few weeks later I shake the bags and if the contents sound crisp, I roll them lightly between my palms to separate the leaves from the stems. It may be necessary to spread the stems apart after taking them out of the bag and remove some of the leaves, which were at the center of the bunch, by hand. The dried herb is then spread on a cookie sheet and allowed to finish drying in a cool (not over 100° F.) oven. This method works for most leaf herbs. No volatile oils escape while the bunches are drying and they are not absorbed because the herbs do not come in contact with the brown paper bag until rubbed off the stems. There is no need to turn the foliage over daily as must be done if it is dried on a tray.

Garden basils were common in England in 1597, when John Gerard wrote his "Herball." He described lemon basil, calling it "citron basil," as well as sweet basil. Concluding the second page devoted to basils in his folio volume he says:

> "the smell of Basill is good for the heart and for the head. That the seed cureth the infirmities of the heart, taketh away sorrowfullness which commeth of melancholy, and maketh a man merry and glad."

Lettuce-leaf basil has leaves which can grow as large as a man's hand. It is not as branching as sweet basil and yields a greater amount of green herb for drying. Purple basil, now offered as Dark Opal basil, is extremely ornamental and has a slightly tea-like scent and flavor. The blossoms are pinkish instead of white. If the leaves are put into white vinegar it turns a bright ruby shade. It is a plant of which you will be proud to say with Gerard, "it groweth in my garden." It combines well with pink flowers, in the border or in bouquets.

Another desirable feature of purple basil is that it does not attract Japanese beetles. The scent of green basil will bring them winging to wherever you are working with the herb. If they bother the plants in the garden, the invaders can be repelled by dusting the foliage with ground lime. This will have to be washed off before the herb is used for cooking or drying but it is not poisonous. Green basil has a more popular flavor than the purple-leaved herb but both have their supporters for a place in the garden and the cuisine.

Borage (Borago officinalis)

Height. 2 feet

Leaf and blossoms. Typical of its family, borage, like anchusa and pulmonaria, has blossoms which open pink and turn blue as they mature. Leaves vary from three to four inches long and two inches wide at the base to the narrow leaflets on the flowering stems. The exquisite blue, star-shaped flowers nod above the rather coarse prickly leaves. Silvery hairs about the watery stems and pointed sepals give the effect of a misty haze through which the blossoms are seen. When the flowers are picked, the petals slip away from the black cone of stamens which form the centers of the blue stars. It is the blue corollas which are candied for decorating cakes or floated in cool beverages for a light cucumber flavor. Young leaves may be chopped fine and added to salad but the herb does not dry well.

Culture. An annual of easy culture, borage can be planted directly in the garden. It will usually self-sow to obviate the need for starting it anew each year. Some of the volunteer plants are handsomer than those deliberately planted. It is an ideal herb for the beginner, because the fat black seeds germinate quickly and the friendly, nodding blossoms reward the gardener from July to September.

If you thin the seedlings to stand ten to twelve inches apart instead of transplanting them, they will come along faster. But it is possible to move borage when it has only four true leaves in the seedling stage. If young plants are potted in peat or clay pots they may be set out in the garden without disturbing the roots. Also, in a window box, borage blooms in miniature,

without reaching its full stature and the blossoms are charming
when seen from underneath. It is as though you look up into
their impish faces if you set them on a windowsill or the high
wall of a sunny terrace.

Borage interplanted with strawberries is not only a very pretty
sight but it is said to help the growth of the fruit, thanks to
the shade of its foliage. A nice combination in the herb garden
is a planting of borage in front of red bee balm. The curious,
furry leaves hide the leafless part of the *Monarda didyma* stems
and the light blue flowers look well with the brilliant red whorls
of balm.

Small holes in the leaves of borage when it is subjected to
drought indicate damage by flea beetles. They may be dispersed by a nicotine spray or, if you prefer to use herbs to
treat herbs, water with an infusion of fresh catnip leaves steeped
overnight in a pail of water. Catnip has a volatile oil which
is eschewed by many insects and it can be captured in the
sprinkling can in this way. Japanese beetles sometimes discover
the delicately flavored blossoms. They can be discouraged by
dusting the plants with ground lime.

Uses. German cooks grow borage to have the young leaves
for salad greens to give a cucumber coolness to a tossed salad.
It is not an herb to dry, for when you take the moisture out
of the leaves you have no flavor left. The blossoms can be
floated on gin drinks: they will change color in contact with the
alcohol. In the more leisurely days of fox hunts and stirrup
cups, borage was included in the claret cup to temper the
warmth of the wine and because it was a "cordial" flower—it
cheered the spirits. As bee forage, the long season of bloom
makes it extremely serviceable.

Scatter the blue stars on a dish of sliced tomatoes if you
want to win praises from your guests. If you want to make
candied borage flowers, brush them carefully with a water-color
brush dipped in beaten egg white, coating both sides, and then
dust them with powdered sugar. They are spread on wax
paper to dry and may be stored in a tin box after two or

three days in which they are open to the air so that the egg white and sugar may harden. Violets and rose petals are candied in the same fashion. You can make a floral wreath of them with strips of angelica, which have been drained of the preserving syrup and allowed to crystalize. These may also be used as a green garland between the blossoms, on a white cake.

Borage Cup

In a large tumbler, put a tablespoonful of sugar, a slice of lemon, two slices of orange, and half-fill with shaved ice. Then add claret to the top of the glass. Put into a shaker and pour into a chilled pewter mug. Float stars of blue borage flowers on top.

Comment. Borage is part of a large family of handsome, blue and pink-flowered plants which grow easily in all parts of the temperate zone. One was an important dye plant, *Anchusa tinctoria,* a biennial from the roots of which a reddish brown dye was obtained.

Caraway (*Carum carvi*)

Height. 2½ feet

Leaf, blossom and seed. In its first season, the biennial caraway makes a mound of threadlike leaves similar to those of carrots but with a smoother texture. The color is a deeper green and the leaves are shinier than those of carrots. They are also aromatic, though not as spicy as the seeds. In May of the second year, and sometimes in late summer of the first year, if the plants were started in a greenhouse and potted before being set out, the flowering stalks shoot up and are topped with umbels of miniature white flowers. After the light brown, half-moon-shaped seeds ripen, the tops and roots die. The seeds are one of the first crops of the herb garden in its second summer.

Culture. Where caraway is grown on a large scale, it is planted with regular farm-seeding equipment and harvested with a combine in the same way as dill. In the garden, it is sown in furrows and the plants are thinned to stand 6 inches apart. As a plant that sheds its seeds easily, caraway has become naturalized in some parts of this country. But since there are also poisonous members of its family, such as the deadly, cut-leaved poison hemlock, it is not a good idea to go about nibbling what you hope may be caraway. The faint fragrance of the caraway's leaves is a fair clue even if the plants are not in seed.

Caraway is one of the many herbs which can be planted in the fall for a headstart on gardening in the spring. It is possible, but not advised, to transplant caraway the first year. But if the seedlings are potted when their first four true leaves appear they do not suffer too much from shock in moving. As with other members of the carrot family, *Carum carvi* has a deep tap root. The plants will tolerate partial shade in summer as the blossoms are usually finished by the time the leaves are fully out on trees. The crowns are extremely hardy and remain clothed with leaves most of the winter.

Habitat. Caraway is a native of Europe, sometimes becoming naturalized in the U.S.

Uses. The dried seeds are used to flavor rye bread. A liqueur called Kummel is manufactured from the oil of caraway extracted by distillation. Seeds are also used to flavor sauerkraut. And in olden-times, caraway seeds were sugar-coated: the comfits were eaten to promote digestion after a hearty meal.

Caraway Beets

Boil young beets in their skins. Peel under cold water and slice. Melt ¼ cup butter for two bunches of beets, and add ½ teaspoon caraway seeds. Pour over hot beets and serve with a garnish of parsley.

Comment. Caraway and other edible seeds of the Umbelliferae (proper name of the carrot family) are subject to attack by aphids when they are ripening. They do not have a protective husk about them and other boring insects can penetrate the green seeds. This is one reason for relatively difficult germination of seed of this family. Sometimes microscopic insects have eaten the heart out of them.

Collected seeds should be scalded with boiling water before being spread out to dry for culinary use. This will remove the germinating power but also destroys any hidden insects. Drain the seeds on fine wire and spread out to dry in the sun for several days. Bring them in at night so that they will not absorb moisture from the dew. When a few seeds can be ground fine with a wooden mallet, they are sufficiently desiccated to store whole in an air-tight jar.

Chamomile, German (*Matricaria chamomilla*)

Height. 18 inches

Leaf and blossoms. The finely divided foliage is a shiny green. The blossoms are disk-like yellow flowers with small white projecting petals at the base; the center of the flower becomes conical as the plant matures. The typical bloom has ten to twenty white rays, but sometimes all the white petals are lacking.

Culture. German chamomile is an annual, while the low, ground cover Roman chamomile (*Anthemis nobilis*) is perennial. Sow seeds of the annual herb where the plants are to remain and thin to four to six inches asunder. It is possible to start the chamomile in flats and then pot the young seedlings: they can be placed in the garden as soon as the ground can be worked.

Habitat. *M. chamomilla* was considered indigenous to Germany, hence the common name, but modern botanists believe the stands appearing in the wild in Europe are escapes from botanical gardens. It is said to be naturalized in North America but I have never seen it, though several other species of matricaria, such as *M. inodora* or scentless, false chamomile are common in New England.

Uses. The dried flower heads are used to make chamomile tea. If the blossoms are dried by hanging them up in bunches in brown paper bags, they can be steeped in hot water to make an amber colored beverage. The popularity of the tea in Hungary gave rise to the name Hungarian chamomile: a mildly analgesic beverage often given to children in Europe and South

America for stomach aches and teething pains. Chamomile tea
is somewhat bitter and thus was considered a punishment in
the story of "Peter Rabbit." This is not the chamomile used for a
hair rinse.

Chervil (Anthriscus cerefolium)

Height. 2 feet

Leaf, blossoms and seeds. One of the most dainty annuals of
the Umbelliferae, chervil has finely divided, richly aromatic
leaves of soft golden-green: the thin leaflets are so segmented
that they seem to be fringed. In May the umbels of petite
white flowers may be inconspicuous on a single plant, but a bed
of chervil makes an exquisite pattern of green and white lace.
The leaves are the portion used in seasoning, often as a substitute for parsley. The flavor of them is slightly licorice, remi-
niscent of tarragon. I have called it the poor man's tarragon
because you can grow it from seed and tarragon must be purchased as a plant.

Almost as soon as the blossoms open, they begin to elongate
to form narrow, sharply-pointed fruits. These ripen and turn
black to resemble long black splinters when ready to be collected for storing or planting at once for a fall crop of chervil.
The single white fleshy tap root, typical of the carrot family
or Umbelliferae, is as thin as a mouse's tail.

Culture. The first requirement for starting chervil is to obtain
fresh seed. Sow it on top of the soil, rake it in, and tamp it
down slightly. Chervil which is allowed to self-sow in soil rich
in humus produces the best plants. Fine ones will spring up
on the compost pile when seed heads are cast there in mid-
summer.

Fall-sowing will help assure you a crop large enough to use the
leaves fresh and have some to freeze. The plants started from
seed sown in early September germinate in a week and stay
green all winter. They can be collected until the ground
freezes hard and will be one of the first sources of green in
the spring. Otherwise seed planted in warm weather will mature

in about six weeks and run to seed. The plants should be shaded part of the day if you wish to keep them from suffering bleaching from the bright summer sun. Successive sowings provide a continuous supply of chervil for the kitchen. It is also a good windowsill plant as it stands more shade than most herbs. Transplanting is not advised unless absolutely necessary. If the seedlings are potted very young they will produce good foliage but must be cut often to prevent their flowering and seeding.

Habitat. Originating in southeastern Europe, chervil may be said to like cool climates.

Uses. As chervil is usually included among the *fines herbes* it has many uses for flavoring. The leaves may be frozen in small packages to provide a winter supply of the ferny green for salads, fish sauce and seasoning cooked vegetables. No blanching is necessary before freezing. Just wash the leaves, pat them dry, and place them in small plastic containers in the freezer. Plan to mince them fine while still frozen because they get limp as they thaw.

Omelette aux Fines Herbes

2 eggs	2 tablespoons cream
pinch of salt	1 teaspoon fresh chervil
dusting of pepper	½ teaspoon fresh chives
1 tablespoon butter	½ teaspoon fresh marjoram

Mince the herbs with a knife on a chopping block. Break eggs into a small bowl and add cream. Beat slightly to blend. Place butter in a heavy, flat frying pan. Put over heat and roll the melting butter around the pan. Pour eggs into the pan just before the butter begins to smoke. Cook over a quick fire until bubbles around the edges show the eggs are getting set. Lift the edges with a fork, with which you have beaten the eggs, and let the liquid run against the heated pan. When most of the egg mixture is beginning to firm, sprinkle with salt and pepper and *fines herbes*.

When you fold in the herbs, lift the edges of the omelette as you would to fold the four corners of a napkin. Turn once to brown the top and slide onto a heated plate. It is better to use a small pan and make one omelette at a time than to try to make a larger quantity. Do not wash the omelette pan. Wipe it dry with a paper towel and keep it just for this purpose.

Coriander,
Coriandrum sativum

Coriander (*Coriandrum sativum*)

Height. 2 to 3 feet

Leaf, blossom and seeds. The rounded basal leaves of coriander are similar to those of anise, but further up on the flowering stems the leaves become linear. The foliage of this badly maligned annual is said to smell like crushed bugs. Actually, the odor is pleasantly sharp and the herb is quite charming in bloom. A slight plant which branches only at the top, coriander carries decorative flat umbels of small pinkish blossoms. The flowers are followed by light brown fruits which seem too large for the delicate plants, although they measure only $\frac{3}{16}$ths of an inch in diameter and are not heavy. The round, ridged seeds, or fruits, split in two when cracked. It is the inner kernel which is used in cooking. The leaves are favored by Central American and Far Eastern appetites in salads and soups. The Spanish name "cilantro" means coriander.

Culture. It is one of the first annuals to flower in the herb garden. Seed may be sown in early spring so that there is little to be gained by trying to start it indoors. Coriander is a hardy annual, sometimes volunteering from last year's planting, if all the seeds are not collected. The plants need little thinning as the foliage is scant when flowering begins. Several sowings will provide a succession of blossoms and seeds.

Tamp the seeds down well with a light covering of soil, since they readily float in a hard rain. The herb does not sprout for almost two weeks.

Habitat. Southern Europe is given in *Hortus II* as its point of origin. Actually it is grown commercially in India and Pakistan and appears in Chinese groceries in this country as a favored green much as we feature parsley.

Uses. The seeds which become spicier as they dry were once chewed to sweeten the breath and promote digestion. Comfits with coriander as the kernel inside the sugar ball were popular old-fashioned sweets. Crushed seeds are used in pickling spices, sausage seasoning and for flavoring cookies, ginger-bread and tobacco products in this country. The oil of coriander is a secret ingredient in the flavoring of at least one kind of whiskey.

The fruits are supposed to be not only soothing to the stomach but also stimulating to desire: it is considered one of the aphrodisiac herbs. The entire plant, when young, is used in preparing chutneys and for adding to soup in middle-eastern cookery. Egyptians add it to meat loaf, a really delicious twist for a familiar dish, if used with discretion. In Latin America it is mixed with salad greens.

Coriander Honey Bread

1 cup black coffee	3 teaspoons baking powder
1 tablespoon shortening	½ teaspoon baking soda
1 cup dark honey	1 teaspoon cinnamon
2 cups white flour	pinch of powdered cloves
1 cup rye meal	1 teaspoon ground coriander seed
pinch of salt	

Add hot coffee to shortening and honey. Cool and add dry ingredients. Beat well and place in a greased loaf pan. Bake 1 hour at 350° F. Keeps three weeks in a tin box.

Comment. Coriander seeds contain enough pungent oils to repel insect attack. So it is seldom necessary to scald the seeds before drying them. The whole plant may be uprooted, clipped off at the base and thrust into a large brown paper bag. Then the ripe seeds will roll off the stems easily: just manipulate the bag gently. If you let the plants dry too much before you harvest the seeds, you will be confronted with small bits of brittle stems which are hard to extricate. Actually, if yours is a small planting of coriander, simply hand-pick the little beige balls from the umbels. Dry them in the sun for two or three days before storing.

Dill, *Anethum graveolens* (Philip W. Foster)

Dill (*Anethum graveolens*)
Height. 3 feet

Leaf, blossoms and seeds. The blue-green feathery foliage of annual dill makes a soft background for the smaller herbs. When the plants comes into bloom, it is hard to find any of the compound, thread-like leaves for culinary use. The plants seem to be all hollow stems and graceful umbels of tiny yellow blossoms. Though tall, dill is not an obtrusive plant, holding its light brown, elliptical, rather flat seeds gracefully erect.

Culture. When pickling time comes, herb gardeners get desperate requests for dill. The people who ask for it would find it so easy to grow in shallow drills in the vegetable garden. It germinates in a week and matures in six. To have a patch of delicate ferny green in the herb garden, merely scatter the seed on top of freshly turned soil in early spring. Transplanting is a waste of time and thinning is seldom necessary if the seeds are spaced evenly.

Succession planting throughout the summer provides fresh leaves for garnishing and seasoning and flower and seed heads for pickling. Where the ground can be left undisturbed at the end of the growing season, dill will self-sow to perpetuate itself. Lewis Gannett, author and book critic, planted seed of dill from Louis Adamic's garden 30 years ago. He has not bought seed since but each year a bright spot of color in his vegetable garden is provided by volunteer plants of dill. If it comes up in a row of beans, it can be pulled out easily. If it stands between the rows it adds beauty to the scene.

Habitat. Originally introduced from Europe, dill has naturalized in some parts of the United States.

Uses. Dill has many culinary uses besides the traditional one of being put between layers of cucumbers in brine to make dill pickles. The leaves provide a pleasantly strong seasoning for fish, potatoes, salads and sauces. The seeds are sometime substituted for caraway on rye bread. Swedish cuisine includes fresh dill leaves in potato salad and to garnish lamb.

Lamb with Dill Sauce

Take two pounds of breast of lamb, rinse quickly in boiling water and put it into a stewpan, covering with more boiling water. Bring to a boil, skimming off the froth. For each quart of water add a tablespoon of salt, three or four black peppercorns, a bay leaf and some sprigs of fresh dill. Cover and simmer for two hours, until tender. Serve cut in pieces with a garnish of dill sprigs and accompanied by this sauce.

Dill Sauce

Melt 1 tablespoon shortening in a small pan and blend in two tablespoons flour. Moisten with lamb stock and simmer to make a medium sauce, stirring frequently. Add 2 tablespoons chopped dill leaves, season with salt, pepper and a dash of cider vinegar. Beat one egg yolk and pour some of the sauce into it, still beating. Return to remainder of the sauce and cook 1 minute, stirring constantly.

Comment. Dill has many ancient associations with women, children and witches. The seeds "sunned in oil, as we do with roses, provoketh carnal lust," says Gerard, the 16th century herbalist. Writers on plants of The Bible have stated that the anise of Scripture must have been dill, the error caused by poor translation of the generic name Anethum. The seeds increased the flow of a mother's milk, said the physician of Tudor times. Colonial housewives made a tea of them to soothe pains of colic in babies. The name dill is derived from the Saxon verb *dilla*, to lull, because of its sedative action upon the nervous system. With trefoil, vervain, St. John's-wort, dill is said to "hinder witches of their will." What a pity to call these seeds, which are planted the world over for their flavor, "dill weed."

Fennel (*Foeniculum vulgare*)

Height. 5 feet

Leaf, blossoms and seeds. Dill and fennel have almost identical thread-like foliage but close examination reveals quite a few differences in the nature of the plants. While dill has a blue-green cast, fennel is definitely more glossy and yellow-green in leaf. The leaflets are roundish instead of flat as in dill. They are also longer and larger. In fact, fennel is a much more stalwart plant, taller than dill with branching stems at the base. The shiny stalks are slightly flattened, translucent tubes with whitish sheaths where the side branches join the main stems.

The large yellow umbels have fewer spokes than those of dill, but are broader and flatter. The petals are so tiny that they are hard to detect around the prominent slightly yellow ovaries. Light tan, ribbed seeds are not as flat as dill seeds and have a sweet anise or licorice flavor.

F. vulgare dulce, or finocchio, makes dense plumes of leaves about two feet in height. It should not be allowed to flower if the swollen basal stems are to be eaten. They are surrounded by earth as they enlarge to egg size and blanched while still growing in the garden. Finocchio is an annual. Both varieties take a week to ten days to come up in the garden.

A form of *F. vulgare* with bronze leaves is sometimes perennial or biennial and is grown for ornament and seasoning.

Culture. In some soils fennel is quite long-lived which causes it to be considered biennial or perennial. It is not winter-hardy in New England and so must be treated as an annual. The best plants are grown from seed sown right in the garden in full sun. Six to ten inches is enough space to allow between seedlings when they are being thinned. The immature plants thus culled from the row may be used in cooking. *F. vulgare* should be placed well to the back of the bed where the tall stalks may be propped up against a fence or tied to stakes if it is to be allowed to bloom and set seed.

The airy plumes of fennels, green and bronze foliaged, can also be used to advantage in the perennial border to screen the dried tops of early flowering plants, like foxglove, of which you want seed. Coarser finocchio should be relegated to the vegetable patch where its late crop will fill in the space used by lettuce or cress planted in the spring. It is frost resistant and should be planted in July to follow other early vegetables. The bulbous stems remain in an edible condition for several months in cool weather. They appear in the vegetable market in October and November.

All of the fennels need a rather rich, well-drained soil. Seed of the taller fennels are difficult to obtain. Packets marked "sweet fennel" will usually prove to be finocchio. Plants of bronze fennel are offered by herb nurseries, for it can be potted when young for safe transplanting. Fennel and dill will adapt to

conditions in a window box to make good indoor herbs if they
are started from seed in mid-summer.

Habitat. California roadsides are stunning in August with
clumps of golden-blossomed fennel. It has become naturalized
there, possibly after escaping from the gardens of the Mission
fathers of the 18th century. It is an Old World herb that
has become quite thoroughly westernized. In North Carolina it
is also a roadside wildling along the coastal area.

Uses. Fennel has leaves and seeds of similar warm licorice
taste, not unlike the flavor of French tarragon. They are popular
in salads and for a seasoning and sauce for seafoods. The seeds
are used to spice rolls and other hot breads. In England, fennel
tea, made from the seeds, is considered a pleasant change from
black tea. The Russians favor the leaves, minced fine, scattered
over salads, boiled potatoes and fish. At the Hotel Metropole
in Monte Carlo, a choice fish called *la loupe* is grilled over
burning fennel twigs to give it a smoky aroma. Finocchio may
be par-boiled and eaten as a vegetable or sliced thin and eaten
raw like celery.

Mackerel with Fennel Sauce

Place a cleaned mackerel in a shallow frying pan with
enough cold water to cover it. Add salt, a little vinegar and
five sprigs of fresh fennel. Bring to a boil quickly and let it
boil hard for a few seconds. Turn down and simmer over low
heat for fifteen minutes. Drain the fish on a cloth and scrape
off the skin carefully. Serve with a garnish of parsley and
lemon wedges on a heated platter. Pass fennel sauce made
by adding two tablespoons of chopped fennel leaves to a
pint of white cream sauce, made with ½ cup of cream and
1½ cups of chicken stock, thickened with 3 tablespoons of
potato flour.

Finocchio has such a short season in the market that it is
a shame to waste what feathery tops are still attached to the
bulbous stems. Cut them off before slicing up the white portion of the pot-herb and put them in a blender with a cup of
salad oil. Blend and store in the refrigerator in a screw-top
jar. This oil of fennel makes a good sauce for boiled fish, a
delectable seasoning for broiled mushrooms on which it is

dribbled before putting under the fire, and an unusual dressing for cooked spaghetti or other types of pasta.

Comment. Longfellow described the herb as being significant in promoting longevity and courage. But he was not the first poet to laud fennel. The use of fennel for eye troubles is mentioned in the ancient poem by Macer:

> "By eating herb of Fennel, for the eyes
> A cure for blindness has the serpent wise;
> Man tried the plant; and, trusting that his sight
> Might thus be healed, rejoiced to find him right."

Since it is similar to dill in appearance, fennel seems to have picked up some of dill's reported attributes, such as increasing the flow of milk in nursing mothers and relieving distress of infants' "wamblings." William Coles, herbalist, records that fennel leaves and seeds "are much used in drinks and broths for those that are grown fat, to abate their unwieldinesse, and make them more gaunt and lank." At last a slimming herb!

Nasturtium (*Tropaeolum minus*)

Height. 10 inches

Leaf and blossoms, seed pods. It is a familiar annual with succulent, rounded leaves and tubular yellow, red and orange flowers which end in a spur filled with nectar. The old-fashioned single nasturtiums have been hybridized to produce double and quite stunning color variations in bloom. The unripe seeds of the flowering herb can substitute for capers in home-made pickles. The leaves have a spicy flavor and pleasant crunchiness in salads.

Culture. Full sun and not-too-rich soil are prerequisites to plentiful blooms: in rich ground the leaves are more abundant than the flowers. Sow seeds where the plants are to remain. For the herb garden the dwarf forms make an excellent edging— they are quick to bloom, providing color in six weeks from seed. Nasturtiums are tender, succumbing to the first frost.

Habitat. Indian cress was the name given to nasturtium by Gerard in 1597 because it came from the West Indies: it was introduced to the Old World in the 16th century via Spain and France.

Uses. In his "Garden of Pleasant Flowers," a part of the great work called *Paradisi in Sole,* 1629, John Parkinson calls nasturtiums Indian cresses or yellow larkes heeles. He noted that the scent was so pleasing that he felt the flowers should be placed in the middle of some carnations to make a "delicate Tussimussie." This is where we get the charming name for a nosegay made of herbs and flowers called a tussie-mussie, today.

Pickled Nasturtium "Capers"

As nasturtiums go to seed, pick the green fruiting bodies and soak three days in cold salted water. Stir once a day. Heat, slightly, the pickling solution made of white wine vinegar, sliced shallots, a teaspoon of chopped horse-radish root, salt, pepper, cloves, mace and coarsely crushed nutmeg. Drain the caper-like nasturtium pods and add to the pickle. Put into a sterilized bottle and cork tightly. Can be used as a substitute for imported capers in tartare sauce.

John Evelyn, in *Acetaria, a Discourse of Sallets,* published in 1699, in the 9th edition of *Kalendarium Hortense,* includes Indian cresses as important for salads. He was sure that something so "moderately hot, and aromatick" must quicken the "torpent Spirits and purge the Braine." The buds were candied in those days to keep all winter. Today the leaves are eaten raw in salads and the buds cooked.

One of the latest wrinkles in companion planting is to circle fruit trees with nasturtiums to discourage aphids. Though they are themselves subject to this pest, it was found by a scientist at the Connecticut Experiment Station that the yellow color of the blossoms caused flying aphids to avoid plants growing above them.

Orach (*Atriplex hortensis*)

Height. 3 feet

Leaf and blossom. French spinach or orach is a stunning annual. The shield-shaped, wavy leaves of beet red have a mealy texture similar to those of its relative, lamb's quarters, also a pot-herb. The blossoms are insignificant but the foliage compensates for that.

Culture. Sow seeds where the plants are to remain. Thin to stand ten inches apart. In hot weather orach needs watering even though it is a member of a genus sometimes called saltbush because some of its species are grown for forage in the desert. It will self-sow if the seeds are left on those plants which are not cut for flower arrangements. In close proximity to the silvery wormwoods, the red leaves are very handsome.

Habitat. The English herbalist Gerard reported that it grew in most "fruitful gardens" and Dioscorides, the first century herbalist, recorded that it was eaten boiled as a salad, which means it must have grown in Greece and Italy at that time. There are shrubby species native to California and Arizona but they are not as ornamental as red-leaved garden orach.

Uses. Orach is more appreciated as contrasting foliage in the herb garden, today, than as cooked greens: the red color of the leaves washes out in cooking. It is valuable in flower arrangements because of the glow its leaves have when light shines through them.

Comment. The herbalists believed that orach had a cleansing quality and if laid upon swollen glands in the throat, either raw or "sodden" (cooked) it cured the condition. Whatever its medicinal reputation in the old days, the herb provides a bright spot of color even without showy blossoms. Goldfinches are attracted to the garden by the ripening seeds. They look like huge butterflies hovering over the plants picking out the flat brown fruits.

Parsley (*Petroselinum hortense*)
  Height. 2 feet
  Leaf and blossom. Curly parsley, of the mossy green, crisped leaves is satisfactory for garnishing and seasoning, but there is another variety which has more flavor: *Petroselinum hortense filicinum,* called Italian parsley. It has larger, flat, segmented

leaves and thick, fibrous roots. The plants reach a foot in height the first year, shooting up to two feet as the yellowish green compound umbels form the second summer. Parsley is biennial but is usually grown as an annual and most people are astonished to see it bloom when it has gone through a winter. While the flowers are inconspicuous, it is nice to let a few plants develop seeds because they will self-sow to make small plants for potting up for the indoor garden. The root dies after the plant seeds.

Culture. Parsley seeds are among the last to germinate in the herb or vegetable garden though they may be planted as soon as the ground can be worked. Mixing the seed with those of radishes to mark the row helps the impatient gardener. You can pull the radishes and thin the parsley at the same time; the broader-leaved root vegetable helping to shade the young seedlings. It is usually better to sow parsley where it can remain in the garden, but it can be transplanted when the herb has four true leaves. Parsley started in a flat or coldframe in late March will be ready for cutting in early June.

Parsley likes a rich, well-drained loam with plenty of humus. It needs ample moisture when young but does not like sogginess. In clay soil, the deep roots will take a firm hold but can seldom be transplanted safely.

Young plants may be started in August for keeping over the winter indoors. Parsley is one of the most successful window garden herbs if it is kept away from radiators and stoves. Frequent washing of the leaves with tap water helps to prevent insect damage under such artificial conditions. Keep the foliage away from frosty window panes while giving them a maximum of sunlight.

Habitat. Parsley was brought to this country from Europe. Despite the botanists' word that it has become naturalized in eastern North America, I have never met anyone who has seen it growing wild. It would be folly to venture to taste many of the plants of its family which do dot our roadsides. Some have yellowish blossoms and much-cut leaves that are typical of the tribe, but there are some really lethal genera among the Umbelliferae.

Uses. On a weight for weight basis, parsley contains three times as much vitamin C as oranges. It is one of the best sources of vitamin A. Though it is not possible to get a daily quota of these vitamins by munching the garnish of parsley on a dinner platter, a generous sprinkling of chopped parsley on potatoes and vegetables is a lot cheaper than pills. The herb also appears to contain a substance which protects its vitamins even through the dehydration process thus making dried parsley too a good source of vitamins. The herb is rich in available iron, containing 1.42 mg. per ounce.

Comment. The flat-leaved Italian parsley is a better choice than curly parsley for drying; it is also richer in vitamin C. The vitamin content varies according to the soil and climate. Parsley grown in India contained twice as much vitamin C per 100 grams as that grown in the United States. Parsley may be frozen, either as whole leaf or chopped.

Dried Parsley

Parsley is the one great exception to the rule of not using heat in excess of 100° F. to dry leafy herbs. It can be placed on wire screens in a hot oven (400° F.) for five minutes until it becomes crackling dry. The leaves should be spread thinly and turned once to prevent scorching. When thus crisped, the leaves will crumble away from the stems: just rub them over the coarse screen wire or press through a large-mesh strainer. They must be crisp before they are bottled because the dried leaves readily take up moisture again. If you prefer, you can dry parsley on an open dish in the refrigerator in order to get an even richer color: the trouble is that this process takes up a lot of space. It also takes a week or more to become thoroughly dehydrated.

Pennyroyal, American (*Hedeoma pulegioides*)
Height. 1 foot
Leaf and blossom. In walking through open meadows in New England, it is often possible to smell pennyroyal before you see it. The slight plant is a bit similar in leaf and habit to basil but on a more delicate scale. Every part of it is filled with the characteristic aroma of its essential oil, Oleum Hedomae. The

few bluish flowers are in whorls: tiny blue, slightly hairy, two-lipped tubes circle the stem, projecting from the axils of the leaves.

Culture. Pennyroyal collected in the wild, as seeds or young plants, is worth getting started in the herb garden. Cultivation improves the plants which will self-sow for many years. Brushing against it makes weeding a fragrant job. You won't find American pennyroyal in any catalog. The perennial English pennyroyal, *Mentha pulegium,* is offered as a plant by herb specialists, but the little wildling has to be your own discovery.

Habitat. Pennyroyal is found in dry places from Canada south-ward through New England. It is usually in the company of meadow violets, wild strawberries and black-eyed susans.

Uses. The U.S. Dispensatory says that American pennyroyal is a gently stimulant aromatic which may be given for colic and a sick stomach. It makes a pleasant tea, either fresh or dried, when steeped in boiling water. And it proves a soothing morning beverage after a night out.

Comment. Pennyroyal may some day be studied to isolate the insect repellent oil which has proven itself over centuries through empirical uses. A handful of the herb rubbed on the face and arms will protect the gardener from mosquitoes and small flies.

Perilla (*Perilla frutescens*)
Height. 3 feet

Leaf and blossom. Perilla is called beefsteak plant because of its dark red, glowing foliage. In some ways the herb resembles a red coleus, but it is definitely an annual. The leaves are large, wrinkled, deeply indented on the margins, broadly ovate, about three inches long by two inches wide. The surface is covered with whitish hairs above and purplish ones on the under sides. Even the square, grooved, hairy stems are wine-colored. The plants are very erect, branching when the incon-spicuous blossoms form: pinkish tubular flowers only ¼ inch long. As the petals drop and four round seeds form (mottled purple like tiny spotted birds' eggs) the calyx turns from purple to green. The racemes of small flowers seem to glisten as the sun sparkles on the shining white hairs which coat the sepals.

Culture. A tender annual, perilla must be sown from seed when the ground is thoroughly warm. It can be started indoors, as you would sweet basil, for it transplants easily at all stages. It will succumb to the first frost and sometimes does not get a chance to set seed in northern New England. But the seeds are resistant to freezing and will self-sow freely if matured. Once you get perilla going in the garden, it will perpetuate itself for years. Volunteers are easily moved so that you can place the burgundy foliage where you want it as a contrast to green plants, or against gray stone walls.

Habitat. Perilla is native to Asia and has been cultivated and selected for different forms in China and Japan. *P. frutescens crispa* has ruffled leaves while the typical form is flat-leaved.

Uses. As quick drying oil used in the manufacture of paint, perilla has an economic value but it is also a culinary herb. In Japan a green-leaved perilla is grown for salads and seasoning.

Twenty years ago I wrote that perilla had no seasoning properties. But, in the course of editing a magazine on herb gardening, I have learned a few things. The chef of the Japanese Embassy in Washington, D.C., contributed an article to *The Herb Grower Magazine* on herbs in the embassy garden. Among them was perilla which he called "shisho" and used in making tempura. Both leaves and seeds of the herb are used in their national dish. The seeds alone are salted and served after sweets. Sometimes, too, the preserved seeds are used as the salty core in Japanese candies. "Shisho" seeds are eaten raw as an accompaniment to a fish entree. Purple perilla is put with pickled plums, including the tender leaves and round seeds which are also fragrant.

Comment. With most Japanese seasoning plants, such as honewort, called "mitsuba" and used in soups, the fragrance spoken of is not our idea of a sweet or spicy odor. It is more of a green herb perfume with a tang of bitterness. They also put into soups a much-used tree leaf called "sansho"—very similar to our native prickly ash—which we would not think has a very pronounced "fragrance." The Japanese also cook the blossoms of "sansho," *Zanthoxylum piperitum* with sake and soy sauce or just boil them briefly and pickle them to serve with pork. We have fields of "sansho's" near relative Z. *americanum* growing in our area but people would never think of using the leaves and blossoms, because it is such a prickly weed tree. The flavor is similar but it is a case of what is abundant is scorned and what comes from afar is desirable. The English call it the "angelica tree of America."

Pot Marigold (*Calendula officinalis*)

Height. 18 inches

Leaf and blossom. The pot marigold or calendula is the single-flowered, old-fashioned plant with yellow to deep orange blossoms. It has two or three rows of flat rays surrounding a brownish disk made up of many tiny florets. The branching, grooved, hairy stems bear widely alternate, clasping leaves. Their texture is oily and glandular which accounts for the bitter, aromatic scent. When the almost perennial plants, which are treated as annual in the herb and flower garden, are full-grown they bloom for many months. The flowers open in the morning but close at sun-down so they are not good for indoor bouquets. Frost-hardy, pot marigolds are among the last reminders of summer in the autumn garden.

Culture. Seed sown in early spring germinates in ten days. Young plants should be thinned or transplanted to stand a foot apart: crowded seedlings do not make shapely plants. The pot marigold needs plenty of sun and not too rich soil. It can be potted to bring indoors for the windowsill garden if the old seed heads are cut back. It will flower again in January and can stand a very cool situation as long as it does not freeze.

In our garden, rabbits have developed a fancy for the foliage. It is often necessary to dust the plants with dried blood powder, available now at garden centers. Both rabbits and woodchucks are kept away from flowers by the odor of the prepared powder which washes into the soil with rain. It must be renewed after this but it helps to give the blossoms a brighter hue as it supplies minerals to the earth.

Habitat. *Calendula officinalis* is one of several species which grow in lands bordering the Mediterranean Sea from the Canary Islands to the Middle East.

Uses. The petals of pot marigold were used to color butter, cheese, custards and sauces. A yellow dye can be extracted from them. Dried petals put in mixed herb tea add color and flavor to the brew. In World War I, the juice of the fresh herb mixed with enough alcohol to prevent fermentation was believed effective for healing wounds. By the "Doctrine of Signatures" (in which every plant used for medicine was thought to have some outward sign of its proper application) the yellow petals of pot-marigold indicated that it was good for treating jaundice. This theory was popular until the 17th century.

Comment. To dry the flowers, spread the individual petals on clean paper, in a dry place, out of the sun and wind. Turn them often, keeping the petals from touching each other. When crisp, store in air-tight containers.

It is important to explain that the African or Mexican marigold with tightly packed ruffled petals of orange and yellow and finely cut leaves, is different from pot marigold. The flower which is now being studied for its remarkable effect on weeds and worms in garden soils is of the genus *Tagetes,* and is from the New World. The Old World pot-marigold of medicinal and culinary use is actually what we know as *Calendula.* Parkinson explained the name as being taken from *Kalendes,* meaning the first day of the month, which is when they were thought to flower. The English, he said, called them "eyther Golds, or Marigolds." In medieval times the plant was associated with the Virgin Mary and from the use of it in church decoration, it was given the prefix Mary. African and Mexican marigolds were featured in religious ceremonies in India, for the former, and Latin America for the latter, and the Church quickly affixed a Christian association to pagan plants.

Safflower (*Carthamus tinctorius*)

Height. 3 feet

Leaf, blossom and seed. With its broadly ovate leaves, two to two and one-half inches long, safflower, or false saffron, is dark green and shining. The leaves have margins studded with sharp, prickly orange hairs. While not a true thistle, safflower might be said to resemble one in foliage and flower receptacle. The reason for growing this erect, not very beautiful annual, lies in its blossoms. The flowers are made up of clusters of spiny, green bracts, topped by dense tufts of deep yellow florets which turn orange as they mature. By the end of August the ripe seeds resemble curious white teeth with dark stains on the ends. It is from them that safflower oil is obtained. The dried blossoms are used as a substitute for the expensive saffron gathered from an autumn crocus.

Culture. Plant seeds directly in the garden when the earth is warm. Thin to stand six inches apart after germination which takes about ten days. Safflower does not transplant well. The herb thrives in poor, dry soil in full sun; it is therefore valuable as a crop for arid regions. In our garden it has to be protected from rabbits until the spines develop on the tips of the leaves, because the young plants are succulent and tender.

Habitat. Native to Europe, safflower is grown as an oil crop in California and our Southwest. Sunflowers which are native to this country have been cultivated and improved in Russia as a food and oil crop in similar fashion.

Uses. Now that the term "polyunsaturated" has become a popular advertising slogan, safflower oil is being included in mayonnaise, margarine and salad dressing. The herb gardener values the dried petals for coloring chicken gravy or as a substitute for saffron when cooked with rice. They make a splendid source of vegetable dye for silk and wool used in embroidery and handweaving: safflower gives two shades—yellow and red—according to how it is processed.

Comment. A plant found in Egyptian tombs, safflower is one of our most modern herbs. Over 350,000 tons of seed are grown in this country for oil.

Clary Sage,
Salvia sclarea

Sage, Clary (*Salvia sclarea*)
Height. 4 feet

Leaf and blossom. The huge, heart-shaped, wrinkled leaves and showy blue and white blossoms, of intense perfume, make clary sage a favorite ornamental herb. Generously proportioned basal leaves, often a foot long, are topped by shining spikes of blue and white flowers with pinkish bracts beneath them. The tall flowering stalks and widely overlapping leaves give the effect of a slim flower maiden standing erect in a flounced, hoop skirt.

A plant of clary sage becomes so large by the second year that it needs a background location. In the small herb garden, the biennial crowds out shorter plants. Blossoms start forming in early July and continue for more than a month on ever-elongating flower stalks. The bluish corollas are very conspicuous; the two lobes forming a wide arch or sickle.

Four round, brown seeds are similar to those of garden sage, but they have a slippery, gelatinous quality when wet. This phenomenon suggested to the herbalists that if seed of clary was put into the eye it would help to slide out specks of foreign objects lodged there. Hence the name "clear eye" or clary sage.

Culture. Clary sage must be grown from seed which may be planted in the garden. It takes only a week to come up. The fat, furry seedlings are easy to detect. Give clary sage full sun, good drainage and sandy loam. The hairy leaves show an adaptation to arid conditions, as the thick down upon them reduces the evaporation of moisture. I have seen a large patch of clary sage blooming in an abandoned vegetable garden at Cape Cod. It was a gorgeous sight in late June, almost as if it were growing wild in the sandy soil where every seed, of a plant allowed to bloom and self-sow, must have come up. In a wet place clary will rot very quickly.

In my garden fall-sown plants come through the winter better than clumps which have not bloomed the first year from seed. If given a head start by being planted in a flat in the greenhouse in early spring, the herb will often bloom in August of its first season. Some of the handsomest clumps come from volunteers. Thin or transplant to leave two feet between mature plants. Where drainage is excellent, some specimens of clary will remain perennial if the seed heads are cut off.

Habitat. Clary sage is one of the native plants of Europe. There *S. horminum,* an annual or biennial also called clary sage, has been used for eye troubles. It has showy purple bracts which are more colorful than the blossoms of the slim plants. A pink form has been introduced recently in flower catalogs. The purple and pink bracts are so intensely colored that they brighten any border and are especially favored for long-lasting bouquets. Mexican *S. chia* has farinaceous, or mealy, seeds which are considered an important food by the Indians. Chia is used as a tea, served cold, complete with seeds swimming about in it, in parts of the Southwest. The nutritious quality of the seeds is said to enable a man to work longer hours with little food if he partakes of them. A variety of clary sage, *S. sclarea turkestanica* has all-white flowers. It is useful in a garden planned for moonlight effects.

Uses. A plant which brings beauty and birds to the garden can be valued for its blossoms alone. But clary sage has a culinary reputation. The young leaves dipped in batter and fried make what are called "little mice" in Switzerland. The leaves are not pungent like those of garden sage, the well-known seasoning, but the flowers have a pervasive odor which is not entirely sweet. Some people consider it offensive, but the perfume industry uses it to tone down the raw scents of synthetic fragrances. Goldfinches frequent the plants allowed to go to seed, eating the ripening fruits. Sometimes called "muscatel sage," *Salvia sclarea* was added to wine in Germany to give it a musky bouquet.

Clary Sage Fritters

Add a pinch of salt to 1 cup of flour. Separate an egg, beating the white until frothy. Stir ½ cup wine or beer into the sifted flour and add the slightly beaten egg yolk. Fold in egg white. Dip small leaves of washed and patted dry clary sage into the batter. Fry in deep fat. Leaving a small handle of stem on each leaf facilitates dipping it into the batter. Remove from fat as soon as brown and puffy and dust with powdered sugar. If they are to be served with cold ham, omit sugaring.

Savory, Summer (*Satureja hortensis*)

Height. 18 inches

Leaf and blossom. A slender, branching annual which should be grown in a mass to be effective, summer savory is one of the important culinary herbs. The individual leaves are narrow, with uncut margins, about one inch long by three-eighths inch in width; paired on the stem, but without stems of their own. Small, pinkish-white flowers barely protrude from the sharply pointed, green sepals. The round, brownish seeds are easily detected because there are no hairs within the throat of the calyx. In August, the foliage turns a purple-bronze, making the drift of tiny blossoms resemble a dusting of powdered sugar on the plants.

Culture. Summer savory germinates in about ten days from seed sown in the garden. Little is gained by starting it indoors. It is better to plant more than you want and use the thinnings in salad, risking the first sowing as early as the ground can be worked. Successive plantings, a month apart, will provide fresh summer savory and several cuttings for drying. The plants can stand to be as close as four to six inches apart, because most of the branching is at the top. This tends to make them top-heavy. The thin stems should be hilled up when the plants are three to four inches high to keep the tops from being battered into the mud by heavy rains. I have seen summer savory used as an edging for a bed of taller herbs by placing low, wire loop fence on either side of the plants. They soon hid the support and made a light green, very attractive border.

Habitat. A native of Europe, summer savory could naturalize in our gardens, if conditions were right for volunteers. The annual self-sows freely when some plants are allowed to go to seed and the young plants are sturdier than those sown in rows. But so much of the plant is cut for culinary use that there is little chance of leaving any for seed.

Uses. Savory, as its name implies, is one of the most compatible of cooking herbs. The leaves are used either green or dried in salads, soups and stews. Savory is particularly good with string beans, but it does well too with poultry, white fish, meat loaf and chicken soup. It blends with stronger herbs and is often included in the mixture called *fines herbes* and in an herb bouquet. The French call it "sarriette" and cook a sprig with new peas.

Many people insist that the fresh herb will relieve the pain of bee stings if rubbed on them right away. I have had no luck with this ancient remedy, but then I am rather allergic to stings. Stems of savory, from which the leaves have been stripped after drying, make fragrant fire-starters as the tinder is scented.

Comment. Savory is another herb to delight the dieter. Gerard says, "It maketh thin; and doth marvellously prevaile againste winde: therefore it is with good success boiled and eaten with beanes, peason and other windie pulses." Though his remarks were made in 1597, summer savory is used today with beans.

Dried Savory

Clip the plants down three or four inches in late June to cause them to branch out. Dry these clippings by spreading them upon a wire screen, in a darkened corner of an airy room. After three or four days crisp them in a cool oven, not over 100° F. Then the leaves will crumble away from the stems as you pass them through a coarse strainer. Bottle in an air-tight container.

Whole plants cut for a late harvest should be pulled up and the roots cut off. Then wash them and hang up in bunches to drip dry. Put each bunch, about the amount you can hold in one hand, upside down in a large brown paper bag. Close the mouth of the bag around the stems with an elastic or string. Let the bunches dry completely in the bags—whether it takes a week or a month. When ready to finish processing, rub the bag between your palms and the leaves will drop to the bottom. If they are not crisp enough to crumble through a strainer of large mesh or grind in a mortar with a pestle, complete drying in a cool oven and bottle.

Drying herbs in a brown paper bag

Sesame (*Sesamum orientale*)

Height. 3 feet

Leaf, blossom and seed. Sesame has unbranching stems with close-set alternate leaves. They are ovate, often four to five inches long with entire margins and pointed tips. The tops of the much-veined leaves are smooth but the undersides are granular feeling from glandular hairs. The whole plant is covered with short white hairs which are widely scattered on the upper part of the leaves. The square stalks are deeply grooved in the center of all four sides.

Pale pink blossoms of sesame are interesting from the time they are in bud until the fruit sets. The petals are united into a five-lobed tubular corolla about an inch in length. Before they open, the ends of the blush-colored buds are crimped. At the base of the flower stem, where it is joined to the main stalk, there are curious little round yellow projections which may be nectar glands. The seed pod gives rise to the phrase "open sesame" for when the thin, oval, cream-colored seeds are ripe, the four-grooved, felty receptacle splits open with such violence that the seeds are ejected.

Culture. If the ground is thoroughly warm, sesame seeds will sprout in two days. Blooming starts when the plants are less than a foot tall and continues over a long period. Seeds can be given a head start in the greenhouse if you pot them for removal to the garden in late May. Otherwise sesame does not transplant well.

Plants grown from seed sown in a sunny, well-drained part of the garden are always sturdier than those which have been moved. Mature plants need only ten inches between them as they branch very little. The roots are shallow and small in proportion to the tall plant and so staking is necessary if the soil is sandy.

Habitat. Sesame is one of the oldest cultivated crops which originated in the tropics and has spread around the world.

Uses. Often called "bene," *Sesamum orientale* yields an oil, called "tahini" in the Middle East. The seeds have become popular in this country as a flavoring for crackers and hot breads.

A confection of honey and sesame has always been popular in China, and in our southern states "bene" candy is traditional. It is made like peanut brittle. The roasted seeds are stirred into melted sugar which hardens to a golden brown glaze. You can toast sesame seeds in the oven by placing them in a shallow pan with two tablespoons of butter; stir and turn them often to insure even browning. While the whole plant is without fragrance, sesame seeds have a nutty aroma when cooked.

In Africa and Asia the oil from the seed is used in cooking. One of the most valuable things about sesame oil is the fact that it can be stored much longer than other vegetable oils without becoming rancid. It is rich in vitamins and minerals. The residue left from the extraction of the oil can be used as a protein supplement for cattle and poultry. There are two kinds of sesame seed oils available from importers of middle eastern foods. One is a clear thin oil and the other is a thick paste-like product called "tahini."

Comment. Sesame is being tried as a crop for southwestern states, since it can be grown on land previously used for cotton. The problem is in harvesting: the seed pods shatter when the stalks are cut; then too, pods on the lower part of the stems ripen while the top of the plant is still flowering. Some plant breeding is being done in Texas to develop a strain which will mature evenly and hold its seed through mechanical harvesting. For the home gardener, the best way to collect the seed is to cut the herb as soon as the first pods begin to pop open. Place the stalks head down in a brown paper bag. The seeds will drop out and can be placed in a tin box or air-tight jar after a few days of drying.

Teasel (Dipsacus fullonum)
Height. 6 to 8 feet

Leaf, blossom and seed head. In the first year of growth, the flat rosettes of spatulate leaves give no hint of the eventual height of the biennial. The leaves are coarse in texture with scalloped edges. The second year brings rapid changes. The leaves become sharply pointed with spines along the undersides.

At the prickly stems, the leaves join to form a basin which actually holds water. Darwin observed that ants and other insects ascending the stems to steal nectar from the flowers were often drowned in the leafy wells, which gave the plant its common name of venus basin or Our Lady's basin. He judged that the plant received some nourishment from the decaying bodies caught in the water, which was absorbed through the bristly hairs on the stems.

Teasel flowers, which ring the conical but prickly heads, are short-lived but very interesting. Surrounding the two to four inch heads are bracts, which in wild teasel, *D. sylvestris,* curve gracefully up beyond the cone. As bees and hummingbirds visit the lavender tubular flowers, which develop first in a ring around the middle of the spiny head, the flowers drop off and new rows of bloom open above and below them. Pollen is transferred from one set of blossoms to those on another plant by bees. Many, short, rod-like brown seeds form in each teasel head which is composed of sharply-pointed scales which separate the flowers and project beyond them. The distinguishing mark in cultivated or fuller's teasel, is the way in which these scales are hooked backwards. It gives the whole head a blunt appearance and makes touching the cones a less painful procedure though the leaves and stems of both species are equally prickly.

Culture. Sow the seeds where plants are to remain. They will stand partial shade but the finest teasel is cultivated in rows in full sun. If you include the herb in a planting of other herbs, place it well in the back and plan to cut it before the seeds are ripe enough to scatter when you do. Teasel can become quite a prickly pest if allowed to self-sow freely. The seedlings are easy to scratch out with a hoe the first year but when the deep tap root is formed, the biennial plants are difficult to extirpate. They are also heavy feeders so it is a good idea not to plant them continuously in the same part of the garden.

Fuller's teasel, *D. fullonum,* is called by early botanists "Manured" teasel because it was cultivated, in England, for the dried heads which were necessary to the woolen industry. The idea was that if you fed it well, the wild teasel would sport heads with curved back scales that would be useful. It seems unlikely that a change of species could be effected by farming practices as both teasels come true from seed. One may have been a sport, or chance seedling from the other, which in turn bred like plants from its own seed. A study of the chromosomes of teasels would clarify the picture but this is work for microscopic analysis.

Germinating quickly from fresh seed, D. *fullonum* takes a full summer to establish the basal rosette and deep root which will support the stout flowering stem the next July. It is a plant which needs no staking and when cut the flower heads stand stiffly erect without any special effort to dry them. They turn brown as the seeds ripen.

Habitat. European in origin, teasel was recorded as growing about moist hedges and by roadsides in England in 1824, by Sir James Edward Smith. D. *fullonum*, he said, was "scarcely wild" but he repeats the old idea that it might be just a luxuriant growth of D. *sylvestris,* as it "requires very richly manured soil to preserve its characters, and useful properties." In upper New York State fuller's teasel has become naturalized where there were fulling mills which used the heads to raise the nap on woolen and felt cloth. After wool or felt yard goods were woven or compressed into sheets, in the case of felt, the fuzz had to be raised in another process called fulling.

Uses. The dried heads of teasel have an ancient history of employment for fulling cloth. A large beam fitted with teasel cones can be seen at the Smithsonian Institution in an exhibit of weaving arts. It is similar to the beam of a loom; cloth was passed over the revolving teasel heads so that the curved back spines could raise the nap without spiking holes in it. If the vegetable pick met resistance, it would break off whereas a steel spine would tear the wool. The life of a teasel head was but three days and then the machine had to be reset with cored teasel heads. Now a plastic teasel has been invented which may

make the herb obsolete in the woolen trade but it will take
several years for all the machinery to be converted to it. So the
fuller's teasel is still imported from France in large quantities.

The straight-spined wild teasel is useful to pull off the rolled-
up fuzz on nylon sweaters. The heads of it were used as bottle
brushes at one time. Gypsy comb is another name for the herb.
The stiff, pointed cones of *D. sylvestris* with their graceful
bracts lend a stunning look to dried arrangements. They can be
sprayed gold for Christmas decoration. Whole stalks with the
large center cones and candelabra-like side branches and seed
heads are works of art in nature. They should be cut as soon
as the blossoms fall and before the seeds mature enough to
shatter. They can be dried by standing them up in the garage
or leaving them out in the weather. Teasel stalks are practically
indestructible, but you need stout gloves on to handle them.
Seed of wild teasel is sold as a tonic bird food in pet shops.

Comment. Advocating growing teasel is almost like urging
people to sow thistles. The prickly plant can get out of hand
if allowed to self-sow. On the other hand, when you see the
prices asked for "kits" of teasel heads, from which dried arrangements are to be made, in gift shops, you know that you will
have plenty of use for the surplus. Teasel is not well known
and yet anyone who makes dried arrangements immediately
sees its virtuosity.

Woad (*Isatis tinctoria*)

Height. 3 feet

Leaf and blossom. Woad is a biennial of the mustard family.
It has smooth leaves which almost encircle the upper branching
stems. They are about four inches long with entire or slightly
undulating margins, sharply pointed at the tip. The smooth
texture and bluish bloom of the leaves resemble broccoli.
Mustard-like yellow, four-petaled flowers give way to flat black
seeds which hang on their wiry stems for a long time. The
flowers are pretty in masses at the back of the herb border in
May.

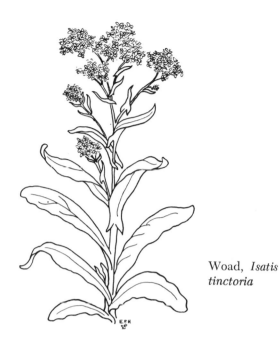

Woad, *Isatis
tinctoria*

Culture. Late summer is a good time to plant woad because
the hardy rosettes of basal leaves get a good start before winter.
Spring sown plants should be left where they are started, with
space of a foot between them. Seedlings can be transplanted if
the volunteers are moved while the ground is still moist. Some
clumps remain perennial if the seed heads are cut early, but
the best plants are those which come up by themselves around
the old roots.

Habitat. Europe and Southwest Asia are the original homes
of woad.

Uses. As one of the most ancient sources of blue dye, woad
has a long history of travel across the northern countries of the
world. Apparently the herb was the chief source of not only
blue but black and green dye in pre-Roman Britain. Azure,
plunket and watchet were the paler hues obtained from it; a
very long immersion in the dye vat produced a rich dark blue.
Indigo has supplanted woad as a source of blue vegetable dye,
but woad was even added to the vat when indigo was first

used to dye blue. Both woad and indigo must be fermented before they will give up their color to water and lime solutions.

The leaves are collected in the fall or spring before the blossoms appear and put in a closed container where they rot to a pulp. This is an odoriferous process but many craftsmen attempt it, in order to give woolens the range of blue only woad creates. The color is not evident until the cloth is exposed to the air. I have seen yarn dyed with woad according to directions given in the helpful book *Natural Dyes* by Sallie P. Kierstead.

Comment. Woad provides such cheerful yellow flowers that it is worth growing even if you are not interested in its link with the past. But if you are you can trace its history to the time of the Picts who painted themselves blue with it to frighten the Romans.

A delightful monograph, written in 1927, by Rendel Harris, *A Primitive Dye-Stuff*, attributes many of the English family and place names to woad. Describing a painting in the National Gallery of the Widow Wadman, he speculates upon who her late husband may have been and how his name was derived from the term "woadman," the person who cultivated woad. Quoting the *History of Somerset,* Mr. Harris relates that the cultivation of woad was in the hands of itinerate "wadmen" who moved from place to place planting the crop in newly broken ground because it was so exhaustive of the soil. Playing games with the history of woad, he finds the English "woad" had a Dutch counterpart "weed" and finally pursues his enquiry back to the Egyptian "watch" meaning blue or green.

A garden can be as fascinating as a crossword puzzle if you have herbs to lead you back through history and etymology.

Wormwood, Sweet (*Artemisia annua*)

Height. 6 feet

Leaf and blossom. A little known herb with intensely fragrant foliage, sweet wormwood deserves much wider popularity. Perhaps it would achieve it if called by the other common name, Chinese fragrant fern. The delicately patterned, pinnate leaves are sweet-scented. They are also green rather than the silver-gray of most wormwoods. The plant has a Christmas tree shape, wider at the base, tapering as it grows tall, with tufts of tiny leaflets crowded in the axils of the branches. The erect, widely-branching stems are grooved, and, as the plant matures, they turn purplish. Small yellow blossoms are rather inconspicuous. Each tiny floret is so enclosed in the green calyx that only the tip shows. But the character of the plant is what gives it beauty; graceful, feathery, almost asparagus-like in appearance.

Culture. Sweet wormwood is easy to grow from seed, but because of its size the annual needs a place all its own: it is too tall for small beds. You can put it in bare spots of the garden where early bulbs have died down. Young plants move readily. So it is easy to pick up volunteers from last year's seeding and place them where you need a green filler. Transplanting has a dwarfing effect which is welcome if you wish to plant a bare spot left by colchicum foliage which has died back. Sweet wormwood will flower under almost any conditions and self-sow to perpetuate itself once you start it in the garden. It does best in full sun. For the informal garden it is valuable as a green foliage plant. In the flower border it offers a pleasant contrast to zinnias and marigolds.

Habitat. Originating in Asia, sweet wormwood is said to have naturalized in North America. This could be true if you counted the herb gardens in which it is at home.

Uses. Dried leaves of sweet wormwood keep their perfume for a long time. They combine well with the scent of lavender and rosemary in sachets and pot-pourri. For flower arrangements and bouquets, the finely-cut, ferny foliage is superb.

ADDITIONAL ANNUALS AND BIENNIALS

If you pick up the *United States Dispensatory* (which is quite a job in itself, as it runs nearly 2,000 pages), you will find that a good many of our garden flowers are listed therein. Space does not permit details about their herbal virtues but here are some additional annuals and biennials it has been interesting to grow as herbs.

Castor bean, *Ricinus communis,* which we in the north must treat as an annual, has moved from pre-Christian days into the modern world where its castor oil is used to lubricate parts in jet engines. It is extremely effective as landscaping even if the broad-leaved, sharply-lobed, almost tropical foliage succumbs to the first frost. As the seeds are poisonous, it is just as well not to let the plants flower. Biting one of the spotted fruits can be fatal.

Celandine, *Chelidonium majus,* is a naturalized biennial in our section of Connecticut. Its yellow juice was used by the colonists as a remedy for jaundice and warts. In England it is grown, as we do poppies, for its yellow flowers in May and June. It thrives in the shade. The blossoms are small but brightly-colored and the foliage is interesting but you should weed it out if the plants become too numerous.

Fennel flower, *Nigella sativa* is a delightful annual, sometimes called Russian or black caraway because the seeds are used on Russian rye bread. The flowers are curiously constructed and have a capacity for fertilizing themselves. Seed of this herb was taken up in Russian space ships along with onion seeds, and other important crop plants. In the 17th century, this nigella and what was called Roman nigella were interplanted among vegetables to deter insects. Love-in-a-mist, *N. damascena,* has very attractive blossoms with blue or white petals surrounded by hair-like bracts. The foliage is similar to *N. sativa;* almost as finely cut as that of caraway. The seeds of both species are jet black and yet those of fennel flower are much more aromatic than those of the garden flower. Pink and red varieties of *N. damascena* are being introduced in seed catalogs. They will add to the flower arranger's pleasure in a plant that is attractive in fresh bouquets or dried for winter ones. Oil of the seed of both species has had medicinal application.

Fenugreek, *Trigonella foenum-graecum,* is a little clover-like annual with white flowers and buff, pea-like seeds. The oil of the seeds is a source of imitation maple flavoring. Unfortunately the plant lends little beauty to the garden but in the 16th century one writer urged those who wished to "possess a green and delectable Garden, let him then sprinkle diligently all the quarters, beds, and borders of the Garden, with the mixture of water and powder of Fenny-Greek tempered together . . ." So the aroma of the seed evidently kept away "noisom worms and creeping things," of which Thomas Hyll was speaking in *The Gardeners Labyrinth,* 1652.

Foxglove, *Digitalis purpurea,* the handsome biennial with velvety, spotted bell-like flowers on tall stalks is the source of the well-known heart regulating medicine. Though its use for that purpose is not as ancient as many herb remedies, it is administered today in much the same way that was described by Dr. William Withering in 1785—as a pill made from the dried leaf.

Fumitory, *Fumaria officinalis,* sometimes called earth smoke because of the way in which the plants seem to float above neighboring plants in the garden, is an inconspicuous annual until it begins to bloom. The ethereal plant has gray, filmy foliage and intricate pink and rose blossoms that place it in the bleeding-heart family. It flowers most of the summer and is always a conversation piece. Though it self-sows freely it is easy to uproot where the delicate plants are not desired. Dioscorides said that the herb being smeared on the brow with gum will keep hairs plucked from the eyebrows from growing in again.

Hollyhock, *Althaea rosea,* the tall biennial flower with red to rosy blossoms has much of the same soothing substance in its roots that made the marsh mallow, *A. officinalis,* a medicine for soothing irritation of the mucous membranes. So, here is another colorful background herb to grow from seed where plants are to remain.

Honesty, *Lunaria annua,* is not found in the *U.S. Dispensatory* but is the "white satin flower" in Gerard's herbal and Shakespeare's plays. The papery seed pods gave rise to many country

names for the plant such as money flower and silver plate—
"and among our women it is called Honestie," says the great
herbalist. As a plant for the shady garden honesty is a treasured
herb. There is magic in touching the drab outer husks of the
permanent seed cases and finding the bright, translucent disks
under their covers. Flower arrangers delight in the dried seed
heads.

Honeywort, *Cerinthe major,* has smooth, spotted leaves and
yellow flowers which bloom from May until September. It is an
interesting member of the borage family because it lacks the
rough foliage of most species and has yellow rather than blue
and pink flowers. The leaves and flowers of the ancient medicinal herb, which self-sows freely after once being planted in the
garden, make long-lasting bouquets. The herb may be annual
or biennial.

Larkspur, *Delphinium ajacis,* seems too pretty a flower to
have been the source of a cure for head lice, but that is the
history of the annual. In some countries it is still used for this
purpose. Sow the seeds in the fall and you will have sturdy
plants the next spring. It does not like hot weather.

Pansy, *Viola tricolor,* is the "heartsease" of yore and was
formerly recognized as a medicine in the *U.S. Pharmacopoeia.*
The flowers of many species of viola were candied for a sweet-
meat and thought to be soothing and therapeutic to the heart.
Pansies are treated as biennials by professional growers who
start the plants in late summer for next spring's bloom. The
blossoms may be used with those of larkspur to add color to dry
pot-pourri.

Prickly poppy, *Argemone mexicana,* is a native annual of the
Southwest whose acrid juice was used in treating skin disorders.
A plant for dry soil, it provides showy white flowers in August.
Though far from its native climate, the herb self-sows in my
garden.

Scarlet Pimpernel, *Anagallis arvensis,* with its reclining habit
and bright blossoms which close with approaching bad weather,
is called "poor man's weatherglass." Though somewhat poison-

ous, it shared in the herbalists' lists of cosmetic plants, the distilled oil being used to clear complexions. The annual, with its shy scarlet, and sometimes blue, flowers quickly becomes naturalized in a garden.

While some of the showiest biennial herbs are definitely medicinal, and sometimes poisonous like foxglove, rampion is neither. But it has legendary connections with fairy tales and witches. The unfortunate Rapunzel of Grimm's fairy tale was bought by the enchantress, who owned a garden filled with beautiful flowers and herbs. Rapunzel's mother longed for some of the rampion which she saw in the garden and assured her husband she would die if she didn't get it. The sorely beset man clambered over the high wall to the garden and stole the rampion. It tasted so good in salad that the woman longed for more. The second trip was a disaster. The witch caught the husband and released him only on the promise that the child his wife was expecting would belong to her. Naming her Rapunzel, the German word for rampion, the witch shut her up in a tower.

Rampion, *Campanula rapunculus,* has edible roots and tender, rounded basal leaves but they are not as extraordinarily delicious in salad as the tale would suggest. The biennial herb is more desirable in the herb garden for the color its bell-like blue blossoms give to the scene in June and July.

CHAPTER IV

Some Perennial Herbs

Annuals and biennials furnish a flower garden with bright colors and an herb garden with many of the most used seasonings, but it is the long-lived perennials which make gardening with herbs a carefree experience. Hardy lemon balm, sweet cicely, lovage, sage and thyme with their foliage of light green, blue-gray, dark woodsy green and pebbled silvery hues offer texture and color interest even when the plants are not in bloom. In England, where herbs have never been set aside from flower gardening, you see large plantings of lavender, nepetas, scented geraniums and santolinas mingling with wide strips of showy garden flowers to give balance to their borders, especially when a section of high color fades. They give grace to their situation, whether it is a rock garden, rectangular formal flower bed or gently curving strip close to the house where they stand in front of evergreens.

Fortunately, propagation of many of the hardy perennial herbs is possible by means of seed. The English offer a greater variety of herbs in their flower catalogs because they have known the beauty of herbs for hundreds of years. American seed houses tend to list herbs among the vegetables, although more and more are being "discovered" here and given a place with new flower offerings. For some herbs, such as French tarragon, which does not set viable seed, it is necessary to start with plants, but tarragon is easy to increase by root divisions made in early spring. For others, those so fine-seeded as to be difficult to handle—such as species of thymes—it is advisable to purchase plants and then make your own separations the second season. The tender perennials are increased by cuttings or off-shoots of mature plants.

Since these fragrant and ornamental herbs comprise a wide range of plant families, it is impossible to generalize. So the individual species are described with their own particular vagaries noted. As many are the official, or original medicinal speces, of the genera, they can be said to be less fussy and demanding than horticultural varieties developed from them.

Aloe (*Aloe vera*)

Height. 2 feet

Leaf and blossom. *Aloe vera* has thick, translucent, strap-like leaves, with awl-shaped soft spines on the margins. The tapering leaves are arranged in a fan shape basal clump and when young they are spotted with white streaks. The rather thick skin covers a transparent jelly-like substance which "bleeds" if one of the six to twelve inch long leaves is broken. The gel in the leaves is a source of healing for cuts, burns and other skin blemishes. For this reason, it has been a popular kitchen windowsill plant and I have dubbed it the first-aid plant.

A. *vera* develops a number of off-shoots or basal buds which can be pulled off the parent root to make new clumps. It usually takes three years for the plant to bloom: a leafless blossom stalk rises above the fan-like clump to bear yellow or reddish racemes of bell-like flowers. In northern climates it does not bloom freely in indoor culture.

Culture. A pot-plant, too tender to live outdoors except in tropical climes, A. *vera* asks very little of the gardener. It needs good drainage but very little watering. Though the juice of the leaves relieves sunburn, the plant does not flourish in direct sunlight. In fact, it will sunburn: the flesh turns reddish if exposed to the sun but quickly recovers if moved away from it. Cold affects it the same way.

In good potting soil, with brick dust or limestone added, the plants can be coaxed into bloom by feeding with soluble plant food. The small plantlets that form at the base of the main stem can be removed to start new clumps. In summer, aloes can be set out under the shade of a bush, either in their own pots sunk up to the rim or directly transplanted into the earth. If the weather is warm the fleshy herb can stand quite a bit of watering, artificial or from rain, but if chilled when wet aloe quickly rots.

Habitat. Though it probably originated in the Middle East, *Aloe vera* came to this country from the Caribbean islands. Africa has many species of native aloes but *A. vera,* or *A. officinalis,* as it is sometimes called, is not indigenous there.

Uses. The emollient substance within the leaf of *A. vera* is used directly on the skin, where it dries immediately to form a protective coating, for burns and abrasions. Some research has been done with the herb for treatment of radiation burns. The whole leaf steeped in water has been used as a soothing drink for a variety of ailments in tropical countries. As a rub, the juice has been placed upon the limbs of children in Mexico to protect them from insect bites.

The dried leaf has a long history as a bitter medicine for cathartic purposes. In recent years the external use has superseded the internal drug applications. A firm in Fort Lauderdale, Florida, which uses the plant extensively, has recently been granted permission to use a picture of the *A. vera* as the trade mark of its Aloe Creme Laboratories products by the U.S. Patent Office. The raw gel of the leaves has been stabilized to retain its effectiveness in the burn ointment, sunburn lotion, shampoo and cosmetics marketed by this company.

In Florida and California aloes are used as landscape plants. The clumps are much larger when grown outdoors in frost-free areas than they ever become as houseplants.

American aloe, *Agave americana,* is sometimes confused with *A. vera* though the former is much tougher in leaf and matures into giant plants. The herbal uses of agave are many: from fiber, found in some species, to an intoxicating drink made from others, but it is not as useful to the cook as our first-aid plant.

A. *vera* is a boon to slight burns from contact with a hot iron to inadvertently touching a shelf in the oven. Just break a small piece of the leaf off one of the outside blades and slice it open. Apply the juice to the injured area and all pain and redness will quickly cease with one or two applications.

The modern convenience of the ancient medicinal herbs is not described in contemporary books, but the early herbalists, Dioscorides, writing in the first century, and John Gerard, in the 16th, speak of its use for wounds and even for preventing falling hair.

Comment. It is interesting to note that this species is being tested for growth under conditions simulating the rarified atmosphere believed to be characteristic of the planet Mars.

Anise-hyssop (*Agastache anethiodora*)

Height. 3 feet

Leaf and blossom. The smooth, dark green, sharply-ovate leaves are covered with a soft gray down on the undersides. They are attached to the main stalk, or side branches, by short stems, in opposite pairs. The edges of the leaves are acutely toothed. The densely whorled terminal spikes of bluish-lavender are showy in August: they attract many bees because the yield of nectar, in the small, two-lipped blossoms, continues throughout the day. The leaves are richly scented of anise.

Culture. Sow seeds where the plants are to remain. They may stand as close as one foot apart without crowding because the side branches are not very bushy. Young seedlings can be moved almost up to flowering time, which is helpful as the plant self-sows freely if the flower heads are allowed to ripen seed. Anise-hyssop is never a nuisance in the garden. If you find volunteers you can move them into the background of a bed where their good color in August is an asset. Fall-sowing is helpful in getting the herb established, as it likes cool weather and can stand partial shade. Seeds will lie dormant over the winter to sprout first thing in the spring. It takes two years to blooming if started from seed planted directly in the garden, in early summer. In rich soil clumps are sometimes large enough to permit division of the basal rosette in early spring but generally it is propagated by seed.

Habitat. Though once introduced by a seedsman as Korean mint, *A. anethiodora* is native to the United States and Canada. Apparently it is found in similar form in Asia because the seed was collected in Korea during the war for the strain so-named.

Uses. The anise-scented leaves invite experimentation as an ingredient of herb tea. Principally grown as a bee flower by honey merchants, anise-hyssop could be classed as a garnishing and beverage herb: its aromatic foliage is used with fruit cups and in cold drinks. It may be dried to increase the bulk of potpourri mixes.

Lemon Balm, *Melissa officinalis* (Philip W. Foster)

Balm, Lemon (*Melissa officinalis*)

Height. 2 feet

Leaf and blossom. Lemon balm is a hardy perennial closely resembling mint in appearance, habit and cultural requirements.

The leaves are heart-shaped with a deep veining which gives them a somewhat wrinkled look. The texture is thin and translucent. Sparse hair is found on the upper sides of the leaves and along the stems. Small two-lipped blossoms hide under the paired leaves; when in bud, they are a creamy yellow, but when fully open they are white and less conspicuous. The foliage has a fresh scent of lemon.

Culture. Balm is one of those garden friends which is always with you once it gets a start. In some sections of New England it has become naturalized around old house foundations. This does not mean that it is a nuisance plant, although it does self-sow profusely in moist seasons.

The seed can be sown very early in the spring directly in the garden or in flats for setting out. The herb will thrive in full sun or partial shade. Fall-planting affords the best germination if fresh seed is used, because nature keeps the life-giving grains under optimum conditions until the weather is ready for spring growth.

Lemon balm can be divided in the basal rosette stage—in late March or early April: just lift a clump and slice it apart with a shovel. After flowering, the herb sends out short runners which remain green most of the winter; these runners make new plants readily if they are separated from the old clump. If the plant has been cut back severely in August to harvest the leaves for herb tea, the new growth that develops at the base can be propagated to make three plants for one, in early fall. If you leave the blossom stalks standing all winter, a ground cover of small seedlings will be noticed around its base in the spring. Fortunately, there is always someone who wants a start of such a fragrant, obliging, easy-to-grow herb.

Habitat. Europe and Asia.

Uses. Just smelling the fruity leaves of lemon balm is cheering to the spirits, even if you don't believe the old herbalists who said it should be added to tea for this purpose. An exchange student from Chile showed me how to make tea with the leaves of fresh herbs, using lemon balm as an example, so that it would have a good dark color as well as the aroma of the leaf.

He put a lump of sugar on a long-handled meat fork, held the sugar over a flame until it carmelized on all sides, and then placed it in a tea cup with several sprigs of fresh lemon balm and added boiling water. He removed the leaves after they had steeped to the right stage for drinking. The tea made a refreshing but not too stimulating drink. In South America all sorts of lemon-scented plants are used for tea, even the leaves of the lemon tree itself.

During World War II we used herbs in canning fruits and vegetables. A leaf or two of lemon balm was found to be delicious with preserved pears. Today, the fresh sprigs are put in iced tea as a garnish: dried leaves are steeped with black tea and mint to make a base for punch; some tips are put in waxed paper bags to freeze for chopping up and adding to winter fruit cups. Rubbing fresh lemon balm on wooden furniture gives it a good gloss and delicious fresh scent. The oils in the herb foliage do the wood as much good as commercial lemon oil polish. If it is a partially upholstered chair, the scent of lemon balm will keep a family feline from scratching the cushions with her claws. A spray of lemon grass oil is sold for this purpose and the scent is very similar.

The platforms on which bee skeps (straw hives) stood were scoured with branches of lemon balm in the 17th century to attract any errant swarm. Today bee keepers grow lemon balm for its high yield of nectar.

Comment. Golden lemon balm, *Melissa officinalis variegata,* which I saw in English flower borders, seems to go quite green here during the heat of summer: it shows the bright glow of its golden markings only in early spring and late fall. But cuttings taken into the greenhouse for propagation have good variegation. Perhaps, there is something about the amount of sunshine that affects variegated plants. In England, where they have so much less than we do, I have seen golden lemon balm, golden comfrey, golden rue and even a variegated dandelion. Miss M. Brownlow, The Herb Farm, Kent, kindly sent me three plants of golden balm which have been perfectly hardy even in sub-zero winters.

Bay, Sweet (*Laurus nobilis*)

Height. Becomes a small tree in warm climates.

Leaf and blossom. The leathery leaves of *Laurus nobilis* are highly pungent even when dried and supply the bay leaves of the condiment shelf. I have never seen the tree bloom, because it is only a pot plant in northern climates. The new leaves are a delightful light green and are produced plentifully in late summer. Bailey describes the flowers as borne in umbels in the axils of the stems, yellow in color, followed by black or dark purple berries. It is a broad-leaved evergreen shrub or tree.

Culture. As a trouble-free aromatic tub plant, sweet bay is interesting to grow, but you need a cool room in which to keep it over the winter. It requires rich soil mixed with plenty of humus or peat. In summer the pot can be set outside in the shade. The old leaves do not fall until the new ones develop, so the small tree has no time of dishabille.

Southern nurseries propagate *L. nobilis* by suckers taken from mature plants, but this is almost impossible with a potted bay. Though it develops many stems, they are not easily removed from the root stock with any portion of root attached. It is necessary to take cuttings which sometimes require more than a year to root. I have tried both old wood and new shoots for cuttings and found them equally recalcitrant. Constant mist of the type used by nurserymen to fog cuttings of evergreens daily would probably be a good solution to the knotty problem of rooting this plant.

The other difficulty which besets the plant under less than ideal conditions is scale. For this an oil spray applied twice a year is helpful. A wash of baking soda in water has been reported to be effective by a lady in Kentucky who cleaned up her plants by regular application of it. If you start with a healthy specimen and keep it away from other plants infested with scale insect, you will have no trouble.

Habitat. Sweet bay is so common along the coast of Southern Europe that the scented wood is used in cabinet making as the inlay material for designs.

Uses. Bay leaves gathered from your own growing plant are quite different from the gray, dried bits found in grocery store packages. A whole leaf may be added fresh from the true laurel shrub to soup, stews and fish stock for a wonderful flavor. It is stronger than the dried herb which is of undetermined age when you buy it. Bay is one exception to the rule of using more fresh herbs than dried in cooking. It is often part of the *herb bouquet* which is dipped in a pot of boiling broth and then removed before serving. Never waste the prunings taken from a large plant to bring it in in winter. If laid under a fire as kindling they give off a pleasant incense.

Comment. Laurel or bay is the classical herb of literature. The new stems are pliant, reddish brown, and easily bent so that it must have been from them that the laurel wreaths were fashioned. Our word baccalaureate comes from the custom of crowning young doctors of medicine with laurel leaves and berries, bacca lauri, which in turn led to the word bachelor. The only problem with growing *L. nobilis* as a houseplant is that you become so fond of it that you might also fall under the spell of the stories told about it since the time of Nero. It seems that during epidemics Roman emperors moved out into the country where the laurel trees grew because they thought that breathing air scented by the trees was a protective measure. Also, if the trees were frosted and died in a hard winter, their death was considered an omen of disaster.

The East Coast bayberry, *Myrica caroliniensis*, is quite different in leaf but was used similarly by the colonists. It has a gray waxy berry which yields the material for bayberry candles. Thoreau used the wax to remove pine pitch from his hands. Myrica is a hardy shrub which can be grown in inland gardens but, unless you have male and female plants, no berries will form. Nevertheless, the fresh green leaves have a delicious pungency.

On the West Coast, California laurel, *Umbellularia californica*, is a larger tree than either of the other bay plants. It has long, pointed leaves of strange scent which is known to have a depressing effect upon those who inhale it. I didn't believe this when I picked a few leaflets in Hidcote Gardens in England, but later I felt strangely dejected and realized I was still holding the sprig in my hands and sniffing of it.

Bergamot, *Monarda didyma*

Bergamot, or Bee Balm (*Monarda didyma*)
Height. 3 feet

Leaf and blossom. A very handsome, aromatic herb with ovate, opposite leaves, bergamot or bee balm, shows its kinship to the mints when it sends out spreading stolons in the fall to make a base for the next year's tall flowering stems. It is a hardy perennial with larger leaves than the true mints. Then, too, the leaves are slightly downy in texture. The long, narrow, tubular blossoms, in tiered whorls, have wide-curving, sharply-lobed lips which seem designed for and certainly perfectly match the ruby throat of the hummingbird, their constant visitor. A few long-tongued moths also pause at the blazing red fonts, but they are mainly attractive to the swift, small birds.

Culture. *M. didyma* is propagated by divisions of the clumps in the spring. It is not a plant which sets much seed, and so if you want the art shades of pink, magenta and mahogany red which have been developed by nurseries, it is essential to buy plants. Bergamot spreads rapidly in good soil and it is wise to lift the clumps in the spring, remove any woody and blackened portions of root, and then set the runners out in a new spot. If you cover the runners with compost in the fall you can keep a patch of bee balm flourishing for several years without shifting plants about. Some winter-killing occurs where the new runners heave out of the soil. Give them a mulch of garden soil or compost to prevent this.

Monardas provide vivid color in the garden in August and are therefore very desirable for their long-lasting blossoms. Unfortunately, the flowers do not last long when picked. The plants will grow equally well in full sun or partial shade.

Habitat. A truly native herb, *Monarda didyma,* is listed as occurring from Quebec to Georgia by Bailey, but the lavender *M. fistulosa,* or wild bergamot, is more frequently seen along roadsides in New England, than farther south. It may be that the red bee balm was common in earlier days before the spread of population uprooted many choice wild flowers. *M. fistulosa* grows most profusely in limestone areas and when it is accompanied by patches of naturalized wild marjoram, with its pink blossoms, it is a lovely sight. I was saddened last summer to see the road crew of the state highway department scything down great patches of the two herbs in full bloom on a sharp bank where they prevented erosion in the most colorful fashion.

Horse-mint, *M. punctata,* grows throughout the southeastern states and has a special charm because of its whorls of yellow blossoms spotted with purple and the pinkish bracts touched with green. The herb is a source of thymol, which is also found in *Thymus vulgaris,* and has been proven to be an antibacterial essential oil.

Lemon bergamot, *M. citriodora,* was sent to me from the

mountains of North Carolina by a cousin of Thomas Wolfe's. I can say now "it groweth in my garden." It has white flowers and dark green, citrus-scented foliage. It is not as free-flowering as the other Monardas but it adds interest to the collection.

Uses. The colonists substituted leaves of bergamot, or Oswego tea, as they called it, for black tea in pre-Revolutionary War days. They learned the use of the herb from the Indians. Jane Colden, 18th century botanist, named it red mint. The number of names a plant acquires through the centuries often indicates the closeness with which it was connected with the lives of people. Bee balm suggests that the plant attracted bees, particularly bumblebees in the case of *M. didyma.* Today's gardeners find that if the herb is tucked under a garden hat the scent of the leaves disperses mosquitoes and small gnats that bother them. It is an herb to dry for pot-pourri, not so much for the bulk of the leaves as for the color of the flowers.

Comment. Bergamots are the exception to the generalization that herbs have rather small blossoms. Its flowers are handsome, long in bloom and valuable in the herb, flower or wildflower garden. To keep the colors pure, it is necessary to propagate from divisions of spreading roots. Self-sown plants vary in shades if different species are grown in close proximity.

Burnet, Salad (*Sanguisorba minor*)

Height. 18 inches

Leaf and blossom. Perennial salad burnet forms charming rosettes of toothed-edged pinnate leaves which vary in hue from blue-green to lime. Though not at all woody, the crowns are almost evergreen. Individual, almost round leaflets, seem to be gathered at the midrib which causes them to fold in half. The cut edges and wrinkled centers of the leaves give the whole plant a crisped appearance. Drops of dew are pinioned on the points of the leaflets, even in mid-day, to give a sparkle to the plant when the sun strikes it. Though not scented, salad burnet—particularly the tender, young leaves—tastes like cucumbers.

Salad Burnet, *San-guisorba minor*

In May, the thimble-shaped flower heads are tipped with rosy, tufted pistils which are the female part of the blossoms. Later they become bearded with drooping yellow or white strands suspending the pollen sacs. The stamens develop only after the pistillate upper florets have been fertilized by pollen from another plant: though they are not much visited by insects, the wind whips the light grains from one flower to another.

Burnet seeds are pale brown, diamond-shaped, furrowed and pitted; so light as to be easily blown about the garden, and rough enough to catch on the fur of passing animals. This is one of the most lowly members of the rose family but not without a charm of its own.

Culture. One of the simplest herbs to grow from seed, salad burnet does not need rich soil. It can be sown where the plants are to remain and the thinnings of the row can be transplanted to other locations. Self-sown plants can be moved when young but mature clumps have a deep root which makes them difficult to move. In wet seasons clumps of two and three-year old plants will sometimes succumb to crown rot over the winter. So, it is a good idea to let some plants go to seed to perpetuate the planting as it is impossible to divide salad burnet. Give the plants full sun. Seeds germinate in about ten days. Flowers do not develop until spring of the second year.

In parts of California and New Jersey, burnet has been seeded
on a large scale to supply forage for sheep and game birds
on land that is too dry for grass crops. In such situations it
may be necessary to fertilize the plantings, but in the garden
no feeding of the clumps is advisable. It is better to keep new
plants coming along rather than to try to prolong the life of
old clumps. The first year specimens are more attractive than
flowering plants. They make excellent edging for a vegetable
garden bed and can be treated as an annual there.

Habitat. Salad burnet is native to Europe and Asia, but there
is a handsome species found in North America with tall spikes
of white blossoms and toothed leaves, S. *canadensis,* attractive
enough for perennial flower gardens.

Uses. The young leaves are more tender and flavorful for
salads than those of the flowering period. Then the blossoms
should be cut back with some of the foliage removed to encourage new growth. People who cannot eat cucumbers will be able
to enjoy the flavor without any of the distress that vegetable
causes. Simply snip salad burnet among the greens in a tossed
salad. The flowering tops and foliage may be steeped in vinegar
to give the same flavor to the greens in winter.

Burnet Vinegar

Fill a glass-topped quart mason jar with freshly gathered
clean leaves of burnet. After washing them, drain well or pat
dry with paper towels. Pack them loosely to within two-
thirds of the top, and then pour over them cider vinegar
which has been heated but not allowed to boil. Seal with a
rubber ring under the lid and store for two or three months
in a dark closet before using.

Catnip (*Nepeta cataria*)
Height. 3 feet
Leaf and blossom. Catnip is a hardy perennial with velvety,
heart-shaped leaves which are neatly scalloped on the edges
and arranged in opposite pairs on square stems. The pale pink
blossoms with purplish dots inside the corollas form dense
whorls along the branching stems. The fragrance of foliage and

Catnip, *Nepeta cataria* (Philip W. Foster)

flowers seems to be a combination of balm and mint. It is attractive to cats, but only if the plants are disturbed. The old saying that if you sow it the cats don't know it, but if you set it the cats will get it, is true. Plants grown from seed are rarely disturbed by felines unless they brush against them, but a freshly transplanted clump can bring cats from all over the neighborhood.

Culture. Catnip is an all-season plant blooming successively from July to late September. Start it from seed sown in early spring or as soon as it ripens in September. It should be cut for drying when the first flower buds form, so that it will become bushy and offer a second or even third cutting. The dense downiness of the leaves enables it to survive very dry summers, but plants which have been allowed to go to seed will not usually live through the winter as well as those which have been cut. It is such a free-flowering plant that even if you cut all the leaves you want for herb tea and catnip toys, there will be some seed heads to stand through the winter. Goldfinches will visit the dried heads even when the snow is on the ground. Where ripe seeds can fall upon open ground, a good crop of self-sown catnips will be assured.

Leaves are larger and more tender where the plants grow in partial shade rather than in full sun. There are several species of nepeta which are used in flower gardens as edging plants because of their neat, gray-green foliage and spikes of lavender bloom. *N. mussini* is the mat-like perennial with blue blossoms in May. It does not exceed twelve inches in height. It is easily grown from seed or divisions of mature plants. *N. grandiflora* reaches two feet tall with lavender blossoms lasting from June to September, if the faded blooms are cut off. It can also be clipped to make a hedge of gray, fragrant leaves. Propagation by division of root stock in the spring or fall is the best way to acquire enough of it for borders. Curiously, cats are not attracted to the other species of nepeta which are more ornamental in the garden than *N. cataria.*

Habitat. Plain catnip is believed to have originated in Europe and Asia while *N. mussini* is credited to the Caucasus and Iran by L. B. Bailey.

Uses. It is interesting to see that some of the most familiar old herbs, such as catnip, known in folklore as soothing to ladies if taken in tea, but stimulating to cats if eaten fresh or dried, are getting scientific scrutiny. Thomas Eisner of the Department of Entomology at Cornell University described tests made on a variety of insects exposed to the vapors from a small tube filled with pure liquid nepetalactone, a terpene isolated from the herb. The majority avoided the tube and kept turning away from it when it was pointed at them. So it is speculated that the growing catnip plant contains certain insect repellent oils. Certainly catnip plants are relatively free from insect damage. If you steep fresh catnip in the water used for sprinkling plants you can send flea beetles scurrying and, if you do it often enough, it will discourage other insects and ants from the garden.

Roman Chamomile,
Anthemis nobilis

Chamomile, Roman *(Anthemis nobilis)*

Height. 12 inches

Leaf and blossom. Bright green, finely-cut leaves in double rows of narrow, linear segments, with solitary flower heads, either with or without rays distinguish the perennial chamomile. The white petals around the yellow disks are conspicuously notched at the tips. Foliage has a delicious apple scent. Many small rosettes of tufty foliage are attached to others to make a flat carpet when the plants are not flowering.

Culture. Chamomile is propagated by seeds or divisions of the low clumps. If the chaff-like seeds are obtainable, they may be planted in the garden in fine, well-drained soil in full sun. Do not cover the seed except to firm it into the raked seed bed and dust a little fine sand over it. English growers say that chamomile should be given a lime-free location which is unusual for herbs. If you want to have a dense ground cover it is worthwhile to prepare the bed with peat moss incorporated into a mixture of sand and soil to encourage it to produce runners. Clover and grass must be weeded out of the chamomile patch or it will shade and depress the foliage in wet weather until patches of decay appear.

Plants sometimes flower the first year from seed, but blossoms should be cut off to encourage spreading. Where the ground does not freeze hard for long periods, chamomile can be used as turf. In our garden plants must be covered with salt hay to keep them evergreen.

Habitat. Originating in continental Europe, chamomile has become naturalized in England but, unlike some of its relatives, it is not common in this country.

Uses. Where chamomile winters well, it invites use between paving stones: its scent when crushed is sweet. Mrs. Grieve, the author of *A Modern Herbal*, says of a chamomile bed, "The more it is trodden on, the more it will spread."

It takes two seasons to obtain enough blossoms to dry them for Peter Rabbit's tea—with its bitter flavor—or for a strong infusion to brighten blond hair. The flowers keep coming all summer so you have to remember to pluck them when you can. (If you put them in a brown paper bag the heads will dry on the stems and can be rolled off at a later date.) In Mexico and South America *manzanilla* tea, as they call chamomile, is a popular tisane. It is bitter but soothing and digestive. Like most herb teas, it should be brewed in a covered glass or china pot to keep the volatile oils from dissipating. The herbalist Culpeper recommends it for a bath infusion to remove weariness from aching joints.

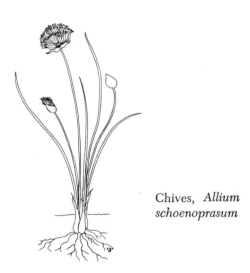

Chives, *Allium schoenoprasum*

Chives (*Allium schoenoprasum*)
    Height. 12 inches
    Leaf and blossom. Botanists speak of chive, but gardeners would never be content with just one plant of the round-leaved,

mildly onion-flavored, grass-like herb; so to us they are always chives. The bulbs or stools (botanists again), are not separate and distinct as with other species of Allium but grow in clusters. From them spring clumps of hollow, light green leaves which are cut for seasoning. In May, very pretty purple flower heads, composed of dozens of individual flowers, appear in elongated spheres. It is possible to let some of the blossoms decorate the plants and still gather leaves for the kitchen. Chives are hardy and live for many years if treated properly.

Culture. All onion family plants need good soil and full sun, and chives are no exception. If the foliage is cut regularly, the plants should receive feedings of liquid fertilizer: apply once a month to chives growing in pots. In the garden, bone-meal may be scratched into the soil alongside the clumps early in the spring, after the seed heads are cut off in June and again in September for renewed growth. Though I have a positive compulsion to rescue the chives sitting on grocer's stands in the spring and put them in the garden, I know there is a limit to how many chives a garden can support: if allowed to bloom and drop their black seeds, the volunteers spring up in awesome numbers around the old clumps.

If given proper care, chives will last a long time indoors and still be in good condition to set out in the garden later. In fact, the key to keeping chives attractive and usable for a long period is the way you cut them. To shear the whole plant ever closer to the bulbs is wasteful. The cut stems turn to stubble, and so the roots are not able to store up food through leaves which manufacture it for them. If you select side spears and cut them to the base of the clump, you will have enough chives for salads, cream cheese dips and garnishing without disfiguring the plant.

Chives may be grown from seed if you are willing to wait a full season to have anything to crop. Otherwise, it is best to divide old clumps in March, or to buy young plants which have been started in a greenhouse. If you start from seed, sow it thickly in a row and do not thin it until the next spring; if you want to save time, plant the seed in August and mark the row well so that you will not weed out the grass-like spears when they first come up in the spring. If you wish to bring chives in for the windowsill garden, let the roots freeze for a month or two first or pot them and put them out to freeze as you do for bulbs you wish to force.

Habitat. The Russians claim to have most of the useful Alliums as natives of their country but, of course, onions, chives, garlic and leeks have moved with man wherever he has travelled. Leeks are mentioned in The Bible and seed of onions have been taken up in space ships by present day Russians. The eighteen inch tall, larger-leaved variety of chives, known as Siberian chives, may well have come originally from Russia.

Uses. Few people need suggestions on how to use chives. It it is the one herb, other than parsley, that you meet in restaurants. A Swedish friend, who does catering, makes a delicious carrot dish by grating the roots coarsely before cooking with just enough water to prevent burning. She adds a lump of butter before putting them over the fire in a heavy covered sauce pan. When the carrots are tender and the water is boiled away, she sprinkles half a cup of finely-cut chives over the quart of carrots just before serving. The green specks are a pleasant contrast to the orange chips of carrots and should be mixed well with them.

Minced chives have been marketed as a frozen food. The oniony spears do not dry well by the usual methods of unheated air ventilation used for most leaf herbs. They can be brought to a crisp and typically chive-flavored dry state if you spread the leaves on a layer of table salt (not iodized) on a cookie sheet, covering them lightly with more salt, and pop them into a cool oven (not over 200° F.). In ten to fifteen minutes the leaves are dry enough to crumble, and the salt has taken on a nice onion flavor. Both can be saved and stored in air-tight jars, either separately or as chives salt with bits of the green dried herb in it. A useful kitchen aid, nice gift idea and not so heavy on the breath as commercial onion salt.

Chives, Garlic (*Allium tuberosum*)

Height. 2 feet

Leaf and blossom. Garlic chives or Chinese chives, as they are sometimes called, are flat in leaf but grow in clumps similar to chives, though the bulbs are individually attached to a rhizomous root. They have the flavor of garlic and offer the convenience of chives in that the green tops can be cut continually from early spring until their late August flowering. The two-foot tall stems bear flat umbels of white florets which are sweet-scented and very attractive.

Culture. *A. tuberosum* is a heavy feeder and demands shifting to new soil or lifting and dividing every third year to keep the clumps neat. The clump is more open in growth and therefore the bulbs separate more easily than do regular chives which have to be cut apart with a trowel when they are old. Flowers should be cut back as soon as the seeds form because if allowed to self-sow, the strong-scented, grass-like seedlings will soon crowd out other plants. Some may be potted to bring indoors if you have failed to heed this warning. They do not need as long a rest period before forcing as do plants of *A. schoenoprasum*.

Habitat. Garlic chives came from east Asia and a very similar species, *A. ramosum*, which blooms in May is a native of Siberia. It has the same tall flowering stalks as *A. tuberosum* with six-petaled florets making delicate white stars in bunches. The individual petals are striped with purple, whereas in *A. tuberosum* the rose lining appears only on the buds.

Uses. The leaves invite frequent snipping for salad seasoning and garnishing and for both cold and cooked dishes. The green, knobby seed heads have been used for seasoning too, even for rubbing a wooden salad bowl to leave a trace of garlic flavor.

Cicely, Sweet (*Myrrhis odorata*)

Height. 3 feet

Leaf, blossom and seed. The leaves of sweet cicely, sometimes called giant chervil, are heavily segmented in a fern pattern similar to that of chervil but they are larger and the texture more velvety. The whole plant is intensely aromatic with a sweet licorice taste.

The two to three foot tall flower stems rise above the graceful clumps to bear showy umbels of white lacy blossoms. Even the ripening fruits do not spoil the beauty of the plants because new leaves unfold constantly to fill in where the flowers are cut back as the umbels yellow in maturity. The seeds are striking when they become jet black. They hang in pairs from the spokes of the umbels, attached at their sharply pointed tips and are lined with deep grooves from end to end. Cicely is one of the last plants to be browned by frost in late autumn.

Culture. Though seeds take about nine months to germinate, sweet cicely can propagate freely by self-sowing in soil rich in humus. Ripe seeds should be planted as soon as they are collected in August. The young two-leaved seedlings can be moved to stand two feet apart in the spring. After a year, cicely develops one or two deep tap roots, about two inches thick, that penetrate the ground to a depth of a foot. These can be dug and split with a knife or sharp spade to make two for one. The fall is the best time to move mature plants.

Sweet cicely makes an excellent foundation planting for the north side of a house where the delicately cut foliage does not receive sun all day. The bed should be dug two spade depths and compost or peat moss added to give plenty of humus. If seeds are planted in flats for potting before they are placed in the garden, they should be frozen first to facilitate germination.

Habitat. A European herb, sweet cicely has an ancient history as a seasoning and fragrant foliage plant.

Uses. In olden days the roots of cicely were eaten as a vegetable or parboiled to be served cold in a salad. The leaves are so plentiful that there are always enough for garnishing or mincing to add to cooked foods. This herb is not usually dried or frozen for winter use simply because it lasts so long in the garden. There is always good picking from the time the first tender green fans unfold in April until the snow covers the bushy clumps in December. The licorice tang seems to have the

same quality as that of French tarragon for removing the fishy
smell and taste of seafood. One gardener observed that the
scent reminded him of fresh trout. Children like to chew the
ripening green seeds before they turn hard and shiny black—
just like licorice candy. The blossoms can be cut for bouquets
where their accompanying foliage is desired for softness and
fragrance.

Comfrey, *Symphy-
tum officinale*

Comfrey (*Symphytum officinale*)

Height. 3½ feet

Leaf and blossom. The hairy leaves and pendant, bell-shaped
lavender flowers proclaim the herb's relationship to anchusa,
borage and pulmonaria. Lush clumps of broad, pointed leaves,
often up to two feet in size, are rough-textured, and, in some
species, almost prickly, on succulent grooved stems. Flower
buds first show a deep purple color but open to a pale mauve.
S. *officinale* has yellow, rose and white-flowered forms. Their
graceful positioning is not apparent at a glance but closer in-
spection shows that the curled-over heads are really very pretty.

Comfrey is a modest pot-herb, one that has been used for

cooked greens. It has so much vigor that it needs careful placing in the garden. It is not a plant for small beds or knot gardens. In the background of a wide border of perennial herbs, or well-spaced in a row along with rhubarb as a permanent boundary for the vegetable garden it has a cheerful aspect.

Knowing comfrey's problems in a small herb garden, I was astonished to see that English flower gardens included many clumps of the herb. But it was a more ornamental species, *S. caucasicum,* called blue comfrey, with plentiful pink and blue blossoms resembling a rather large hairy mertensia plant. It blooms for two months in early summer if the faded flowers are cut off. The foliage has the same slippery juice in leaf and stem that makes *S. officinale* useful for a medicinal herb tea or poultice. The greens can be used as a spinach if cooked in two waters and flavored with chives.

Russian comfrey, *S. peregrinum,* is taller, reaching four to five feet, and has blue and pink blossoms but they are not as showy as the English border comfrey. A variegated form of comfrey with creamy white markings on the leaves was seen at the Oxford Botanical Garden in England. The Herb Farm, Seal, Sevenoaks, Kent, England, offers hardy, strong-growing blue comfrey, *S. caucasicum,* which has to be started from roots.

Culture. It is possible to grow *S. officinale* from seed if you can obtain it. But collecting it—even from your own plants—is difficult because the brownish-black, shiny, almost smooth, ir-regularly shaped, nut-like kernels which form as the petals fall from the flowers, also drop out of the five-pointed green calyx as soon as they ripen. Root divisions are easy to make if you can brace yourself to chop the clump apart with a sharp spade or a cold chisel: almost every split piece of the white slippery root will form a new crown if planted right away.

Symphytum species will grow in full sun or partial shade. They can stand a good deal of moisture. In fact, it is hard to discourage the plants once you have them so that care should be given to placing them in the garden.

Habitat. Comfrey is native from Russia to the Middle East.

Uses. The leaves and roots of comfrey have been valued for centuries in England and Europe for their healing properties. The herb is one vegetable source of vitamin B12 and contains calcium and other minerals. The new growth makes a bland cooked green which is not at all hairy when chopped fine.

It was the root which was dug, peeled and dried to make the medicinal tea used to cure broken bones which gave the plant the folk-name knit-bone. In recent years a substance called allantoin has been isolated from comfrey which does have drug properties for internal and external disorders. There are face creams on the market containing allantoin because it is beneficial to the skin.

As a row crop, Russian comfrey is cultivated for greens for feeding sheep and for dried forage for horses, particularly race horses. In California, on Snow-Line Farm, owned by Thomas C. Kendall, herb grower par excellence, we saw a 40 x 40 foot planting of comfrey which was cut fresh to feed two sheep from early spring until slaughtering time in the fall. The most tender, delicious lamb chops resulted from the animals raised almost entirely on comfrey greens, at a cost far below market prices. The plants were cut frequently, even if the sheep could not keep up with them, to encourage new tender growth. Old leaves with woodier stems were put on the compost where they added bulk and moisture.

Costmary (*Chrysanthemum balsamita tanacetoides*)

Height. 3 feet

Leaf and blossom. The leaves of costmary are more attractive than the blossoms. As with many herbs, the foliage is larger before flowering. Each basal leaf stands erect on a short stem, and is five to six inches long by two inches in width with rounded teeth along the edge. The light green color and slight bloom upon the surface suggests spring in its freshness. Though the leaves feel quite smooth, they have a slight hairy covering which is glandular and releases the scent of mint when any part of the foliage is touched. This is unusual for a member of the chrysanthemum family and accounts for the qualifying word *balsamita*.

Tanacetoides refers to the small yellow button-like flowers without rays which resemble the blossoms of tansy in a wan, sparse fashion. When the plants develop the three foot tall flowering stems, the leaves along them are but two inches in length: the stems require staking if you let the plants bloom.

Camphor plant, *Chrysanthemum balsamita,* is of slighter growth and intensely camphorish odor, with yellow flower buttons with a few short white rays. It does not make as large a clump and the leaves are narrower, more evenly measured in width from stem to pointed tip, whereas costmary leaves are broader at the top than at the base. The whole plant has a grayish cast while costmary is green.

Culture. As species of chrysanthemum, costmary and camphor plant need the same treatment. They should be divided in the spring, and portions of their spreading roots should be reset for increased vigor. They are not usually grown from seed though they both set seed after flowering in July. It is easy to start the plants from divisions, given a place in the sun: in good soil they will quickly regain the size of the parent plant.

Habitat. No one seems to be quite certain where these herbs originated but the old names alecost for costmary and maudeline for camphor plant suggest that they have been carried from Europe to England and thence to America.

Uses. Both herbs invite pressing because the blades are so flat and it was this characteristic that led to their use as markers in books, particularly The Bible, which is the reason costmary was called Bible plant. The fragrance of both herbs is retained in the dried leaf. They may be cut to keep the rather ungainly flower stalks from forming and all the clippings dried for sachets and pot-pourri. Just put the leaves, still on their stems, in a large brown paper bag, close it and forget it until you are blending herb leaves and rose petals for the basic pot-pourri mix. Some people use the mint-flavored costmary leaves in iced tea which is a logical application of them: they were called alecost because they flavored ale in England. Mint geranium is a synonym which only adds to the confusion of genera and species of mints. Costmary is neither mint-like in appearance nor geranium-like in texture or habit of growth.

Comment. In the 18th century Philip Miller, author of *The Gardener's Dictionary* (1731), dismissed costmary as "formerly in greater request than it is at present, many people were fond of it in soups with other herbes . . ." Yet I have known Italian neighbors who swished a leaf of costmary around in the butter in which a scrambled egg was to be cooked. I admit I find the flavor too sweet to use in this way and the scent of the leaf like that of mint chewing gum.

The old writers differ on whether the mary in the name refers to the Virgin Mary; but the other name for camphor plant, maudeline, is supposed to refer to Mary Magdalene. John Parkinson in 1629 sums it up by saying that costmary and camphor plant "make sweete washing water; the flowers also are tyed up with small bundles of Lavender toppes, these being put in the middle of them, to lye upon the toppes of beds, presses etc., for the sweete sent . . ."

Three other species of chrysanthemum belong in the herb garden because of their insect repellent properties as well as the beauty of their flowers and foliage. They are feverfew, *C. parthenium,* with yellow-green, crisp looking leaves which are broadly pinnate and snipped about the edges so that they seem to curl back. The foliage has a spicy scent, typical of chrysanthemum but the root does not spread the way the genus usually does. The perennial plants may be increased by seed—usually self-sown—divisions or root cuttings made early in the spring or fall. They are two feet tall when adorned with white-petaled yellow heads of bloom from June to September. In partial shade the foliage is larger and more ferny looking. It needs rich soil or new ground in which to allow volunteers to replace old plants.

Pyrethrum, *C. cinerariaefolium,* has more finely-divided, grayish foliage in basal clumps with daisy-like heads on two-foot stems. It is not reliably hardy in New England and, therefore, the more showy garden form *C. coccineum,* or painted daisy, is usually grown in its place. Both plants have insecticidal properties in the blossoms which have flattened centers and, in the case of the last, attractive rosy, red rays. Many horticultural varieties have been developed from the perennial which originated in the Middle East. In the drug trade the powder of the dried heads is called Persian pyrethrum while that of *C. cineraaefolium,* is known as Dalmatian pyrethrum though the plants are indigenous to Japan and Yugoslavia, and now are largely grown in Kenya. All species need good soil and plentiful sun to produce many flower heads.

Feverfew was used medicinally for tea to relieve the discomfort of fevers. The fresh leaves steeped in rubbing alcohol, which is then dabbed on forehead and arms when working in the garden, will give protection against small black flies. Heads of the pyrethrums can be dried and powdered for use as a contact poison for insects, or, as with catnip leaves, steeped in the water to be used for sprinkling plants. It is one of the safest bug poisons because it is not toxic to humans.

Geraniums, Scented *(Pelargonium* species)

Height. Aside from some climbing species, most geraniums do not exceed two feet in height, except where they are grown outside the year round, as in their native South Africa, or in California.

Leaf and blossom. There are many greenhouse varieties of pelargoniums. The most familiar to herb growers is rose geranium, *Pelargonium graveolens,* with its broadly cut leaves of a rose-like perfume. The flowers are small, separate pinkish, or pink-veined with purple, and the foliage is the most significant aspect of the plant. Peppermint geranium, with its velvety, grape-like leaves and small white blossoms is *P. tomentosum.* Lemon-scented, *P. crispum* has the most conspicuous flowers of the group, on quite long stems, which are a deep rose color. Here again it is the leaf texture, crisped and of a fruit fragrance, which distinguishes the plant. Nutmeg and apple geraniums have small, almost rounded, soft gray leaves with the scent of spice or apple.

Culture. Propagated by cuttings rooted in sand in full sun in the window garden or greenhouse, pelargoniums often grow too large in the garden to be returned to the house in the fall. The lemon geranium takes longer than most to root, sometimes three months. It needs more water while growing than do the larger-leaved species. Cuttings of geraniums should be made six weeks before frost so that the plants may be potted before the source material is lost. Drainage is important to pelargoniums. The average potting soil mixture should have sand or fine grit added to it. It does no harm to the plants to have the pots small enough to dry out daily between waterings. Blooms will be encouraged by undersize pots, and there will be less danger of root rot.

To avoid confusion, I should also mention another group. Cranesbill geraniums are the hardy plants, some of which are native to North America, which had some herbal use by American Indians. For the shady area of the herb garden, *Geranium maculatum,* with its broad clumps of palmately-lobed leaves on wiry stems and single, rose-purple flowers, an inch across and borne in great profusion, is a bright spot of color from June to August. The more dainty herb robert, *Geranium robertianum,* has deeply-cut, softly hairy leaflets which are pleasantly fragrant. It needs semi-shade and sufficient clear ground to self-sow as it is annual or biennial.

Uses. Returning to the storksbill or pelargonium clan, peppermint, rose, or apple and nutmeg geraniums furnish the basis for tiny bouquets called tussie-mussies. The fresh leaves invite experimentation for garnishing fruit cup and salad. If leaves of rose geranium are put in a pint jar with granulated sugar the sweetening will take up the perfume flavor to be added to any dessert you prefer. Apple jelly flavored with rose geranium leaves is an old-fashioned delight. When it is cut up into fancy shapes and served directly on the fresh leaves as an accompaniment to broiled chicken, as I have enjoyed it at lunch with Helen M. Fox at her home in Mt. Kisco, it is a work of art. The jelly is usually tinted with red vegetable coloring to give a more rosy hue.

Comment. The way one group of plants can develop scents similar to other flowers and fruits, as in the scented pelargoniums, is one of nature's great mysteries. Certainly, perfumes have powers for remedial action against bacteria and affect the psyche to the extent of raising the spirits and stirring appetite and memory. If all other means of gardening were closed to me, the fragrant mimicry of pelargoniums on a windowsill would carry me through the year, provided I had cuttings, a bit of sand, soil and adequate sun. They do not go dormant in winter as do the large flowered show, fancy or Lady Washington types.

Germander (*Teucrium chamaedrys*)

Height. 12 inches

Leaf and blossom. The dark green, glossy, ovate, toothed-edged leaves on straight stems make a miniature hedge when the small plants are set close together. It is hard to decide whether to keep germander clipped to give a formal effect or let the pretty pink or mauve, two-lipped flowers form in August. The tubular, downy corollas are arranged in few-flowered whorls on loose spikes. The fragrance of the foliage is rich and piney.

Culture. Germander may be quickly increased by layers or cuttings. It is slow to germinate from seed; it takes careful handling until the young plants are set in a permanent place in full sun, four to six inches apart. The almost evergreen tops should be protected with leaves or straw to keep them from dying back to the roots each winter. This is the only reason teucrium is not an ideal substitute for the miniature box which it resembles. But, if you can keep a small row garden or nursery for growing divisions of germander, made from the plants which have been heaped with earth the previous fall, so that just the tips of the branches show, you will have plentiful replacements. Layering the stems to cause them to root down is a good idea for many of the more expensive, shrubby small herbs. The whole clump can be lifted and many rooted side branches removed when you want more.

Habitat. The garden germander comes from Europe. We have a native species, called wood sage, *T. canadense,* which is taller, has light pink flowers and can become a spreading problem plant in the garden. It has been used as a dye plant and is not lacking in beauty but the creeping, underground stems must be controlled like those of mint. Another species, called *T. fruticans,* is a tender greenhouse plant with gray, pointed leaves and large, blue flowers which in no way seem like those of garden germander. A creeping, less glossy, green but equally aromatic form, *T. chamaedrys prostratum,* makes a fine ground cover for full sun if you have the patience to keep it free of weeds and grass. It blooms in July and is a very good rock garden plant.

Uses. An ancient remedy for gout, once included in a formula called Portland powder, germander is now used only for ornament in herb and rock gardens. It is almost evergreen except in Northern New England. The foliage is attractive and can be clipped to make designs in small gardens which are divided into geometrical patterns. In miniature bouquets either the fragrant leaves or pretty pink flowers will last a long time. It was one of the strewing herbs of the 17ᵗʰ century.

Comment. Teucrium is a very interesting genus for its very different but ornamental perennials. Parkinson says: "The Germander, from the forme of the leaves like unto small oaken leaves, had the name Chamaedrys given it, which signifieth a dwarfe Oake."

Good King Henry (*Chenopodium bonus-henricus*)

Height. 18 inches

Leaf and blossom. The undersides of the leaves and stems are covered with a mealy, glandular pubescence. The arrow-shaped foliage of this perennial can be used as a cooked green. It is a little bitter but when combined with spinach or sorrel it makes a good pot-herb. The flowering spikes are composed of many, small greenish-yellow blossoms which are usually cut off to accentuate the leaves. Otherwise, it blooms continuously and will self-sow if allowed to seed.

Culture. Mature plants may be divided in the spring: lift the clump and make root cuttings. If grown from seed, the first year greens are more tender and useful for perennial spinach than those of plants which begin to flower.

Habitat. Good King Henry is a European herb brought to this country by the early colonists who were anxious for green vegetables which could be gathered in early spring and late fall.

Uses. It is more of a curiosity in the herb garden than vegetable garden crop because of its perennial nature and elegant name. As one of the chenopodiums, it has earned the name blite, not because it is a problem in the garden but because the word is derived from bliton meaning insipid. John Evelyn says: "It is well named, being insipid enough."

Comment. Actually it is an herb that is more fun to read about than to grow.

Horehound (Marrubium vulgare)

Height. 2 feet

Leaf and blossom. The deeply-veined, almost round leaves and square stems are so thickly covered with down that the whole plant appears more gray than green. At the tips of the new leaves the pubescence is as thick as wool. The small white, sharply-lobed, tubular blossoms are arranged in dense whorls. Both leaves and flowers are rather widely spaced on bent-down branches. The calyx has sharply-pointed teeth which, when dry, become as prickly as burrs: they are likely to catch on the fur of passing animals and thus the seeds are widely distributed. The woolly nature of the herb enables it to live in hot dry situations as the heavy beard acts as an air-conditioning system for the leaves. When very little water is available to the roots,

Horehound, *Marru-bium vulgare*

the down on the foliage reduces the transpiration of moisture from them.

Culture. Horehound is one of the easiest herbs to start from seed. In fact, it is generally propagated only by seed because the plants do not permit division of the roots very readily and are too soft-stemmed for making cuttings easily. It may be planted directly in the garden in the spring or early fall. Young plants should be thinned or set out at least twelve inches apart, in full sun. They will often bloom the first year and if allowed to set seed, the volunteers will make fine plants for the next season. They may be moved when small but are difficult to transplant when mature.

Habitat. Horehound is a European herb which has become naturalized in parts of this country, particularly California and Oregon. Silver horehound, *M. candidissimum,* is a beautiful plant to grow in any perennial border for its silvery leaves and more erect habit than *M. vulgare.* To botanists, the difference between the two plants lies in the spreading rather than recurved calyx teeth. To the gardener, the difference is that between aristocrat and plebian. Silver horehound is less common and more difficult to obtain seed of than common horehound. I first saw it in Helen M. Fox's garden where so many choice herbs have been introduced to Americans through her importation of seed and lifelong delight in raising the unusual from seed.

Uses. Horehound cough drops are the first thing that comes to mind when one mentions the plant which the herbalists described as "hot and dry in the third degree." The fact that the gray plant is a good garden subject, particularly for hot dry situations with poor soil, seldom occurs to people. *M. candidissimum* could win its way with any rock gardener because the silver cast of the plant makes a fine contrast to small evergreens. The rather trailing foliage of horehound makes an interesting background in flower arrangements and lasts a long time in water. Horehound candy can be made at home by the following method:

Horehound Candy

Make a strong infusion of ½ cup dried horehound steeped in 2 cups of boiling water in a covered teapot. Strain after ten minutes into a 6 quart saucepan. Add 3 cups granulated sugar and ½ teaspoon cream of tartar. Boil to the hard crack stage—or 300° F. on a candy thermometer. Pour quickly into a buttered rectangular pan. Mark off in squares before the candy is entirely hard and break into pieces as soon as it can be handled. Sifting powdered sugar over the chunks helps to keep them separate when stored in a tin box.

Comment. The Benedictine nuns of Regina Laudis Monastery in Bethlehem, Connecticut, make superb horehound candy. Some of it was shared with Episcopal monks of St. Gregory's Priory, in Michigan. Brother Gerard reported that they eat it on Sunday as a special treat. The Sisters are more austere and save it for those who are ill with coughs. Sounds like the 17th century but horehound remains as efficacious today as it was then.

Horse-radish (*Armoracia rusticana*)

Height. 2 feet

Leaf and blossom. Horse-radish is a member of the mustard family which does not set seed. The root in no way resembles a radish, being long and thick, with pencil-like projections which can be detached to make new plants; in fact, this is the only way to increase horse-radish. It is found growing wild around old house foundations where the plant may have been first planted a century ago and those plants were vegetative divisions of roots from the Old World. Luther Burbank offered a large sum of money to anyone who could provide him with horse-radish seed that would grow. It was one of the many herbs he sought to improve by selection and hybridization but no one took him up on the reward.

Some botanists are still trying to decide which genus horse-radish belongs to, *Cochlearia* or *Armoracia*. The huge leaves account for the name horse, meaning any plant which is large and coarse. The first leaves that come up in the spring are almost fennel-like, darker green than the broad, pointed blades which appear in May.

I have never seen blossoms of horse-radish but Elizabeth Blackwell, the first lady herbalist, pictures it in her *A Curious Herbal,* 1737, as having small mustard-like flowers and seed pods. She says the blossoms are white.

Culture. Horse-radish was growing near our old house (built in the early 1700's) when we bought it in 1951. For a number of years we tried to get the roots out of the area where the herb garden was planted. No matter how carefully the soil was dug, each spring some indestructible horse-radish came up in the same spot. Probably it thought it had a better claim to the land after 200 years than we did. The old roots seemed tough and difficult to prepare so we went to a neighbor who was expert at growing and preparing his own horse-radish, Mark Van Doren, and asked him for advice.

The poet propagates his plants in the fall, lifting old roots and resetting slim pieces of side shoots at intervals of eighteen inches in a trench. He covers the tops of the root cuttings with three inches of soil which has been well-spaded and mixed with rotted cow manure first. To tell which is the top of each root cutting he makes a slanting slice across it so that he knows which end is up.

Half a dozen plants are sufficient for the average family. As they are hardy perennials, it is a good idea to put them at the edge of the vegetable garden. If you want to be as industrious and thorough as Mark Van Doren, you can dig all the roots each fall, resetting only the best young portions for next year's crop. The making of ground horse-radish from the large roots is quite an operation. Our neighbor does it on a breezy day on a table outdoors because the fiery vapors of the peeled roots will bring tears to the eyes. If all the roots cannot be ground in a meat chopper, using the smallest blade, in one session, the others may be left, unpeeled, in water to keep them from discoloring.

Habitat. Horse-radish has been moved from Europe and Asia to North America by man.

Uses. Horse-radish belongs with the bitter herbs used in the Feast of the Passover. It has a nutritional rationale to account for its long cherished place in kitchen gardens. The roots are high in vitamin C, having almost twice as much per 100 grams as orange juice. There is no scent to the leaves or roots until the latter are cut. Then the pungent volatile oil is released. The white root will turn dark upon exposure to the air and the vapors and flavor quickly evaporate. To preserve them, the root is covered with vinegar and stored in a sterilized jar. I have found that the blender is the most comfortable way to make chopped horse-radish. Vinegar is added as the pieces of root, which have been cut in inch segments, are whirled about, a few at a time. Then all the fumes remain in the glass container. The product is not quite as smooth as ground horse-radish but it is very usable.

Isabella Gaylord, culinary editor of *The Herb Grower Magazine* gives us her recipe for:

Horse-radish Sauce

Whip ½ pint of cream very stiff, sprinkling 1 teaspoon of garlic salt over it, as you whip. Fold in 2 tablespoons freshly ground, frozen or bottled (in that order of preference) horse-radish. Keep in the refrigerator until the last possible minute. The contrast of hot and cold does as much for the meat as the contrast in flavors.

Comment. By the medical theory of counter-irritants, horse-radish root was rubbed on rheumatic or palsied limbs, and held against the face to relieve the agony of neuralgia. Dr. W. T. Fernie, writing in 1879, said that it was a corrective for digestion when eaten with oily fish or rich fatty meat, and at the same time would benefit a relaxed sore throat by contact in swallowing it. Who could have a relaxed throat when swallowing horse-radish?

Hyssop, *Hyssopus officinalis*

Hyssop (*Hyssopus officinalis*)
   Height. 2 feet
   Leaf and blossom. Dark green, narrowly blade-like leaves of hyssop are almost evergreen upon erect, square stems which become rather woody in the fall. The blue blossoms are small and mint-like with two-lipped corollas beloved by the bees. The stamens protrude beyond the petals and are colored to

match them. Since individual flowers are arranged in dense whorls along one side of the stems, they achieve a richly colored effect that makes hyssop useful in the herb garden or perennial border. There are pink and white flowered hyssops which are of the same genus and species. The first flowers appear in June and the last ones do not go to seed until November. The foliage is so hardy that it is a favorite shelter from the wind for birds and rabbits in the garden on a cold winter day.

Culture. Hyssop is easily grown from seed which may be started in flats in the greenhouse in March or planted in the garden in April or May. It will flower from seed in the first year, though it is perennial. Plants should stand eighteen inches apart. Large two or three-year old clumps may be divided at the roots with a sharp spade to make several new plants from each one in early spring or fall. Seed of hyssop may be sown in late fall to germinate first thing in the spring. It is often possible to find volunteers about the old plants which have gone to seed. If seedlings are lined out in a nursery bed for the first year, you will know the color of blossoms before putting them in a permanent place.

A hedge of blue, white and pink flowered hyssop makes a delightful border in full sun; it will be more lax in habit if grown under the shade of trees. For more formal beds such as the segments of a knot garden, a combination of blue hyssop alternating with gray Roman wormwood makes an interesting design.

Hyssop is not demanding of soil, so long as it is well-drained. The plants need no winter covering but they must be pruned back to the ground in the spring. The old stems become woody and sharp-pointed, making it hard to weed among them.

Habitat. Not the true hyssop of The Bible, *H. officinalis* is a Mediterranean coastal plant which serves as one of the bitter herbs in Jewish ceremonies. The herb which grew in the Holy Land at the time of the compilation of Holy Scripture is thought to be a species of origanum by students of taxonomy.

Uses. The chief use of hyssop today is for color and design in the herb garden. It was one of Thomas Tusser's "strewing herbs," some twenty plants listed in his *Five Hundred Points of Good Husbandry,* 1577, as proper to spread on walks and floors to tread on to release their scents. Elizabeth Blackwell, almost two hundred years later, says that it is excellent for removing black and blue spots from bruises. This I can vouch for some 200 years later still. A friend who was hit in the eye by a falling green apple made a compress of the leaves steeped in water and held it to her eye when it was cool enough to handle. She suffered no "shiner" at all. Bees visit the blossoms of hyssop in great number. The flowers are numerous and yield nectar over a long period. The scent of the leaves is a matter of opinion. Some people find it antiseptic and pleasant. To me it is musky and strongly resembles the rich smell of civet, as though it had been brushed by a skunk, when you touch it. It is not an unpleasant odor but neither is it sweet-smelling.

Iris, Florentine (*Iris germanica florentina*)

Height. 2 feet

Leaf and blossom. The familiar iris foliage is topped with white, tinged with a shadow of blue, flowers. The plant is slightly more slender than the newer types of named iris but it makes a fine show in May in any garden because it can be seen from quite a distance. The herb is one of the bearded iris group. It is not an edible herb.

Neither this iris nor still another bearing a somewhat similar name, blue flag, should be confused with sweet flag, *Acorus calamus*—which has narrower, yellow-green foliage with a prominent rib down the middle and a curious flower structure like a green finger projecting directly from the leaf about mid-way down. The tiny flowers are crowded along this yellow-green spadix. The rhizomous roots and lower stems which are attached directly to them have edible centers which have long been used in folk medicine. They are nut-like in flavor and make a pleasant addition to salad if cut up in it.

Culture. Divisions of rhizomes are made in August and early

September. Plants should be given a well-drained, sunny location with soil that has not been enriched with animal manures. The best blooms occur the second season after planting.

Habitat. The original home of the old-time iris or flag of the herbalists is lost in antiquity. Wild blue flag that grows in wet places from Labrador to New England is not an edible plant. Confusing its dark green stems with those of sweet flag, *Acorus calamus,* could be dangerous because the *Iris versicolor* or blue flag is somewhat toxic. Sweet flag has become naturalized in low places throughout New England but it is really a plant of the Mediterranean regions.

Uses. Florentine iris, the white flowered form, is one of the sources of the perfume fixative called orris root which is made from the dried rhizomes. While it does not have a strong scent of its own, it has the quality of holding the volatile oils of other perfume plants and is much used in cosmetics and face powders today. Orris may be purchased at drugstores for use in pot-pourri and home-made sachets.

Lady's Mantle, *Alchemilla vulgaris*

Lady's Mantle (*Alchemilla vulgaris*)
    Height. 18 inches
    Leaf and blossom. The perennial, extremely hardy ornamental herb, with the charming name which derives from the fact that

the leaves appear pleated like the folds of a lady's cloak, is neither fragrant nor flavorful. It is in the rose family but the corymbs of small yellow-green flowers in no way suggest the glamour of that favorite. But, taken in multiples, the blossoms have an airy grace and mimosa color. The leaves are velvety and where their toothed edges are folded and exposed to the air, drops of dew collect on them and remain throughout the day. It is one of the most interesting and hardy foliage plants of the herb garden.

Culture. In the garden, lady's mantle will self-sow if left undisturbed after blooming, but starting it from seed is rather slow and difficult. Old plants can be divided after blooming in June and July, and crown cuttings reset to make new clumps. The herb has a deep root, like the rose, with no breaking point for separation. But it is possible to lift the clump and work parts of the basal rosette asunder with some root attached to make new plants in early fall or spring.

Habitat. Species of alchemilla have been reported growing wild in Scandinavia, and as far north as the Arctic regions, so it is no wonder it is adaptable to the coldest situations.

Uses. The blossoms go with almost all the brighter flowers of early summer, last for two months in the garden and can be dried for winter bouquets. Individual leaves are so artistic that they invite pressing for making spatter prints or placing under rice paper to make notebook covers.

It is a favorite with people who collect plants named for the Virgin Mary and the genus name suggests that it was used by the alchemists as well as the herbalists. The latter believed it stopped bleeding if the fresh root was used in an astringent lotion.

Lavender (*Lavandula spica*)

Height. 2½ feet

Leaf and blossom. Lavender has narrow, blunt-tipped, grayish leaves measuring about one and one-half inches long by one-quarter inch wide, covered with a whitish mealy down. The stems are also hairy, woody at the base and branch at angles from the dense, leafy clump. The bluish-lavender blossoms appear on tall, leafless spikes in June. The small but vivid flowers are arranged in dense rings, becoming closer together at the blunt apex of the stem. The two-lipped violet corolla is paler than the ribbed, purple calyx. At the base of each flower is a shield-shaped yellowish bract. The color of the unopened buds is more brilliant than that of the unfolded flowers. They should be cut for drying just as the bottom rows of bloom start to expand their scalloped lobes.

Lavender has many varieties of varying degrees of hardiness. *L. spica* is the true lavender of the essential oil industry and it has been crossed with *L. latifolia* which has branching floral stems and somewhat broader leaves, called spike lavender in the trade. These two species hybridize readily and many of the fancy named varieties are crosses between the two above species. In France, where great fields of lavender are cultivated for the perfume industry, *L. spica* grows naturally at higher altitudes than support *L. latifolia*. In my garden, a strain of true lavender developed or rather separated from mixed lavenders by L. J. Wyckoff, who grew the herb for distillation of the oil in the state of Washington for many years, has proven hardy at temperatures as low as 25° below zero F. The branching-stemmed, taller spike lavender was not able to survive one winter of zero or minus 10° F.

In California it is possible to grow many tender species of lavandula. Miss Edna Neugebauer, chairman of the Southern California Unit of the Herb Society of America has made a large collection. She has planted specimens of her world-wide genera in the herb garden at the Los Angeles City and County Arboretum. From her I received seed of a soft-leaved, greenish foliage lavender, *L. multifida*, many years ago. It is in bloom all winter in the greenhouse and the purple spikes are welcome in winter tussie-mussies. The scent is more turpentiney than true lavender. Though tender, it is easy to grow from seed which forms on plants set out in the garden each summer. Some of the seeds fall to self-sow, I have discovered, about the time to take the old plant indoors again. Sometimes it is easier to pot one of the seedlings than move the mature clump which really has no resting period.

Culture. Lavender is difficult to start from seed, for the grains must be fresh and they need a long, cool germination period. Some of the best seedlings come from dried heads of lavender which have been allowed to ripen seed on the plants. They may be scattered on a freshly dug seed bed in late autumn instead of being carefully rubbed out of the stems and planted in a furrow. Somehow the scattered seed heads shade the young plants with their dry stems and underneath the heap you may have one of the best starts of lavender seedlings ever sown. Few people have the means to be so lavish with lavender seeds, so start purchased seed in flats in a cool greenhouse in early spring. The best results come from sowing them on a half-inch layer of clean sand sifted over the flat filled with regular potting soil. Sphagnum moss or vermiculite, which we usually advise for covering the soil to make a planting layer that is sterile enough for seeding, stays too wet for lavender. Even the seedlings need good drainage or they will quickly rot. The layer of sterile material over the soil helps to reduce damping-off fungus found in the soil.

The first season lavender will grow no more than two or three inches. The young plants need protection from wind during the winter—such as a mulch applied after the ground is frozen. Salt hay is the best material but pine needles can be used if they are removed after the ground thaws. They should not be left to rot into the soil because of their acid nature. Lavender is a lime-loving plant. The proper degree of alkalinity can be created by adding ground limestone where the pH is below 7.

Propagation by cuttings or layered divisions of three-year-old plants is very simple. Cuttings should be made from woody stems which will root in sand or perlite. A dusting of root-promoting hormone powder helps to prevent rotting and speeds up rooting. To make divisions of plants it is necessary to lift the whole clump. Ease the lower stems apart so that they break with a part of the root attached. Do not let them remain out of the soil any longer than absolutely necessary; keep a wet burlap bag at hand to cover the portions of the root not yet set in new holes.

Lavender roots are long, black and rather stringy. Only at the base of the clumps are many small rootlets evident and it is these which produce satisfactory divisions. Separations can be made in early spring, just as the new leaves begin to break or after the plants are cut back for collection of the flowers or removal of seed heads. As it takes two to three years to produce a good stand of lavender plants that will blossom, it is helpful to be able to make divisions of old plants to hasten the process.

The amount of humus in the soil is more important to lavender growth than any fertilizer which has been tested in commercial plantings by Mr. Wyckoff. Some of the finest dried lavender is produced at Snow-Line Farm in Yucaipa, California, by Thomas Kendall who uses tons of compost under a straw mulch for his herb acreage. In the fall, the mulch is pulled away from the base of the lavender plants; then ground kelp, limestone and powdered granite are spread around them. Several inches of compost are added and the mulch is replaced. By spring all of this has turned into humus which suits the plants admirably.

Trimming the plants in August makes it easier to cover them with salt hay or straw in November. It also produces shapelier clumps the next summer for if you trim them in the spring you sacrifice the blossoms in June.

Habitat. Lavandula species are found all along the Mediterranean coast. *L. stoechas* gets its name from the Stoechades Islands. *L. viridis,* a green-leaved sort, comes from Portugal, while *L. pedunculata* is native to Spain. *L. spica* comes from southern France, Italy and Dalmatia.

Uses. Lavender is one herb which has never gone out of use from the first century A.D. when Dioscorides said it was good for "griefs in ye thorax" to the present time when the oil is used to perfume soap, powder and toilet water.

One of the most charming uses of the dried flower stems is as a lavender fan. The longest sprigs are laid upon a semi-circle of organdy with another layer of the material above them. They are fanned out at the top, the stems bunched together to form the handle. The material is pleated to allow for the bulk of the flower heads between the layers and to bring it together at the center to close over the stems. Then it is stitched by hand to close the edges: the larger, lower layer of organdy is scalloped at the top and the upper edged with embroidery. Satin ribbons cover the bunching at the handle with many loops of a bow; the stems are held together by lacing them with the ribbon. The scent of lavender remains for years in the dried flower heads. When the dainty fan is used, the passing of air through the fine organdy brings with it wafts of lavender fragrance. A more delightful gift for someone who is hospitalized would be hard to conceive, unless it were a pillow of scented herbs.

Just smelling the fresh herb is said to relieve headaches, and the old herbalists were certain that it cured everything from cramps to migraine, tremblings and passions of the heart. The oil is believed to be anti-aphrodisiac which might explain its popularity in Victorian days. It is one scent which will overcome mildew odor if the oil is sprinkled in musty trunks.

Comment. It is easy to dry your own lavender just by hanging the cut heads in loose bunches, upside down, in a dark but airy cupboard. Unfortunately many people are discouraged from attempting to produce their own dried lavender by smelling the synthetically perfumed, spent flower heads which are sold at flower shows in small baskets. They have neither the color nor aroma of true lavender and I would ban them if I were in charge of commercial booths.

Lovage (Levisticum officinale)

Height. 6 to 8 feet

Leaf, blossom and seed. The glossy, much-cut basal leaves with irregular margins are arranged in groups of three leaflets about three inches long by two inches wide. They are carried on hollow stems which seldom exceed two feet in height. Suddenly, in June, tall, five-foot high blossom stalks shoot up from the lush clumps. They are crowned with compound umbels of yellow flowers. These turn to brownish, elliptical, ribbed fruits of the same celery-plus-curry aroma of the rest of the plant. If the busy goldfinches leave any seeds to ripen on the heads, they should be gathered for sowing in September because lovage seed loses its viability quickly unless stored in a freezer.

The hardy perennial nature of the plant with its increasingly strong and deep roots makes it a subject for the background of the herb garden or a permanent place in the vegetable patch along with comfrey and other large pot-herbs.

Culture. Lovage is most easily started from seed planted in the fall. It is sown in rows in a seed bed for transplanting to the garden in the spring. It needs rich, well-drained soil and full sun. It will stand partial shade, as at the edge of a shrub planting but the shapeliest clumps are those with plenty of room around them. Mature roots may be dug and chopped apart in the fall: new clumps will form from each piece with a bit of leafy top attached. In hot climates lovage must be given shade part of the day.

Habitat. Garden lovage, originating in southern Europe was also once called *Ligusticum levisticum* which gives a clue to its origin in the part of Italy known as Liguria, now Genoa. The Roman ligusticum evolved into the late Latin levisticum from which it became levesche in Old French. On Middle English tongues this was transferred to loveache (pronounced love-aitch), hence our present day Lovage.

Uses. Lovage may be used in any dish that would be improved by a celery-like seasoning, particularly meat loaf, stew, sorrel soup, fish sauces, roast chicken and turkey salad. The fresh leaves are superb if minced fine and added to green salads or tied with a string and steeped in hot foods during the last few minutes of cooking. For poultry dressing the dried herb is useful. It keeps a fine green color through the dehydration process, especially if it is kept out of the light and crisped off in a cool oven.

Lovage seeds are ground and added to beaten biscuits for a richer flavor than celery seed gives hot breads. If they are to be used in cooking, the seeds should be scalded in boiling water before drying to remove any insects. As you will not want to use a residual poison on herbs intended for culinary purposes, it takes close observation to be sure that the seed heads are free of aphids. If they are infested, they can be pulled down from their great height, while still green, and dipped in soapy water to float off the sucking insects. The green stems are supple for all their towering distance and they can be arched over without breaking them.

Comment. If you want to keep lovage a low plant for harvesting the foliage, cut off the flowering stalks as soon as they appear. To dry the herb, use the paper bag method. Collect leaves with stems long enough to tie into a loose bunch. Wash them and let them hang up to shed all drops of moisture before enclosing them in a large brown paper bag. Tie the opening of the bag around the stems and suspend it from a line or peg in the pantry. A month or more later, you can take it down and process the leaves for bottling. If they are not thoroughly crisp, spread them on a cookie sheet in a cool oven until they will crumble. Then put them in an air-tight container.

Lovage freezes well without blanching. Just pack the leaves in small wax paper envelopes or bags and place them in a freezer container so that you can take out one at a time for a single dish. Once you try lovage you will understand why our children used to say it is called "lovage because you love it."

Marjoram, Sweet (*Majorana hortensis*)

Height. 12 inches

Leaf and blossom. Also called knotted marjoram, the tender perennial with bluntly ovate leaves, smooth at the margins and covered with a downy velvety hairiness, has curious knot-like arrangements of blossoms. The tiny flowers are two-lipped white tubes barely protruding from between a series of soft, rounded, overlapping scales. There are a dozen or more flowers in each hop-like inflorescence. The ripe seeds are minute brown grains which must be handled with care in planting. Sweet marjoram is sown annually though the woody mature plants can be carried over the winter in a greenhouse. They change character under indoor conditions becoming rather lax and much lighter green. In the garden, the plants are erect and have a grayish color.

Culture. Under ideal conditions, fresh seed will come up in twelve days even when planted right in the garden but the weather must be evenly warm and the soil must be screened or raked very fine to just barely cover them. The most economical way to get a number of plants of sweet marjoram is to sow the seeds in a sterile medium such as sphagnum moss or clean sand over soil. They are subject to damping-off fungus soon after germination, so it is wise to soak the plastic flats from below rather than sprinkling from above. If there is evidence of rot at the soil line, a sifting of clean sand or shredded sphagnum between the plantlets will save them.

Seedlings should be transplanted when they have four true leaves. This is usually done inside and the young plants are then hardened off for a few weeks by placing them outside in a sheltered place during the day and returning them to the heat at night. Wind is one of the greatest enemies of small seedlings.

Where there is no frost, sweet marjoram remains perennial and mature clumps may be lifted and divided in the spring. They should be set ten inches apart in rows.

For drying, the herb is severely cut just as the first knot-like buds appear. Two or three clippings are obtainable in a good season. They are frost-resistant and plants can be cut as late as November quite far north.

Habitat. Native to Europe, sweet marjoram has been given a separate genus from the origanums which are closely related and give us the seasoning oregano. A truly perennial herb with leaves larger and attached directly to the stem without petioles, by the name of *Majorana onites*, is described in *Hortus II* but gardeners in this country do not seem to cultivate this native of Southern Europe and Asia Minor. It is much sought but seed so labelled usually turns out to be *M. hortensis*.

Uses. Sweet marjoram is one of the most versatile of culinary herbs. It has a distinctive warm, pleasing taste which enhances many foods without altering their natural flavor. Roast lamb, egg dishes, macaroni and cheese, pea soup, baked fish, green salads and omelets are but a few dishes with an affinity for marjoram. It blends well with other herbs particularly sweet basil, thyme, chives and parsley. For this reason it is often found in the *fines herbes* mixture.

Comment. Since marjoram hugs the ground, its downy leaves pick up a film of earth. The clippings must be washed and drained well before drying. They can be spread on wire trays or screens in an unused bedroom and turned daily to hasten the process. Do not let the sun strike them if they are in a room with windows. If you have no more spare space than I do, in your home, you will let them drip dry in bunches and then put them in the large paper bags until you have time to roll the leaves off the stems. If you like dried herbs very fine, you can pound dry marjoram in a mortar with a pestle or grind it in a meat chopper before bottling. The important thing is to remove as many of the small, sharp bits of stem as possible.

Gerard, in 1597, said sweet marjoram and sweet basil should be watered at noon when the sun shines hottest rather than in the evening or morning as most plants are. Even in his day there was a question about the different kinds of marjoram. He mentions amaracus which is the gray-leaved, marjoram-scented herb called dittany-of-Crete which is grown as a pot plant by herb gardeners. It has pink blossoms in "scalie, or chaffie huskes, or eares, in August," as Gerard aptly describes them.

Marjoram, Wild (*Origanum vulgare*)

Height. 2½ feet

Leaf and blossom. The hardy wild marjoram of England and from there to New England roadsides, is cultivated for its showy pink flowers rather than for the slightly scented foliage. The leaves are smooth, broadly ovate, with a glandular texture. They are carried on short stems in opposite clusters on the rather woody flower stalks. The pink, tubular corollas form broad, flat-topped clusters. Between the blooms are ovate, leaf-like bracts marked with purple. The sharply pointed calyx is tinged with pink, the interior becoming filled with white hairs as soon as the petals drop.

Besides being a hardy perennial and much taller than sweet marjoram, *O. vulgare* is a very different looking plant. The foliage is dark green, downy only on the undersides of the leaves. It makes a thick ground cover in the spring but the flowering stalks are tall and leafy too. The root stock spreads by mint-like runners which become so thickly woven that plants must be divided every few years. For this reason wild marjoram might well be encouraged to naturalize on sunny road banks or sharp slopes where a good soil-retaining plant is needed. It can be clipped by a mower to make a low green cover or allowed to spread and self-sow with abandon.

Culture. Wild marjoram is easy to start from seed or root divisions. The seed is so fine that it had better be sprinkled on top of the soil and firmed in rather than covered with much soil. It may be started right in the garden or in a flat or seed bed in early spring. The young plants are easy to move at any time. They should stand at least twelve inches apart. If you want a strong, colorful herb for dried arrangements, a buffer for grass and weeds, and plenty of blossoms in August and September, wild marjoram is a very good choice. It will withstand partial shade though it blooms less.

Habitat. Origanum means "joy of the mountains" and it is the less hardy *O. vulgare viride* which provides the Greek oregano used for seasoning. The herb may be grown from seed found in a bunch of dried oregano imported from Greece. It seems to be able to stand New England winters if not allowed to go to seed. It has white flowers and lighter green foliage, but otherwise is

very similar to wild marjoram. The flavor is more pronounced
when the herb is dry than when it is fresh.

Uses. Wild marjoram has landscape possibilities around outcroppings of rocks in a lawn where it is impossible to mow right
up to the stone. The herb will hold its own against grass and can
be mowed several times and finally allowed to bloom at the end
of the summer to enjoy the attractive, long-lasting flowers.

The culinary herb oregano, indispensable for pizza and other
Italian dishes, dries quickly in large brown paper bags. The long
stems are cut just as the flower heads form. They are washed
and hung up to drip dry and then enclosed in the bag. Home-
grown oregano has a much better flavor than the imported herb
bought in grocery stores. For one thing it is fresher, greener because it has not been dried like hay in the open, and sometimes
the foreign product is a mixture of other plants which happened
to be growing along with it. In Latin America a species of coleus
is called oregano and used in the same fashion because the flavor
is similar. It is *Coleus amboinicus,* a tender perennial which is
propagated by cuttings and grown as a houseplant in the
north.

Wild marjoram was called bastard marjoram by Gerard while
what we term oregano was "organie" to him. Of the latter he
says that the whole plant is of a sweet, sharp smell and biting
taste. He marvelled that the root endured in his garden while
the leaves remained green "all this winter long, 1597" though
he had heard that it would perish as did sweet marjoram.
Gerard's "organie" came from Candie and was called by the
Italians origano, by the Spanish oregano—so it is nothing new
for herb growers to be able to say "it groweth in my garden."

Comment. It is said that the flavor of goat's meat served in
Greece as a great delicacy comes from their foraging on oregano
which grows on the mountainsides. Colonial housewives used the
tops of wild marjoram to obtain a purplish color on wool and reddish brown on linen. They also made a tea of the herb for relief
of spasms, colic and indigestion.

Mint (*Mentha spicata* and other species)

Height. 2 feet

Leaf and blossom. The species of mint are numerous and often confused by nurserymen. In describing them it is easiest to compare each one to the best known garden mint, *Mentha spicata,* or spearmint. It has bright green, smooth, lanceolate leaves about two inches long with sharply-pointed, widely-spaced teeth on the margins. They are attached directly to the stem in opposite pairs. The flowers form pointed spikes of close-set whorls. Each tiny, five pointed, tubular corolla is a delicate pink color. It is surrounded by a purplish, streaked, shining, hairy calyx about one-third as long as the blossom. The flavor of spearmint is the familiar taste associated with mint sauce and mint julep.

Many hybrids of spearmint have developed which differ slightly in aroma and foliage. Curly mint is one with wrinkled leaves which are sometimes almost heart-shaped. The fragrance is similar to spearmint. The wild mint, *M. arvensis,* which is found along streams in fields looks like a hairy form of spearmint.

Orange mint, *M. citrata,* is a distinctly different species. It is sometimes called bergamot mint because the heart-shaped leaves about two inches long are mottled with purple. Whorls of lavender blossoms comprise the blunt, short, terminal flower spikes. Individual petals, fused into a short, tubular corolla, are round-lobed. The glossy, dark green foliage has a distinct citrus tang which goes well with fruit drinks and iced tea.

The variety of peppermint, *M. piperita,* called black mint, has purple stems and dark green leaves. It is about three feet tall when crowned with spikes of lavender flowers in July. The distinguishing feature of peppermint is the longer leaf stem.

Applemint, with rounded, sessile leaves which are net-veined rather than veined in a feathery pattern, is called woolly mint or dry-land mint, because it will grow with less moisture than all the other species. Botanically it is *M. rotundifolia* which is truly descriptive of the hairy, rounded leaves. It is one of the tallest and sturdiest of the mints. A variegated slightly lower form known as pineapple mint, *M. rotundifolia variegata,* is even handsomer. The vigor of the plant is not as great as those of applemint but it makes up for its lack of hardiness by beauty of leaf which is marked with white. Some sprigs are pure white at the tips. It has a pleasant fruity aroma and substitutes nicely for spearmint in cold drinks. The flowers of both species are pinkish white on branching spikes.

The other very downy mint is *M. longifolia* with narrower, long leaves which are pinnately veined. It is not as pungent as the others though it is said to be the mint mentioned in The Bible so it must be a very early form. What it lacks in beauty it makes up for in spreading ability. It has to be dug out of the bed and reset frequently or it will take over a whole garden. It will grow in dry sandy soil as well as applemint.

American applemint, a smooth-leaved, sometimes variegated with gold form, is *Mentha gentilis.* The scent of the foliage is sort of a cross between that of spearmint and peppermint. Some sterile forms of this herb are replacing spearmint in the commercial production of oil of mint. In the trade this is occasionally confused with *M. spicata.*

Corsican mint, *M. requieni,* is a tiny, round-leaved mint with flat foliage that does not exceed an inch in height even when it produces pinkish flowers. It is not very hardy but can be grown in a sheltered rock garden where the ground is moist. By a pool, it makes a pretty mat of intensely mint pungency and will spread over a rock like a brilliant scented moss. It has to be kept free of competition with larger plants and should be covered in winter with pine needles or salt hay.

English pennyroyal, *Mentha pulegium,* is quite flat also, until it blooms in July. Then, graceful wands of whorled lavender blossoms stand twelve to eighteen inches tall. The leaves are roundly ovate with a citronella scent which is anathema to fleas and mosquitoes. A covering of salt hay, pine needles or even just soil heaped over it helps it to survive sub-zero winters.

Culture. The spreading runners of mint constantly seek fresh ground. For this reason commercial plantings are renewed each year by lifting the roots and resetting them in furrows with soil to cover roots and new shoots. If this is not possible in the garden, root prune the patch by spading the perimeter with a sharp blade thrust down far enough to cut off the stolons (creeping stems which root down). After a few years lift and reset all species of mint.

Manure should not be used fresh on mint plantings. It will encourage a dread rust disease spread by spores which infect new plants placed in the same ground. The great mint fields of northeastern Connecticut were ravaged by this scourge early in the 20th century. Compost and bone meal are the best fertilizers for garden mints.

Mints will grow in partial shade but the large scale crops are now planted in full sun. All species need plenty of moisture and quickly deplete the soil. They should be discouraged from flowering, for the flowers produce natural hybrids which are not likely to be of as good flavor as the original stock.

Habitat. Mints are natives of Europe but the more vigorous species have become naturalized in many parts of the United States.

Uses. Spearmint for mint sauce, mint jelly, tea and juleps, is an aid to digestion and a natural flavor partner but there are other species which invite experimentation. Peppermint oil finds its way into candies, tooth paste, liqueurs such as crème de menthe and medicines. The dried herb makes an aromatic tea without the addition of other tea leaves. Applemint leaves may be candied by brushing the fresh, washed and patted dry leaves with white of an egg and then dusting them on both sides with powdered sugar. They make a natural confection when the sugar and egg white harden and will keep for months. Pineapple mint is a pretty garnish for fruit cup, salads and cold drinks. Orange mint steeped with tea leaves and lemon balm sprigs serves as a delectable punch base. Pennyroyal was a natural as a strewing herb because the odor keeps fleas away. The oil of the herb, or even the dried leaf, cannot be sold in this country because it was once used as an emmenagogue.

Mugwort (*Artemisia vulgaris*)

Height. 3½ feet

Leaf and blossom. Mugwort has dark green, three-cleft, stem-less leaves. They resemble chrysanthemum leaves except that the undersides are zinc-colored with a heavy covering of downy hairs. The leaflets are about one and one-half inches wide by two to three inches long with sharply-pointed tips. The erect stems are dark purple. Thick panicles of small flowers appear to be white from a distance. This illusion is caused by the woolly character of the calyx which almost envelops the densely packed head of tiny yellow florets. After the quarter inch blossoms fade, the browning seed heads are still ornamental. However, they should be cut back assiduously because, if allowed to ripen, the light brown seeds will scatter and drift over a wide area. Thus the herb can become a very bad weed if it grows untended.

Culture. Hardy perennial mugwort may be started from seed sown directly in the garden. Each grain is so tiny that it appears to be only a speck to the naked eye. Under a magnifying glass it is possible to see that it is a ridged brown fibrous seed. Plants should be thinned to stand two feet apart. The roots are spreading, like those of chrysanthemum, only much more invasive. Each piece broken off in cultivating the bed will start a lusty new clump. Mugwort is too weedy for the herb garden. On the edges of a shrubbery it can be kept in check by cutting back the foliage before blooming. It will thrive in full sun or partial shade.

Habitat. One of the European artemisias, mugwort is known as *beifuss* in Germany where the leaves are valued for cooking with pork and goose to render the fat more digestible. White mugwort, A. *lactiflora*, from China is not as rampant and can be used in wide perennial flower borders for its showy, loose panicles of white flowers. Western mugwort, A. *ludoviciana*, has many forms with entire silvery leaves and gray panicles of yellow-centered blooms.

Uses. Western mugworts are useful in flower arrangements and for decorating at Christmas. They also spread but not as viciously as mugwort. The gray foliage is desirable for drying to make moth preventive bags for the closet.

Comment. A leaf of mugwort placed in a man's shoe was supposed to enable him to walk 40 miles before noon without weariness.

Rocambole (*Allium scorodoprasum*)

Height. 3 feet

Leaf and blossom. Also called French, or giant garlic, the herb has flattened leaves which grow in clumps. Before the flowering scapes of the garlic-flavored plant attain their full height they are curved in fascinating circles and then straighten out with pointed, peaked caps at the top which enclose heads of tiny bulbils in July. Instead of the buds opening to blossoms, the heads of purple-skinned bulbils resemble knobs of popcorn. The scales covering each bulbil turn brown and the rest of the foliage dies back to the ground in August.

There is another perennial allium which has the same propensity for producing small onion-flavored bulbils at the tops of the stalks. It is *A. cepa viviparum,* called Egyptian Multiplier onion. The leaves are fat and round like those of garden onion but, instead of blossoms, fairly good-size onion bulbils appear out of the buds. These increase in number over a period of a month until the hollow stalk bends under their weight and they fall to the ground. There, they send up more green onion shoots and develop roots to make new plants. Both the green onion leaves and the top onions may be used in cooking.

Culture. Both alliums are hardy perennials. They need rich soil and full sun. The individual bulbils produce new plants but the roots may also be divided in early spring. Rocambole goes dormant in August when the scapes turn straw color and the conical heads of bulbils split apart. If the weather is wet at the time, each little "clove of garlic" will start to sprout a new leaf. They should be harvested before this happens and stored in a brown paper bag with their heads down. In September, the new green shoots which spring up from the roots may be used like chives. This is convenient because garlic chives at this time is going to seed. Egyptian onion is amusing in the garden and provides top onions for storage and starts for friends who admire the bizarre plant. If you believe that onions deter aphids from roses and fruit trees, you will have plenty of material for encircling them from one plant of Egyptian Multiplier. A friend insists that the rose bush surrounded by chives had no aphids last year while the control plant separated from it by several yards did.

Habitat. Most onions stem from western Asia.

Uses. The early greens of Egyptian Multiplier onion, sometimes called the potato onion, may be chopped like scallions into salads. Large hollow stems can be filled with whipped cream cheese and then sliced for hors d'oeuvres. The top onions keep well if hung up in a cool room during the winter. It is nice to be able to peel one thumb-size onion for sautéing instead of cutting a large globe that will have to be thrown away or stored until used again. If you want green spears of onion in December, all you have to do is plant one of the segments in a flower pot and it will sprout.

Rocambole answers the need for just a little garlic. The bulbils are sometimes as small as a kernel of popcorn but the flavor is as strong as regular garlic. It is not always necessary to peel the bulbil. If you are adding it to spaghetti sauce but want to remove the actual garlic flavor source early, just prick a bulbil with the point of a knife and drop into the oil in which you plan to brown the meat. Fish it out before you put the meat in and only the flavor will remain. A single segment of rocambole is small enough to conceal in a square of meat or chicken heart to feed a dog or cat some preventive medicine for worms. They will not get put off by the smell of garlic if you tuck the little clove into the meat without peeling it. The bulbils keep much better than cloves of garlic. They do not go soft even when stored in a warm place and there is no odor to them unless the skin is split.

Rose, Apothecary's (*Rosa gallica*)

Height. 5 feet

Leaf, blossom and fruit. The oldest and most useful rose of the herbalists is called the apothecary's rose because it has been used in medicine through the ages. It is a shrub rose with single flowers of rich crimson which are intensely fragrant. They are single with prominent yellow stamens which add to the beauty of the blossoms. The foliage is not a glossy green, as in modern roses, but it is pleasant if not thick on the airy bush. *R. gallica* is a species rose. It can be reproduced from seed and has not been changed by grafting or hybridizing. It needs rich soil, good drainage and full sun to attain its true beauty. Unfortunately, it flowers only once a year, in June, so you must gather rose petals while you may if you wish to make pot-pourri, rose petal jelly or jam or to candy the petals.

When the blossoms fall, smooth red fruits, called hips in roses, form to give color in the autumn. They have their herbal associations, too, as they are rich in vitamin C.

Culture. Nurseries which specialize in old roses advise fall planting. The bushes are shipped with bare roots and must be put into the ground immediately. While waiting for delivery, it is a good idea to dig the hole about two feet deep and just as wide, breaking up the sub-soil and adding well-rotted manure and compost to it. The humus mixture in the bottom of the cavity should be rounded in a cone. Over this spread the roots so that they have a chance to stretch out. Then begin to fill in with top soil, tamping it down with a shovel handle as you progress. Finally, mound six to eight inches of earth, compost and manure around the base of the plant. More compost and straw or salt hay should be heaped upon this for winter protection.

In the spring, as soon as the ground is thawed, lift off the mulch and spade in the compost and manure. When growth is established it is time to supplement the nourishment derived from this top dressing with manure water, made by steeping fresh or dried manure in a bucket of rain water.

Over the years, *R. gallica* will send out suckers several feet from the old plant. They may be cut off in the spring to make new bushes.

Habitat. The history of the rose is such a long one that it is hard to pin-point the place of origin. Speaking of *R. gallica* in her beautiful book *Roses,* Anne Ophelia Dowden says, "It has been a cultivated plant since pre-history, and was brought into Europe through Asia Minor and Crete."

Uses. The old roses mean more to the herb gardener than many of the new, less fragrant hybrids. The apothecary's rose deserves first place as representing the humanities of horticulture. Not only the color and scent endear it to the gardener, but the history of its service to man is intriguing. The Romans spread the petals of this and other roses throughout their banqueting halls and hung garlands of blossoms about the necks of guests. Their food and cosmetics were perfumed with oil of roses. The pharmacopoeias of every age since have included *R. gallica* in medicines. Today it is the hips which are known to have nutritional benefits through their vitamin C. During the Battle of Britain rose hip tea took the place of imported oranges. Other roses have larger fruits, particularly *Rosa rugosa*, but none have any more fragrant petals which keep their scent when dried than *R. gallica*. It is the right rose for making pot-pourri.

The mixture of herbs, flowers and fixatives which fill a sweet jar or pot-pourri pot to give fragrance to a room is based on rose petals. It may be stored for years and still retains the mingled perfumes of a summer garden. On a shelf in my dining room are several rose or pot-pourri jars from Rosetta Clarkson's collection of more than one hundred of the fine porcelain treasures. They have two lids and are shaped like ginger jars of the kind shipped from China in happier days. When the inner solid cover is removed, the outer one, which has slits in it, is replaced so that the scent of the contents can escape into the room. If you return both lids to the pot-pourri jar, the seemingly inexhaustible fragrance builds up again in the contents. Leaving it open, you may not notice the aroma too long but just stir the dried petals, herb leaves and spices by shaking the jar and the perfume is there.

Comment. The method of making a blend to fill a pot-pourri jar is more important than the choice of ingredients. Beside rose petals, herb leaves, bright garden flowers for color, dried lemon peel, chips of cedar or sandalwood and spices may be added. The possibilities of varying a basic recipe are infinite. All mate-

Pot-pourri jars (Vincent Bristol)

rials must be dried before blending. Rose petals and some flowers change color somewhat in the process of dehydration but, as the mixture is stirred, they all take on an old rose color except for bright blue bachelor's buttons, delphinium florets, yellow pot marigold or chrysanthemum petals.

All summer long the herb gardener should collect flowers for pot-pourri. It is easy to get a quantity of lemon balm, rose geranium or pineapple sage foliage to dry just before frost but blossoms come and go. Rose petals should be spread on paper or cloth, such as an old sheet, laid over screen wire, so that air can circulate through it, in a room that is not too sunny or too much in the traffic of daily life. They have to be turned daily and, if they do not seem to be getting crisp in three or four days, they must be finished off in a cool oven (not over 200° F.). Leave the oven door open so that you can stir them and see that they are not cooking but merely becoming chip-dry.

The old system of drying flowers in sand or borax can be applied to pot-pourri making. If you can obtain fine, dry sand, spread it in a dress box and lay the petals out one layer thick upon it. Then sift more sand over them to cover and place on that another layer of petals. No more than two layers is advisable. The box is left open in a warm but dry place. This has to be kept away from the family cat. Actually, the litter material used for cats' pans would do just as well as sand or borax but if the material sticks to the individual petals they may need dusting before making into pot-pourri. Whole rose buds, picked just before they open, can be dried in sand, borax or silica gel (which is used in a covered container) to add a special charm. Most recipes give amounts in quarts of rose petals which is more than most people could muster in a single season. I like the simple formula put out by the American Spice Trade Association.

Rose Pot-pourri

6 cups dried rose petals	½ tsp. ground allspice
½ tsp. ground cloves	½ tsp. mint flakes
¼ tsp. ground cinnamon	1½ tsp. orris root

Add spices to dried rose petals. Sift in the ground orris root which may be ordered through a drugstore. Mix in a wide bowl and pack in a large jar. Cover tightly but open the container every few days to stir the mixture. This is a pleasant task and one that will inspire other blends including dried rose geranium leaves, lemon verbena and many other herbs, with the rose petals.

Rosemary (*Rosmarinus officinalis*)

Height. 6 feet

Leaf and blossom. It is hard to describe the loveliness of rosemary, for its beauty stems from its bushy, erect growth, so like a miniature fir tree, as well as its fragrance. The leaves are really needle-like, narrow, dark green and leathery with edges curled under. They are smooth above but grayish underneath. The arrangement in the axils of the woody stems is fir-like and the new shoots are lighter green as in hardy evergreens.

Pale blue, sometimes white, two-lipped flowers crowd the axils of the leafy stems. The upper lobes of the petals are wide-spread and the lower lobes have ruffles on the edges. The downy green calyx, with broadly pointed tips, is one-quarter to one-half the length of the half-inch long blossoms. Since rosemary must be treated as a pot plant where the ground freezes, its normal flowering time in late winter is sometimes delayed until the plants are put out in the garden in the spring. In fact, it will have a few blossoms on different branches throughout the year.

A low-growing variety, *R. officinalis prostratus*, grows faster and blooms more freely than the upright types. In California, this form has become a special planting for banks, along sidewalks and atop stone walls at the California Institute of Technology in Pasadena. The leaves are shorter, and seem to be produced in denser clusters, but more widely spaced on the arching stems. The fragrance is very pronounced in all parts of the plant. It is the typical piney scent of rosemary.

Culture. If you have no facilities for keeping rosemary over the winter on a sunny windowsill where it can be sprayed regularly with a misty vapor to keep the foliage from drying up, it is hardly worth starting the plants from seed. By the end of the first summer, the tender perennial plants are still too small to cut for drying.

Propagation by cuttings is the simplest method to get good-sized plants in a short time. Four or five inch long sprigs from the top of the plant, with a pair of growing tips if possible, are sliced off with a slanting cut. They are stripped of leaves for the two or three inches that will be imbedded in the rooting medium. Clean sand, or perlite mixed with peat moss, may be used for rooting. Dipping the ends in root hormone powder helps to prevent rotting and speeds up rooting. Rosemary will root in six weeks if the parent plant has woody stems from which to make cuttings. The prostrate rosemary cuttings will go right on blooming while separated from the parent plant. Putting a plio-film bag over the pot of cuttings keeps the humidity high and speeds action at the base of the stems. Do not leave the plastic covered cuttings in direct sunlight or the bag will get steamy. Constant mist, such as is used by greenhouse operators is ideal for rosemary.

Occasionally plants may be layered in the garden. In a moist season they will strike roots wherever the branches are covered with earth. This makes it easy to cut off rooted portions of the plant to pot up for bringing indoors in the fall.

In good garden soil, full sun and a season with usual rainfall, rosemary will grow more than six inches in summer. But rose-mary which must be potted never reaches the full height of six feet which is attained where the shrub grows outdoors, as in California, south of Washington, D.C., and in England and Eu-rope. You can keep the plant in the pot all year round, increas-ing the size annually, but I like to put rosemary right into the garden bed. It takes several months to get adjusted to the change but by October, when I must bring it in, I can cut it back for drying and help the plant recover from root loss at the same time. Though frost-resistant, rosemary should be potted before the ground really freezes so that the plants can be kept quite moist until they must be brought into the heat. House condi-tions can be fatal to the evergreen if the tops and roots are al-lowed to dry out. A saucer of pebbles with water reaching not quite up to the bottom of the pot will help to raise the humid-ity when the herb is used as a houseplant. Frequent sprayings of the foliage with fine mist help rosemary over the shock of transplanting.

Rosemary seed is slow to germinate, sometimes taking three weeks. It must be planted in a sterile medium such as sphagnum moss over soil or clean sand over soil. The watering should be done from below so that sprinkling does not wash out the lightly covered seed or wet the tender young leaves. When transplant-ing, after the seedlings have four true leaves, try to choose pots that are rather small for the plants. Rosemary should have its roots somewhat crowded in the pot to force it to bloom.

In the garden, rosemary thrives in full sun. It must be protected from winds for the first week that it is brought out of winter storage. If it has been in a greenhouse it will have a lot of tender, soft-green tips which turn brown if exposed to drying winds immediately it is set out. I try to wait for a warm misty rain to put out the larger rosemaries which have been stored in a deep coldframe all winter. If sudden clearing catches them and me unprepared, I put half bushel baskets over the plants until evening and then let them catch the dew, covering them again the next day if necessary.

The soil should be somewhat limey but it needs very little enrichment. The scent of rosemary is stronger when it grows in sandy, lean soil as on Cape Cod where it has been known to winter safely outside. It is possible to sink the pot, holding a large rosemary, right up to its rim in the garden but you have to remember, for the rest of the summer, to keep the soil around it evenly moist. Rosemary grown on a terrace as a pot or tub plant can stand to dry out once in a while but in the heated house this is often fatal. One grower withholds water from a large plant in a wooden tub that is placed out-of-doors in summer, giving it only enough to survive. Then when it is brought into the greenhouse it invariably flowers all winter. Another herb gardener finds that it is a matter of light as well as water and soil that influences blooms. A large upright rosemary which she places in a bay window in the kitchen each winter flowers only on the side turned toward the glass in February. It is a table Christmas tree for the family before that and they hang it with miniature decorations of an ornamental and edible nature.

Prostrate rosemary may be trained to resemble bonsai. When plants are put in the garden they spread horizontally, and the main stem becomes quite woody. If a two year-old plant is root-pruned and trimmed at the top, when it is lifted for bringing indoors in the fall, it may be planted in a bonsai container. Rosemary will continue to grow throughout the winter, and so you

Rosemary as bonsai

can bend or guide the supple shoots before they become woody. The fragrance of the foliage, the usefulness of every flavorful leaf cut away in the pruning process, and the beauty of the blue flowers which appear in the axils of the leaves make this variety an exciting substitute for the usual bonsai material.

Habitat. *Rosmarinus* means dew of the sea, and rosemary is found growing along the coast of the Mediterranean. Travelers report that its scent can be detected quite far out at sea if the wind is off the land. In California the herb can be grown to its full shrub-like proportions in the calcareous soils. It is also evergreen in Alabama and other southern states, though it is found only in gardens.

Uses. Rosemary is quite pungent as a cooking herb. It is better used fresh than dried. Top a roasting chicken with sprigs of the green herb before you place it in the oven. It will give a richness which is subtle and superb. Tarragon is often suggested for poultry, but, to me, rosemary is the preferred herb for chicken. Individual leaves stuck in slits made in a roast of pork or lamb before cooking permeate the meat with a light touch of the herb's taste. Use it sparingly with eggplant and other vegetables and you will wonder why you have been so timid before. Rosemary biscuits, or dumplings made by grinding a few dried leaves and adding them to the batter are delicious.

A tea, made from the dried herb steeped in boiling water, will clear the head if one suffers from a cold, I learned from an English gardener. The same infusion, sans sugar or honey for sweetening, can be used for a rinse for dark hair. It makes an excellent wave-setting lotion. Hungary water, said to be made from a recipe owned by the Queen of Hungary, calls for rosemary infused in wine. A bath bag of rosemary leaves tied up in tulle or cheese cloth and soaked in the tub gives the water a nice perfume. The ancients would say it strengthened the sinews, but we would merely hope it relaxed the nerves.

Comment. Rosemary is one of the easiest herbs to dry. As soon as the sprigs are cut they begin to desiccate, but they do not shrink as much as most herbs. There is much less moisture in the leaves than in sweet basil, for instance, and the essential oils remain even after the herb is dried. When you strip the needle-like leaves from the brittle stems, after you have had the herb in a brown paper bag for several weeks, your hands will show signs of the resinous oil.

Dried rosemary does not pulverize to a powdery substance. Small bits of individual leaves remain even after the herb is dry enough to be forced through a coarse strainer. If you wish to crush the herb to get a dusting of rosemary powder, you really have to grind it in a mortar. Usually the individual leaflets are left in quarter-inch bits until the herb is used for cooking. Then they can be reduced to smaller size just before they are added to bread or biscuit dough.

Branches of green rosemary were used in bridal garlands in Shakespeare's day. Bridelaces were sprays of rosemary wound with ribbons and carried before the bride in the wedding ceremony. Of the myriad mentions of rosemary in literature, I like the one applying to a gay suitor who said:

> "Well, well, since wedding will come after wooing,
>   Give me some Rosemary, and lett's be going."

Rue, *Ruta graveolens*

Rue (*Ruta graveolens*)

Height. 2½ feet

Leaf and blossom. Rue has lovely blue-green, persistent foliage which remains a lively color when most of the herb garden has gone to bed for the winter. The irregularly-cleft leaves, which look as though they had been marked out by stenciling into four and five-lobed spoon-shaped segments, are as attractive as the color of the foliage. There is a sort of bloom upon them that contributes to the blue cast. The perennial woody, branching main-stems are yellowish. The plant is upright and can be clipped for hedging. The problem in using it this way is that the foliage can cause dermatitis in some people. Just brushing against it when the plant is coming into flower will cause a rash that can be as severe as poison ivy to sensitive skins. The intensity of the eruption is increased by exposure to sunlight. If you are hot and working bare-handed with rue, you may get rue poisoning. If the exposed area is quickly washed with brown soap, or as the old herbalists suggested, covered with oil, no problem occurs.

The blossoms are yellow with wide-spread petals, cupped at the edges. A conspicuous green ovary projects one small white pistil from its center. The surrounding stamens bend over individually to dust their pollen on its sticky surface without benefit of insect intervention. Perhaps, this accounts for the numerous black seeds which develop in the hard, glandular capsules. Seed heads of rue sprayed with gold or silver paint are long lasting decorations for dried herb wreaths or winter bouquets. They remain on the plants all winter in the garden.

Culture. Gardeners tend to live dangerously and few herb collectors would forego the beauty and legendary interest of rue because of its occasional deleterious effect. It is a hardy plant which is started from seed. Cuttings of new wood root very slowly and divisions of plants are almost impossible, because the main stem is single and seldom branches low enough to develop roots by layering. The ease with which it can be started from seed directly in the garden makes it possible to have an abundance of rue from one packet of seed. It should be sown in early spring or late summer. Some first year plants bloom in full sun.

Rue will withstand some hours of shade every day but the thriftiest plants are those grown in the open where the soil is more gravelly than rich. The roots are rather small and close to the surface so the plants tend to heave during spring thaws. This, more than winter-killing, is the cause of losses. They should stand ten inches apart and be trimmed the first year to increase bushiness.

If some plants go to seed, there will be volunteers the next spring to make a succession of rue. The need for a nursery area along with a formal garden of herbs increases where you use many plants of one kind for designs depending on foliage colors. Seedlings of rue found around old clumps may be lined out in the nursery bed until the need for replacement in the border or hedge. If the air and soil drainage are good, rue will live for many years with no more attention than annual clipping off of the flower or seed heads. It is slow to leaf out in the spring. Mature plants may look quite dead until new yellow-green shoots appear along the stems. Then it can be pruned to an even height.

Habitat. Rue is another herb of the Mediterranean. It is in the same family as our citrus fruit trees.

Uses. In the modern garden, rue is considered more an ornamental herb than a culinary one. However, the leaves have been
chopped and mixed with cream cheese for a roquefort-cheese
flavor. One imaginative herb gardener puts a sprig in her martini
glass instead of an olive. The bitter flavor and strange scent of
rue seem unpopular today but it was used as a preventive of disease in less antiseptic eras when judges carried bunches of
rue to the bench to protect themselves from the prisoners' diseases. It has been discovered in recent times that rue contains
rutin, also extracted from buckwheat, which is used to treat
fragile capillaries.

Comment. A variegated rue, very like *R. graveolens*, has proven
hardy in my garden. It shows its creamy streaks on the foliage
better in the greenhouse than in the open. A fringed form with
linear, curling leaves proved too tender even for my cool greenhouse. It is a lovely blue-green plant and I would like to be able
to grow it in the garden but cuttings would not root for me and
the plants succumbed during their first winter.

Saffron, True (*Crocus sativus*)

Height. 6 inches

Leaf, blossom and stigmas. Narrow, green, grass-like leaves
appear in summer. In September the lovely flowers are white to
lavender with prominent stigmas which hang out between the
petals of the floral cup like orange tongues. It is these frail female
organs of the flower which are dried to make the precious and
expensive seasoning and coloring agent. A few of the dried stigmas packed in a small glassine envelope cost upwards from 25
to 50 cents, depending upon the value of the glass jar used for
packaging them. In markets where foreign foods and herbs are
sold, saffron perfumes the store, for the powerful aroma of the
dried, slightly bitter herb comes through paper envelopes where
there is no pretense of fancy jars.

Culture. It is possible to grow the saffron crocus in cold climates but getting it to bloom freely enough to give any orange
strands with which to make saffron rice is another matter. It
needs a longer season than New England affords. The corms

need sharp drainage and where they are cultivated commercially in Spain they are taken up after the third season and divided. Though spring crocuses flourish in our yard, the precious saffron had dwindled away by the third season so that it did not have strength enough to produce blooms.

It is wise to mark the spot where saffron is planted in the spring so that the corms will not be overplanted with something else before the leaves appear just prior to flowering. Actually, the greatest difficulty is buying the correct species. Crocuses are usually available for planting in the fall but at that time saffron would be about to bloom. If you make arrangements with a bulb dealer, a year ahead, you may be able to get the corms in the spring or early summer in time to have them bloom at least once in your garden. It is worth the trouble to see what infinite pains it must take to collect the dried herb from thousands of the plants. No machine could possibly do the harvesting.

Habitat. *Crocus sativus* comes from Asia Minor. The Arabs introduced it as a seasoning and dye plant to Europe. In Eastern Asia the dye is reserved for monks' robes.

Uses. Saffron is steeped in chicken stock for ten minutes before adding to gravy for fricassee chicken. In saffron rice, a few of the stigmas are cooked with the rice. As only two pounds can be collected to an acre, the price per pound of saffron is extravagant.

Pennsylvania Dutch cookery sometimes uses saffron for noodles because it saves an egg, giving as much color as an egg yolk. Special boxes decorated in brown and red were used by the Dutch to keep saffron dry in the kitchen. They are collectors' items, now, like snuff-boxes and pot-pourri jars.

A recipe for saffron cookies by Sidney Duerr shows how little of the herb is needed for color and taste:

Saffron Cookies

2½ cups flour	½ teaspoon baking powder
⅛ teaspoon salt	1 cup butter
¾ cup sugar	1 egg
¼ teaspoon saffron steeped in a small amount of water	

Cream butter and sugar, add egg. Cream until light and

fluffy. Add saffron liquid (about a tablespoonful). Mix well. Sift in dry ingredients. Put into the refrigerator until firm enough to roll into small balls. Flatten them with a fork or small glass with design on the bottom. Bake 7 to 10 minutes at 400° F.

Comment. Fortunately the corms of *C. sativus* are not expensive. So, when you find them order by the hundred, if you have a sunny, well-drained spot to plant them.

Meadow saffron should not be confused with true saffron, despite the similarity of the common name. Meadow saffron is also called autumn crocus but actually is *Colchicum autumnale*. It, too, blooms in the fall, indeed the bulbs bloom without soil. It is true that they cannot be discouraged from sprouting in September, even if left dry on a windowsill but they do much better in the ground. Also, they are expensive and should be treated with care and some respect because the plants are poisonous.

Colchicum is the source of the present-day drug used to treat gout. The substance colchicine, derived from the bulbs, has been used to produce doubling of chromosomes in plants. The flowers of the bulb are breath-taking in the fall when the lavender or white chalices pop through the ground. The foliage is broad-leaved and takes up quite a bit of space when it comes up in the spring. Then, it yellows and dies and the bulbs are forgotten until the white noses of the flower buds push through in September.

Sage (*Salvia officinalis*)

Height. 2½ feet

Leaf and blossom. The pebbled gray leaves of sage linger on the woody stems all winter. It makes a thrifty bush which becomes more handsome with age. The tomentose, entire, deeply-veined leaves are oblong, from two to four inches in length. They are green when young, becoming very hoary by autumn. The main stems are woody the second season but remain soft and tender at the growing tips.

In May, bluish-lavender flowers are borne in scattered racemes.

They are showy, and even after the petals drop the sharply-pointed calices are purple above and greenish below. The strong scent and clear blue color of the blossoms attract honeybees. In fact, the large tubular corolla is so designed to facilitate the work of the bee in pollinating the herb. The round-lobed lower lip of the flower spreads out to form a landing platform for the insect. As it enters the tube about the neck, it cannot avoid tripping the levers which bring the pollen-bearing stamens, hidden in the upper lobe, down upon its bristly back. When it retreats, there is a precious load of fertile gold dust which will be brushed off on the sticky pistil released in the same manner from within the corolla of another plant.

Thus the development of four black seeds is assured by the visit of the worker bee, though the same flower will not pollinate itself.

Culture. The ease of cultivation and long life of sage plants raise the question of why it is not more commonly included in vegetable and flower gardens. In England, the purple-leaved variety and a form with markings of cream and rose color upon the foliage are used for edgings for wide perennial flower borders.

One or two plants of culinary sage will provide enough leaves for use fresh during the summer and for drying for winter for the small family.

Sage seed may be planted in the garden early in the spring. Young plants should be thinned or transplanted to stand two feet apart. As they mature they quickly fill in the spaces between them and need little weeding. Two-year-old plants may be dug and divided after flowering to start new clumps. Wherever a strong stem is pulled away from the old wood, a portion with roots attached will break off.

It is possible to divide the plants in the spring but it means sacrificing some blossoms. A better time is after the clumps have finished blooming and the first harvest of leaves has been made. Cutting back the persistent foliage to within several inches of the roots does not prevent flowering in second-year plants. It helps to produce more leafy stems which must be cut back again after they bloom. Then the second growth may be cut for drying.

Commercial growers set out seedlings, collect a crop the first summer and again the next spring harvest the tops before buds form. They start new plants each year so that they will have softer stems to make mechanical harvesting easier. First-year plants often bloom in August. They should be grown in good soil, full sun and be kept free of weeds. The last cutting for drying, or to prune the plants back in shape, should not be made later than September as the plants need foliage to support the roots through the winter. In the spring, the stems with old leaves still clinging to them can be cut back to several inches from the roots.

Habitat. S. *officinalis* comes from the Mediterranean region. The tender salvias which are grown for their late summer flowers, such as S. *elegans,* with fruit-scented foliage which gives it the name pineapple sage, come from California and Mexico. Helen M. Fox, author of many books on herbs, describes more than 20 salvias in *The Years in My Herb Garden.* She grew most of them from seed and makes a good case for including them in the herb garden for their fragrance. The perennial varieties which are tender must be kept in a greenhouse in winter and propagated by cuttings. Pineapple sage roots very easily in water even when you have cut the fire-cracker red flowers for a bouquet. It blooms too late to decorate northern gardens but in warm climates it is almost a sub-shrub with handsome, somewhat hairy foliage and stems.

Uses. Sage is familiar as a culinary herb when dried for poultry dressing and sausage flavoring. In former times it was highly regarded as a tea for colds. The leaves are pulverized for seasoning but they may be left whole for making herb tea. The constant use of the herb is believed to ensure longevity. The flavor of fresh sage is more delectable than the dry herb. Pineapple sage loses its pungency when dried so it is used as a fresh garnish for fruit cups or cold drinks.

Santolina, Gray (*Santolina chamaecyparissus*)

Height. 18 inches

Leaf and blossom. The gray, toothed leaves of santolina or lavender cotton, as the 16th century writer called it, look more like some sort of coral or rock formation than true leaves. The fragrance comes from a resinous oil which can be felt when touching the leaves. Except at the seaside, where the hoary plant makes a salt-resistant landscape subject against cottages or along brick walks, it seldom flowers. But at The Herbary, in Orleans on Cape Cod, May Sargent has plants of santolina a full four feet in diameter that bloom continuously throughout the summer. The button heads of bloom are conspicuous for their deep yellow color. They are on leafless stems, not very high above the handsome gray clumps.

Green santolina, *S. virens*, has even narrower leaves than gray santolina and paler, lemon-drop flowers in compact heads. It has a slightly different pungency equally appealing in hand and in bouquets. Sandy soil and mists from the sea bring this species to enormous proportions by the seaside.

At the Brooklyn Botanic Garden both santolinas are used among huge boulders in a rock garden leading down steps to the knot garden. They look like miniature evergreens, being as broad as the rock outcroppings. The foliage is persistent and where it does not have a heavy snow cover it remains attractive all winter.

S. pinnata, with more feathery leaves, is a light gray with green tinge and Mrs. Fox calls it more hardy than the others. All three stand clipping and can be shaped into ribbons and bands to delineate a formal design. John Parkinson recommended it for this purpose, in the 17th century, but qualifies his statement with the caution that it will die back in winter.

Culture. The santolinas may be propagated by cuttings taken in late summer and kept in moist sand in a greenhouse over the winter. They can also be layered and this is the most successful way to keep a quantity of the plants in New England. The plants to be layered should be set out in a nursery bed where earth may be tamped down among the spreading branches in the fall to encourage rooting. In the spring the whole plant can be lifted and pulled apart to make vigorous new clumps. Cuttings take two years to reach the size of layerings.

Habitat. Gray and green santolina are plants which came to us from the coastal region of southern Europe. That they arrived in the New World early is witnessed by John Josselyn, traveler and writer, who visited the colonies in 1638 and 1663. He included lavender cotton in a list of plants he found being grown in New England.

Uses. Besides the many landscape applications of santolinas, the cut herb is excellent in flower arrangements. It lasts a long time in water and is pleasantly fragrant to handle. The dried sprigs can be put in mixtures to prevent moths. John Gerard scorned the confusion which existed in the 16th century between this plant and southernwood, saying of the earlier writers, "we leave them to their errors." He added, "It killeth wormes either given greene or dry, and the seed hath the same vertue against wormes, but avoideth them with greater force." No wonder the brave women who tossed about in sailing ships cosseted santolina slips all the way. Children still get worms in our enlightened day and one doctor's remedy was a tincture of gentian violet. Chopping a little green santolina in their salads would be an easier safeguard.

Savory, Winter (*Satureja montana*)

Height. 12 inches

Leaf and blossom. Glossy, almost evergreen, narrow leaves, to an inch in length, are attached directly to the stems. The plant is stiffer than summer savory and darker green. It can be trimmed to make a verdant mound, if the old wood is cut back to within a few inches of the ground in the spring.

Winter savory is often used in rock gardens for its attractive pinkish white blossoms in August on low-growing woody plants.

Culture. The perennial may be started from seed but takes two seasons to reach flowering proportions. Seeds can be planted in the fall in a "seminary" or seed bed which will keep them in cold storage until spring, or they can be sown in flats in a greenhouse in March. Young plants are sturdy and not difficult to handle. They should be pricked out or potted before placing in a permanent location in the garden. Full sun, moderately rich soil and excellent drainage are the main requirements. In partial shade the foliage is softer and not so hardy.

Winter savory is a good edging plant for a knot garden because it can be kept clipped throughout the season. The shearings have value as a dried herb. It needs a light covering of pine needles or salt hay to keep the tops green most of the winter. The tree-like main stem will be thrust upwards if the ground heaves with freezing and thawing, exposing the surface roots. The protection

Winter Savory, *Satureja montana* (Philip W. Foster)

against this should be put on after the ground freezes. If additional plants are needed, just spread out the side branches and heap soil over them. They will be rooted along the stems in the spring. Then, whole clumps may be lifted to pull off sections with a portion of woody stem and fresh roots attached. This is possible in September if the plants have been thus layered during the summer.

Habitat. Savories were brought from Europe and England with the first settlers.

Uses. The culinary uses of winter savory are identical with those of annual summer savory—for green beans, poultry seasoning, stew and soups, whether fresh or dried. It is an easy herb to dehydrate by placing in a large brown paper bag until crisp enough for bottling.

Shallot (*Allium ascalonicum*)

Height. 18 inches

Leaf and blossom. The tubular, blue-green leaves of shallots are narrower and not as tall as those of the onion. However, when in the second season, some of the plants go to seed they have fluffy white balls of blossoms on eighteen inch stems. Usually the plants are dug and some of the cloves reset so that most people never see the full height of the plant or the blossoms. It is the clusters of reddish-brown skinned bulblets which give us the delectable, sweet onion, slightly tinged with a breath of garlic, flavor. They are a little stronger than chives but more subtle than garlic. The green tops may be used like chives in early summer.

Culture. It takes two years to develop shallot bulbs from seed, so the individual cloves are planted in the fall for the next summer's crop. They need rich soil, full sun and good drainage. When the leaves begin to wither the bulbs are almost ready for harvest.

It is just as well not to wait until all the leaves have died down to start digging the shallots. Like potatoes, the clusters of underground bulbs sometimes break off in the digging. No harm is done for these are the ones that will grow tall and seed the next summer. You lift the whole reddish-brown clusters intact, store them in a dry place, not closed up in a can, until it is time to plant tulips and spring-flowering bulbs. Meanwhile the spot in the garden may be readied by forking in dried sheep manure and bone meal because shallots are heavy feeders. If you can rotate the position of planting each year to one where plants of the onion family have not grown before, so much the better.

Habitat. Probably a native of western Asia, like the onion, shallot is connected with the French cuisine more than any other.

Uses. The brown cloves are peeled and usually sauteed lightly, but not really browned, in butter before making gravy, cream sauce or curry to be flavored with them. The tender spring greens are superb snipped into omelette or salad.

Skirret (Sium sisarum)

Height. 3 feet

Leaf and blossom. The shiny leaves of skirret have two patterns. This is true of other members of the carrot family where the seedling leaves look quite different from the mature foliage. Skirret has heart-shaped, young leaves becoming ovate and acute. They are opposite, sessile and smooth, without any particular scent. As the plants run to flower the second season the leaves are pinnately compound and the umbels of small white blossoms rise above them on smooth round stems. But it is neither the leaves nor the blooms which has made skirret renowned as a pot-herb. The tuberous roots are edible and in olden days were dug and stored for winter in sand, as carrots can be.

Culture. If skirret is to be grown for the roots it should be started from seed in the fall or early spring in shallow drills. The ground must be rich enough for vegetable crops and the herb should be planted in full sun. However, the discouraging job of peeling the roots for cooking and their rather tasteless character has made us prefer skirret for its attractive glossy foliage and white flowers in late summer.

As a perennial, skirret may be divided in the spring when the leaves first show above ground. Each section of root will make a new plant. In our garden, rabbits have discovered that the tops are tender and delicious. So I have to dust the foliage with dried blood to keep the rodents away. In a former garden where no bunnies intruded I was able to use skirret as a low hedge for a bed of taller pot-herbs by cutting back the flower stalks as soon as they began to bud. Now the rabbits tend to do the pruning, right close to the ground, but the hardy roots remain and keep trying to produce foilage.

Habitat. Skirret was brought from eastern Asia to enrich the limited choice of vegetables available to Anglo-Saxon England.

Uses. Skirret is more of historic interest than culinary use today.

Comment. At one time Miss Eleanour Sinclair Rhode, English author of many herb books, wrote Rosetta Clarkson asking her if she had seed of skirret. The plant which came to this country from England was not then available as seed there. Now, it is listed by Thompson and Morgan, seedsmen, of Ipswich, England, and is quite a scarce item in this country.

Sorrel, French (*Rumex scutatus*)

Height. 18 inches

Leaf and blossom. A pot-herb sometimes grown as an annual because the shield-shaped leaves are more tender the first season, sorrel should be planted at one edge of the vegetable patch so that it will not interfere with tilling. The roots go very deep, like those of wild dock to which it is related, and the panicles of russet blossoms are not very ornamental until in seed. Then, they are appreciated by flower arrangers but if allowed to drop their fruit about the garden the seedlings will be difficult to pull up the next spring.

Culture. Start from seed in fall or early spring. Plan to renew the row or at least transplant the clumps and divide them every second year. Sorrel likes rich soil but it becomes very thick and tightly bunched making a haven for snails which like to feed upon its leaves. Young plants do not seem to be bothered by them. If the leaves are dusted with powdered limestone, the snails are sent packing. Sorrel survives partial shade; often the leaves are more tender in it.

Habitat. We have a most ubiquitous wild sorrel always with us as a garden weed, but the taller French pot-herb was brought from Europe.

Uses. If you taste sorrel soup made with sheep sorrel, the wild *R. acetosella,* you might wonder why cultivate garden sorrel? The flavor is more delicately acid and just as good in soup as the pot-herb but the wild sorrel does not grow in every yard and it is more difficult to pick and clean. As an accompaniment to spinach, French sorrel is delicious. You can mix the greens half and half, or put in one-quarter comfrey leaves or Good King Henry tops. Sorrels, unfortunately, turn a sad brownish green when heated or cooked in two waters, as is necessary for using them as spinach. The plant is a source of oxalic acid so should not be eaten in quantity, and not at all by people subject to gout. As a sauce it goes well with lamb, veal or sweetbreads.

French Sorrel Soup

2 handfuls of sorrel leaves	2 shallots
4 tablespoons butter	2 cups chicken stock
3 tablespoons flour	2 egg yolks
2 tablespoons fresh lovage	1 cup cream
Salt and pepper	4 tablespoons fresh chervil

Remove midribs of sorrel leaves by folding them and tearing the center rib from the top down. Chop them fine and cook in butter in which minced shallots have been slightly browned. Stir constantly until the sorrel becomes a puree. Blend in sifted flour, minced fresh herbs, salt, pepper and chicken stock. Bring to a boil and pour some of the soup into the egg yolks which have been beaten slightly. Return to the sauce pan and add cream. Stir while cooking over lowest heat only until thickened. Serve hot with croutons or cold with a dab of sour cream topped with chives. If you have a blender the soup may be poured into the cream and egg yolks and whirled for one minute. This saves straining out any lumps or bits of stems before serving.

Comment. Sorrel, salt and vinegar were mixed together to scour copper pans in the days before polishes were available.

Wool sorrel, with clover-like leaves which close up at night, is of the geranium family but contains oxalic salts as do the rumex species. Children often nibble it to allay thirst and it was made into a drink by herbalists for this relief for fevers. Too much of any of the sorrels is harmful to the system because oxalates in combination with calcium build up deposits in the kidneys. But a few fresh leaves in salad give a pleasant flavor contrast to blander greens.

Southernwood (Artemisia abrotanum)

Height. 3 feet

Leaf and blossom. A green artemisia with finely divided, lemon mixed with pine scented foliage with tufts of leaves at the ends of the woody stems, southernwood has many pet names. It has been called old man, lad's love and even maidens' ruin.

It does not seem to flower and the plants can be clipped to make a fairly high hedge about an herb planting if they are in full sun. Partial shade does not kill it but the foliage is not as full and some leaves yellow and drop from the lower branches in damp weather.

Culture. Not having any blossoms, southernwood must be started by cuttings or divisions of old clumps. The latter are easily made in early spring or fall by lifting the plant and pulling off pieces of lower stem which usually come away with a good deal of root attached. Cuttings root quickly in sand and give squat, even-sized plants for setting out in a row.

Where the temperature does not go below zero, the foliage is persistent through the winter and each branch will break with new green buds in the spring. In New England, it has to be trimmed back to six inches to remove the dead parts of the stems before new growth starts. It helps to give a well-rounded look to the plants but sometimes the job is done for you by rabbits who love to sit beside the plants in winter and nibble the tops. If the snow is deep they clip them higher than if it is only a light covering. There is a camphor-scented species. A. *camphorata*, sometimes called lady's maid, for its way of rooting down where the stems branch out and then bend an elbow to the ground to become rooted down. It is very like southernwood in appearance except that it does produce panicles of light green blossoms in August.

Both herbs need good soil, sharp drainage and lifting every three years for resetting. The old wood can be pruned out and layered stems split off to make new clumps.

Habitat. The greenish artemisias come from Europe and western Asia while the silver forms are Alpine or western North American in origin. A really shrub-like southernwood that grows eight feet tall with more wide-spaced leaves of fruity fragrance is not listed in *Hortus II*. It may be what Gerard took to be a result of manuring in his graphic descriptions of southernwood: "The greater Sothernwood by carefull manuring, doth oftentimes grow up in manner of a shrub, and commeth as high as a man. . . ." But, actually, even in poor soil this form attains such stature.

Uses. If southernwood is burned to ashes in the fireplace, it will take any cooking odors out of the house. The leaves prevent moths when placed in organdy bags and hung in the woolen closet. The name lad's love came from its use as an ointment which young men applied to promote the growth of a beard. Gerard indicated it helped to prevent baldness but when he spoke of its internal "Vertues" he coined a classic in herbalists' terms:

> "The tops, flowers, or seeds boiled or stamped rawe with water and drunke, helpeth them that can not take their breath without holding their neckes straight up. . . ."

Tansy (Tanacetum vulgare)

Height. 5 feet

Leaf and blossom. The fresh, always crisp looking, pinnate, much-toothed leaflets are arranged in a fern-like pattern on smooth grooved stems. The entire leaf is three to four inches long with the greatest width in the middle. In August, the plants are topped with flat cymes of rayless yellow blossoms. Each head is

composed of hundreds of tightly packed florets which never
seem to open but are soon full of chaffy seeds.

T. vulgare crispum, curly tansy, has longer, wider leaves ir-
regularly shaped and broader at the base. The much-cut margins
and uneven arrangement on the stalk give the plant a curly look.
The light undersides of the leaves show up, giving a lighter green
color to the foliage than common tansy. The whole plant is less
tall, bushier and seldom flowers. It has a chamomile-like scent
while *T. vulgare* has a bitter chrysanthemum aroma.

Culture. Tansy is so easy to grow from seed or divisions of
two-year or older plants that the chief problem to the gardener
is where to put it so that it will not spread into areas occupied
by other plants. It self-sows freely, will stand partial shade and
even quite deep shade if the tops of the plants get some light.

Habitat. Tansy evidently has a wide range in the northern
hemisphere. In New England, it is a sign of old cellar holes and
former farm houses when you see it naturalized, holding its own
against grass, nettle and bouncing bet. The early settlers
brought it with them as they did those "weeds," for its many
uses.

Uses. In the days before refrigeration, tansy was kept in the
meat safe or canvas closet where meats were stored, in the cellar,
to keep flies and ants from intruding. I have seen the beautiful
green curly tansy used as a wreath for a platter of potato salad
at an outdoor supper in California. The crisp leaves took the
place of lettuce, which might have wilted in the heat, and also
kept flies from buzzing around the food. It is one of the ancient
strewing herbs, for its scent is more evident when it is crushed.

Tansy pudding, a sort of custard pie with leaves of the fresh
chopped herb for color and flavoring, was served after the
Lenten fast in England. The herb was said to take the place of
nutmeg and cinnamon.

Modern housewives do not curtsey to tansy as one old lady
told me I should do because it had been of such benefit to
women. We use it fresh and dried in flower arrangements. The
green herb placed along doorsills of a country house will keep

ants from finding their way through cracks. One gardener reported that tansy growing around yew trees kept the deer from
eating them during the winter. The seed heads are long lasting
and remain standing until the next spring. Then a great crop
of seedlings will volunteer around the old plants but fortunately
there is usually someone who wants a start of it for naturalizing
on a sandy bank or just growing at the edge of the property so
that the lovely yellow flowers can be cut for bouquets in August.
If they are picked before they change to a tawny color, they dry
right on the stems and keep their color all winter.

Comment. Tansy is considered dangerous if taken as an infusion. It is one of the prohibited herbs for dealers in botanical
drugs. It cannot be sold as a dried herb in drugstores or by mail.
As little as ten drops of the essential oil will produce dizziness
and more could be lethal, if taken internally. It is one of the
embalming herbs of ancient days, when the leaves were placed
about a corpse to preserve it.

Tarragon, French (*Artemisia dracunculus*)

Height. 2½ feet

Leaf and blossom. A plant which does not set viable seed,
French tarragon is one of the most discussed culinary herbs. It
may not be used as often as sweet marjoram in salads, but the
mark of a true herb gardener is to know and be able to grow
tarragon.

The leaves are dark-green, lanceolate, about two inches long
and slightly resemble those of hyssop. The basal leaves are often
three-parted at the tip, smooth and glandular with entire margins. Until July, the new growth is light green and rather succulent but after that the plants become branching and the stems
harden. Strangely enough, the rich aroma is not emitted by the
leaves until they are crushed or wilted for drying. The flavor
lingers on the tongue, a rather licorice taste with a cool overtone
that produces a numbing sensation when the fresh leaf is chewed.

Culture. Since tarragon is so much coveted by gourmets and
must be bought as a plant, it is important to know how to propa-

gate it. There is always someone who wants a start of it, particularly if yours has a good flavor. It needs slightly more attention than do most culinary herbs. Location has a lot to do with its success in the garden. The plants should not be crowded and must have good drainage. More tarragon plants are lost to mildew and rot than winter-kill. The herb will stand 30° below zero F., if it is well grown. No covering of the clumps is necessary even for such low temperatures, if they are spaced two feet apart and kept free of all grass and other weeds which hold dampness about the roots.

Full sun, rich sandy loam and good care are the prerequisites. Tarragon will survive partial shade but it is not likely to give much material for cutting for tarragon vinegar in such a situation. One grower in New England uses potato fertilizer as a side dressing for the plants in the spring and again right after the first cutting is made on the fourth of July. Each year he sets aside a third of his plantation to lift and divide. If you don't untangle the roots of the plant that gained the name, little dragon, from their serpentine habit, they will choke themselves. The key to success with tarragon is to handle it like a chrysanthemum. Each section of root—eased apart from the clump in March or early April—may be reset to make a good-sized plant the first season. It should not be divided annually the way you do hardy chrysanthemums, but every third year. It is slower-growing than 'mums but needs the same good soil, sunshine and lack of overshadowing leaves or moisture from other plants in summer.

French tarragon may be grown from cuttings, but they are slow to root and even slower to grow into plants large enough to supply snippings for salads. They are also likely to winter-kill the first year if little growth has been made before the ground freezes. Some gardeners separate tarragon in September giving it six weeks to get settled before hard frost. After the foliage has branched and the stems have become woody, in August, there is sometimes a renascence at the roots with artemisias, where new shoots are sent out, as in the spring. This is true in a season of normal rainfall but it cannot be counted on so it is safer to wait

until spring to transplant and divide tarragon. It is well to cut
the plants back to within a few inches of the ground in the fall
to save every flavorful leaf for drying, freezing or vinegar. They
will die back anyway.

One correspondent reported on his tarragon in this fashion:

"As I think about it herbs are like true friends—neglect does
not discourage them and if you treat them kindly they are apt
to forget bygones. I have tarragon plants which I have been
moving about and dragging around since I first had correspond-
ence with you people and that must have been since 1939 or
1940. These plants have been moved from house to house in
crates, flats, baskets, anything to hold soil. They have weathered dry summers, glacial till and heavy clay; rugged winters
with no snow and with lots of snow. I have to laugh when
people try to tell me how tender this plant is. Maybe it doesn't
set seed but who needs seed with a plant that is so amiable
about division."

On occasion French tarragon produces panicles of yellowish
green blossoms. This raises great hope in the breast of the gardener who believes that he will now be able to collect the first
seed of it in many centuries. Inevitably his hopes are dashed by
the resulting chaffy material which forms without being true
seed. If you look at it with a magnifying glass, the brown, thread-
like bits within the calices are less promising. Even the fine seed
of artemisias has a definite form which can be recognized. French
tarragon, like horse-radish, has been propagated so long vegeta-
tively that it appears to have lost the power to set seed.

Some seed catalogs list tarragon. This should be qualified, tell-
ing whether it is Russian tarragon, a larger, lighter green, dull-
foliaged plant with almost no typical flavor or some other species
of artemisia. But the purveyor does not know that the culinary
herb is not produced from seed. Russian tarragon is not usually
listed in botanies but its close approximation of French tarragon
suggests that it is A. dracunculus of a particular variety. The herb
is easy to grow, hardy but dull to the palate and in appearance.

Habitat. No one knows just where and when the first sterile
form of French tarragon with its unique pungency occurred.

However, the genus is native to Russia and Siberia. Dr. Edgar Anderson, curator of useful plants of the Missouri Botanical Garden, discusses the proper Latin names for the true tarragon, as herb gardeners call French tarragon. Actually, it may be French more by association than by point of origin. He says that the less useful herb with more vigorous growth and taller, rangier foliage, should be designated A. *dracunculus inodora*. French tarragon is, more specifically, A. *dracunculus sativa*. There is another species, A. *redowski* which Dr. Anderson calls Siberian tarragon. It is the one offered as seed of "tarragon" in some catalogs.

Uses. The antiquity of true tarragon is shown by the story that the Arabs, the fathers of medicine and mathematics, gave a patient a leaf to chew to anesthetise his tongue before taking bitter medicine. The herb has a special way with fish in that it removes the fishy odor when cooked with it and transmutes the flavor to something delectable. Chicken Estragon, as the French call it, starts with lifting the skin of a roasting bird and laying a few sprigs under it before cooking.

Tarragon vinegar is now sold with a sprig of fresh herb in the bottle. It is an important ingredient of tartare sauce. The herb may be frozen to preserve its full flavor and even for making tarragon vinegar in winter.

Commercial growers make two cuttings of the herb, the first while it still has single stems about twelve inches in length and the second from the woodier later growth. Plants can be forced for greenhouse growing if they are potted, placed in a coldframe to freeze for two or three months and then brought into the heat. The dried herb is usually processed from the branching plants in August because they are less succulent and thus dry faster. The paper bag method works for tarragon, too.

Tarragon Vinegar

Some time before the 4th of July, select a dry day and cut the plants back to three or four inches from the ground. If they have accumulated mud, wash them carefully and pat dry with a towel. Stand those sprigs that will fit in a glass canning jar or gallon jug, in a dry container. Heat, but never boil, white wine or malt vinegar and pour over the amount of herb which loosely fills the jar. Bring the vinegar up to cover the herb and to exclude air from the jar. Close tightly so that no fruit flies will get in and let stand for six weeks. If you plan to decant it into small bottles, it may be done at this time.

Sometimes the herb is left in the vinegar until it is used. Otherwise, a fresh sprig of washed and dried tarragon is placed in each bottle before decanting just to show that it is the real thing. The leaf loses its bright green color but still looks attractive suspended in the vinegar.

Comment. The mystery of tarragon was the subject of conjecture by the herbalists. John Gerard repeats but did not believe the strange tale of its origin, in 1597:

"many strange tales hereof, scarce worth noting, saying that the sede of flaxe put into a radish roote or sea Onion, and so set doth bring forth that herbe Tarragon."

For once he was out of words to describe its "Vertues":

"Tarragon is not to be eaten alone, joyned with other herbes, as lettuce, purslaine, and such like, that it may also temper the coldness of them, like as Rocket doth, neither do we knowe what other use this herb hath."

Thyme (*Thymus vulgaris*)

Height. 10 inches

Leaf and blossom. Thyme is a dwarf, shrubby herb with smooth ovate leaves about one-eighth inch wide by one quarter-inch long in the variety known as English thyme. The undersides of the leaves are dark red, especially when the plants are young. French thyme is grayer with narrower leaves which curl under at the edges. This shows the stems more whereas the English thyme gives an impression more of leaves than twigs. Both are covered with pinkish tubular flowers in June.

The leaves of these upright thymes are cut for drying just before the buds appear in quantity, for not only is the flavor stronger then, but after the blossoms open one cannot get near the sweet-scented plants because they are humming with bees.

If thyme is harvested before flowering in early summer, it will bloom later when a second growth has come on. The whole plant of thyme (pronounced "time") is pleasantly aromatic and there are fine degrees of difference between the flavor and scent of different species and varieties. French thyme, *T. vulgaris,* which is easily grown from seed, provides the best flavored dried thyme. The broader-leaved English thyme does not seem to set seed.

As there are more than fifty species of thymus, described in the *Dictionary of Gardening of the Royal Horticultural Society,* it is not possible to go into detail about more than the ten which are commonly grown in herb or rock gardens. Only those which have some definite herbal association or especially appealing characteristics such as lemon scent and variegated marking will be noted here. The best way to study them is to visit a nursery which has a good collection, properly labeled, or a botanical garden which sets them apart under species and varieties. Helen M. Fox gives brief but very clear descriptions of those she has grown over fifty years in *The Years in My Herb Garden.* Another source of information is *Herbs and the Fragrant Garden* by Margaret Brownlow, owner of The Herb Farm in Kent, England. She gives the trade names under which dozens of varieties are sold by that nursery.

Lemon Thyme, *T. citriodorus,* looks very much like English thyme when it has plain green leaves but a golden-edged form is more popular. If you brush your hand over either one of these upright forms they release their pleasant citrus scent. The English grow a form called Silver Queen which is lemon-scented with silver markings on the margins of the leaves but the silver thyme available in this country has the typical thyme pungency without lemon overtones. All three are six to eight inches high and have value as edging plants for sunny gardens.

The large group of creeping thymes are mostly forms of *T. serpyllum* though some are considered distinct species. There is a lemon-scented thyme which makes a mat flat against the ground until the airy, thimble-shaped sprays of blossoms in shades of pink and mauve dance above it in August. It has crept out into the lawn on one side of our garden and continues to hold its own against the grass through mowings and drought. It makes a delightful place to sit upon on a hot summer day.

Caraway thyme, *T. herba-barona,* is a vigorous carpeter which has small leaves tightly spaced on the arching stems. It tends to mound up where it grows though it cannot be considered anything but a creeping thyme. It is an excellent cover on a sandy bank where little else will grow. The species name came from the English custom of rubbing the leaves on the huge barons of beef roasted for banquets. Just a few of the pungent leaves scattered over roast beef before it is put in the oven give the meat a subtle extra in flavor that in no way alters its natural goodness but enhances it. It is the thyme I use most in cooking, not just because it is convenient to the kitchen, serving as part of the rock garden by the driveway, but because of its flavor.

A golden-leaved form of *T. serpyllum* has definitely yellow leaves in spring and fall but in mid-summer it looks so like the species that it may not even be a different variety. *T. serpyllum coccineus* has bright crimson flowers in mid-season with smaller leaves than the above. A more fragile variety, *albus,* with showy white flowers is lighter green with tiny rounded leaves that resent competition even from other creeping thymes. It is particularly good between wide flat paving. If the creeping thymes can get a firm foothold in the soil, as between slate or even cement paving, they will spread out over the water shedding surfaces to look their best. Grass and clover are enemies to the dense foliage because they hold the dew and the herb suffers where it does not dry out quickly after a rain.

Woolly thyme, *T. serpyllum lanuginosus,* has rounded gray leaves that make thick patches of attractive fuzziness in gravelly soil. It stands dampness even less than others because of the dense hairiness of the leaves. The flowers are lavender and very plentiful in July. Still another woolly thyme is *T. lanicaulis* with widely spaced leaves on long trailing stems. The narrow leaves are longer than those of most varieties and the habit of the plant is more spreading. For this reason it permits spring bulbs to come up through its cover, but so, too, will weeds if it is not able to sprawl over rocks instead of plain earth. All of the creeping thymes benefit by rocks to increase the drainage and capture the warmth of the sun. If a good slope is not available for them, at least raise the bed so that they can drape themselves over the edges.

Culture. Thymes are heavy feeders and the spreading sorts reach out for new soil in which to root when they expand so attractively. The soil should be gritty, or reinforced with stone chips to give them a dry surface for the flat foliage and a cool root run. The upright species can be fed by a side dressing of bone meal during the growing season but the carpeters are best left until late fall before mulching with a mixture of compost, sand and bonemeal for the winter. This will work down to the roots during the freezing and thawing or spring rains.

Most thymes flourish in soil that is non-acid but woolly thyme should be mulched with pine needles under such conditions. Throughout the Berkshire Hills in southern Massachusetts where there are limestone outcroppings, wild thyme is found growing in sheets in rocky pastures. It has become part of some lawns where housing has replaced cows in the area. It is a stunning sight in late August when huge patches of the herb are in bloom. The area extends over into New York State, near the former home of Edna St. Vincent Millay, at Austerlitz, where thyme honey was sold by beekeepers. Miss Millay loved herbs. In one of her letters, collected in a book edited by Allan Ross Macdougall, published in 1952, she asked a friend not to send any magazines as gifts because she received so many but she carried them all to the attic unread except for *The Herb Grower, The Bulletin of the Metropolitan Museum* and the *Audubon Magazine,* during the last few years of her life.

French thyme may be grown from seed planted directly in the garden or started in flats and transplanted to stand 12 inches apart. The first year foliage is soft and the whole plant may be cut for drying but the second season the stems become woody, gnarled and almost like little bonsai trees with their gray leaves. There is material to cut before the plants bloom and again after they have gone to seed. Flowering occurs in June and since the pungency of the herb is sufficient to withstand drying even after it is past its peak of flavor you can cut the rows to prune off the seed heads. Bees will see to it that you have seed heads. In sandy soil French thyme sometimes self-sows. The creeping varieties do not need to be sheared even though they look a little shaggy for a few weeks after the blossoms fade. The heads seem to be absorbed by the mat and new growth creeps right out over them.

All thymes may be propagated by divisions, especially if some earth has been hilled up over them in the fall. The creepers have no limit to the number of plantlets which can be pulled off a two-foot wide clump if you do it when the ground is moist early in the spring or fall.

Habitat. Thymes seem to be widely dispersed throughout the temperate climate but more species are native to the Mediterranean region than anywhere else. Some have the name of the islands from which they come in the species designation such as *T. azoricus,* one of the many one to two inch high thymes grown in rock gardens.

Uses. *Thymus vulgaris* has an ancient history as a medicinal and culinary herb. The oil is still the basis of a patent cough medicine. Thymol is known to have anti-bacterial properties of considerable potency. In cooking, thyme is thought of in connection with seasoning clam chowder and, of course, for poultry dressing. The fragrance will suggest many uses in day to day living; especially lemon thyme which is delectable in bouquets and has also served as an herb tea.

Comment. Just as anyone could use more time in his life, the herb gardener never can have too much thyme.

Valerian (Valeriana officinalis)
Height. 4 to 5 feet
Leaf and blossom. Also called garden heliotrope because of the perfume of the fluffy white blossoms, valerian has neat, pin-

nate leaves which make basal clumps only ten inches tall. Suddenly, in May, the plants develop almost leafless blossom stalks to four or more feet in height which carry the pinkish white flowers. After the blossoms fade the feathery seed heads should be cut back or they will self-sow as far as the downy pappus on each seed will carry it. It is rather an obliging plant for the background of the perennial flower garden because the blossoms last several weeks. Then the plant can be cut back to a neat basal clump again. It will grow in quite a bit of shade. Some gardeners find that the herb attracts cats which love to nibble the leaves and roll against them.

Culture. It is possible to start valerian from seed or off-shoots of the rather spreading roots. Seed may be sown as soon as ripe in late summer or in the early spring. Young plants should be thinned to twelve inches apart. Root divisions are made before or after flowering.

Habitat. Naturalized around old house foundations, valerian attests to the endurance of the women who brought their medicinal plants from across the ocean. They and some of the hardy perennials like garden heliotrope flourished in the new land.

Uses. As a drug plant valerian has not continued to enjoy a place of prominence that it enjoyed in colonial days. It was the strangely-scented root which was brewed into tea for hysterical female complaints. The oil of valerian does have an effect on the central nervous system.

Red valerian, *Centranthus ruber,* has entire smooth leaves and rosy red blossoms similar to those of true valerian. It was considered a perennial salad green in France but it has become almost a wild plant in England where it grows in old stone walls such as the escarpment around Windsor Castle. It is not as hardy in this country as garden heliotrope but very decorative wherever it lives.

Woodruff, Sweet (*Asperula odorata*)

Height. 10 inches

Leaf and blossom. It is hard to think that the dainty little woodruff, called waldmeister in Germany where it grows wild in the Black Forest, is a close relative of the coffee tree. The decumbent, medium green foliage of woodruff is composed of square, brittle, slightly hairy stems with many whorls of stiff, glossy, lanceolate leaves. In May, the pure white, four-lobed blossoms look like tiny stars against the green ground cover. The margins of the leaves have many rigid hairs which make them feel as though they were tiny saw teeth. A few round ciliate seed pods develop in June but the plants are not very fertile.

Sweet woodruff is a fine ground cover, especially under flowering crabapple trees. It will grow in the sun but the foliage is a darker green and more plentiful where it gets shade at least half of the day.

Sweet Woodruff,
Asperula odorata

Culture. If there is no ideal woodland site for the herb in the garden, a heavy mulch of well-rotted leaf mold or peat moss should be. incorporated into the bed in which the plants are set. It is not grown from seed but can be multiplied easily from sections of creeping stems broken away from the old clump. Cuttings root quickly in moist sand or perlite. Woodruff remains evergreen in a dish garden or terrarium in the house. In the garden it is green until the snow covers it, as much of the growth of the stolons is made during the fall.

Habitat. Reports of sweet woodruff growing wild in this country usually turn out to be a case of mistaken identity. At some stages of growth it resembles bedstraw, *Galium verum,* but that plant grows much taller and the whorls of leaves do not have the sweet perfume that woodruff develops upon wilting or drying. It, too, is native to Europe and Asia, but bedstraw has become widespread in this country.

Uses. The perfume, like a whiff of new-mown hay, that wood-ruff exhales upon being cut suggests that it would have been a great strewing herb. However, Thomas Tusser, the 16th century writer, leaves it off his list of strewing herbs and puts it among those things to be distilled, with a note "for sweet waters and cakes." To this day the German custom of placing sprigs of the herb in white wine to make Maiwein is continued here and abroad. You can buy it bottled in the cities in the spring. A Maibowle composed of Rhine wine flavored with leaves of woodruff cut just before the blossoms have opened, was part of the May day festival in Germany. It was regarded as a spring tonic and there may have been some basis for this as woodruff contains coumarin which is used as a blood thinner. Herb tea made from dried waldmeister is a delightful drink, just as the foliage is excellent for adding bulk and fragrance to pot-pourri. Gerard, again, had a good word to say for the herb which grows sweeter with the keeping:

> "The flowers grow at the top of the stemmes, of a white colour and of a very sweete smell, as is the rest of the herb, which being made up into garlands or bundles, and hanged up in homes in the heate of summer, doth very well attemper the aire, coole and make fresh the place, to the delight and comfort of such as are therein."

To my delight, when I looked up the above in the first edition of Gerard's *Herball,* I found that he grew the blue woodruff which is an annual. He called it *Asperula caerulea,* or "blew Woodrooffe" and described it perfectly. The white woodruff grew under hedges and in woods almost everywhere in the England of his day and the blue woodruff was found in many places in Essex. Sweet woodruff he said was put into wine to make a man merrie as it was good for his heart and his liver. There is no easier way to take it than in:

Maibowle

Any good, light, white wine should go into the punch bowl—Sauterne, Moselle, or Rhine wine—about a quart of it, and be stirred with ½ cup brandy. Add simple syrup to taste and toss in slices of pineapple, orange, lemon and a good handful of wild strawberries, the biggest you can find. Add a large chunk of ice and crown it all with white stars and leaves of sweet woodruff. In fact, it is of better flavor, if the latter soaks in the wine an hour or so before the fruit and ice are added. You may add a pint of cold champagne at the last minute to give sparkle. Not too sweet herb cookies or pound cake flavored with caraway or anise seeds are more suitable with a Maibowle than cheese and crackers.

Wormwood (Artemisia absinthium)

Height. 3 feet

Leaf and blossom. There are many kinds of wormwood with the same bitter taste and musty smell but the official drug plant is A. absinthium. The leaves are silvery, two or three-parted in segments that resemble those of chrysanthemum but much grayer over-all. Panicles of small yellow flowers appear in late July, almost hidden from view by the hairiness of the calices and bracts, as the actual blossoms are only ⅛ inch across.

The artemisias are as numerous as the mints but they do not seem to hybridize as readily because the bitter blossoms are less frequent and have little attraction for honey bees. Small wasps seem to be their best visitors. A. absinthium is the source of the intoxicating and dangerous drink absinthe which was banned even in France when it was found to be damaging to the brain. It is usually the first wormwood the herb gardener attempts because it can be grown from seed.

That is the best way to get it started because it is one species which does not spread by runners. First year plants are more ornamental than those which run to seed the second summer. But they can be cut back to make two-foot tall shrubby plants.

Culture. The silvery artemisias show by the silky down on the foliage that they are able to withstand drought. In areas of the world where rainfall is as scant as 2½ inches per year, such as the mountains above Hunza, artemisias are found growing wild. This shows that they need full sun, good drainage and little feeding in the garden. *A. absinthium* and *A. dracunculus sativa* do not mind a clay soil but they must not be wet all the time.

Most of the fine-leaved, highly ornamental wormwoods are easily propagated by root divisions made in early spring or fall. In some cases, such as *A. pontica* or Roman wormwood, it is necessary to discourage the spreading nature of the roots by spading around them in the spring as you do with mints. Asbestos shingles which are 12 inches deep, sunken in the ground to two-thirds of their height, make fine root barriers and can edge small raised beds.

Like the santolinas, the wormwoods make excellent plants for seaside gardens because they withstand hot sun, drying winds and salt spray which does not affect their hoary leaves.

Habitat. Beach wormwood, *A. stelleriana,* grows wild in pure sand right on the dunes facing the sea on the Eastern Coast. It has very deep roots, reaching down to moisture so that any attempt to divide a clump to bring home a piece usually ends in disaster. This silver treasure should be left to propagate itself where it is most beautiful. Plants can be purchased from nurseries which specialize in herbs.

A. absinthium is a European wormwood with a long history of medicinal use. Even today the essential oil is the basis of a much advertised liniment. The United States has its share of handsome gray plants that are included in the 280 species of the genus. Fringed wormwood, *A. frigida,* is found on dry plains and rocky soil from Minnesota to Canada and south to Texas.

The American Indians used the attractive foliage, which sticks straight out from the two and one-half foot tall stems like thorns, for a fumigant in severe illness and chewed it for indigestion.

Another western artemisia is *A. ludoviciana,* sometimes mistakenly called Silver King wormwood, but it is a much more sprawling plant than the lovely variety *albula* which is Silver King. All forms of the *A. ludoviciana* species have entire, narrowly ovate leaves, some of which have two "ears" projecting at the sides. In the species are three forms, one of which begins to flower in July and becomes decumbent as the heavy blossom clusters, almost hidden by the bracts and calices, pull it down. The very tall, ghost-like, whitish form is larger in leaf and the blossoms appear in August on six to eight foot tall stems. Silver King does not come up until late in the spring and makes a low basal grouping until August when it seems to suddenly show up with many side branches bearing woolly, narrow leaves that are excellent material for arrangements, either fresh or dried. It must be planted in the background because at maturity it is three feet tall though it appears to be much lower most of the season.

Another European wormwood, *A. pontica,* called old woman or Roman wormwood, has lacy leaves of great delicacy. If its manners were as good as its appearance it would be a delight in the herb garden.

Cudweed, *A. purshiana,* brings us back to this country for the source of a ground cover type wormwood which is six inches tall until the white-woolly blooming stems appear in late summer. It can be clipped, as can Roman wormwood, to make a low edging. The common name of cudweed came from the idea that cattle browsed on it but this seems unlikely as it is bitter and not very good at holding its own against grass. It is found in British Columbia, California and east to Nebraska.

A. schmidtiana nana is called Silver Mound in the nursery trade. It comes from Asia and offers one of the handsomest, silky, shimmering plants, for a sunny rock garden or low accent in the herb garden, imaginable. It makes a twelve inch high beauty spot which is comprised of linear leaves in tufts along the soft gray stems. Plants are easily propagated by divisions of the clumps in March and April but later than this they have more tops than roots. It is a good idea to keep lifting and dividing Silver Mound, not only because you cannot have too much of it but also because the smaller plants are less likely to break down in the center in mid-summer under the weight of silvery heads of bloom.

A. argentea from Madeira has the same gleaming silver tufts of hair-like leaves on taller stems which reach two and one-half feet when the plants bloom. It, too, needs full sun, perfect drainage and frequent separation of its woodier plants.

Uses. Since bitters and bitter herbs are out of fashion with modern palates, except in the ubiquitous martini which cannot be made without the essence of wormwood, the main use of artemisias is foliage effect in the garden. Vermouth is made from several species of wormwood but their use in medicinal teas has gone out of style.

With a number of gray plants in the garden it is possible to avoid the between season doldrums in a perennial flower border. The wormwoods also provide material for dried arrangements and their curving stems invite shaping into herb wreaths.

Tops clipped from Roman wormwood, where it is used to outline patterns in a formal bed, and general prunings from other species make good materials to dry and put in net bags as moth preventives. I have found that some birds use sprigs of herbs among their nesting materials. A hapless robin which made three attempts at nest on a precarious support under the eaves of the house, lost them all just as each was being lined with feathers and grass. Among the twigs, bits of string and other curious stuffs included in each were leaves of wormwood picked up in the garden after I cut back *A. absinthium.* They might have helped to prevent the hatching of lice with the hatching of the young. Wormwood, of course, was a vermifuge; when taken internally it dispelled worms.

The sage brush of our western states, A. *tridentata*, is collected for the distillation of the oil which is used to perfume candles and soaps for the tourist trade. It is not hardy in New England, unfortunately, though the plants are pretty enough to be an addition to the garden.

Comment. Leaving the description of perennial herbs with wormwood is not to end on a note of bitterness but, rather, it points out the historic place of herbs in our lives. It is mentioned twelve times in The Bible and can be appropriately used in landscaping church yards.

OTHER PLANTS OF SIGNIFICANCE AS HERBS

"Surely, it makes a garden more romantic and wonderful to know that Wallflowers, Irises, Lupins, Delphiniums, Columbines, Dahlias and Chrysanthemums, every flower in the garden from the first Snowdrop to the Christmas Rose, are not only there for man's pleasure but have their compassionate use in his pain."

Mrs. C. F. Leyel, editor of Mrs. Maude Grieve's *A Modern Herbal,* in two volumes, first published in 1931 and reprinted even up to today because of its complete information on over a thousand plants which have economic, medicinal or culinary value, wrote the above in the introduction to the 888 page work. Leafing through it we can find justification for adding many colorful flowers to the herb garden. There is space to mention but a few here. However, it will give you an idea of the fascination to be found in the study of why plants were cultivated by man in the first place.

Aconite or monkshood has been an official drug plant. Agrimony and alkanet are grown today for home dyeing. Butterflyweed was called pleurisy root and used for respiratory disorders by the Indians. Bedstraw, both yellow and white, served to curdle milk in making cheese and the use of the leaves for stuffing mattresses gave rise to the legend that the herb was used in the Manger by the Virgin Mary. Betony, both the

green-leaved *Stachys officinalis* and the lovely, furry gray betony
called lambs' ears, had their place as home remedies; being
placed on cuts and ulcers to facilitate healing and so were called
woundworts. Brooms, both cytisus and genista species, were
employed not only to make the famous besoms but also yielded
a green dye from the young tops. Even the familiar ground
cover bugleweed, *Ajuga reptans,* was considered a remedy for
hangovers, while calamints, said Gerard, "maketh a man merrie
and glad."

There has never been a time in history when people did not
need plants to cheer them and even one's commonest weeds
become respected herbs if you know their background of service
and sentiment which caused plants which we consider wild-
lings to be carried across the ocean with the early settlers.
Celandine, with its bright yellow petals and orange juice in the
white stems, which suggested to early physicians that it was a
specific for jaundice, is something I weed out of every garden
bed. I do it with some deference and leave a little to seed
along the edge of the woods.

Chicory with its azure flowers is the glory of our roadsides
in late summer. I grew the pink and white flowered forms from
seed distributed by the Royal Horticultural Society to members
only to find they both occur in stands of the herb not far from
home. Chicory has been cultivated as a salad green in Europe,
and, of course, the root is a substitute for coffee and is sometimes mixed with certain blends of it.

Coltsfoot with its dandelion-like blossoms on naked stems
in April brightens the stream banks. It was the hoof-shaped
leaves which were used in herb tea to treat coughs. If you
read the five pages devoted to the dandelion in *A Modern
Herbal* you will put aside weed killers and enjoy the golden
blossoms in the lawn, even letting some go to seed to attract
indigo buntings who use the down for their nests.

Deadnettle is not a nettle at all but a low, sprawling member of the mint family with pretty silver-striped leaves and
showy white or magenta blossoms which brighten the ground

under shrubs if used as a carefree ground cover. It was used to stop bleeding in olden days.

Handsome elecampane, called horseheal for its use in veterinary medicine, has become naturalized in wet meadows in New England. If invited into the garden it provides a tall accent of bright yellow in July when the large rayed flowers stand six feet tall above the enormous felty leaves.

Ferns, too, belong in the herb garden, not just because fern "seed" can make you invisible but for their time-honored roll as a vermifuge. The true flax used to make linen is an annual but the perennial *Linum perenne* produces seeds with some of the mucilaginous quality that made flaxseed valued as a demulcent when steeped in tea. Linseed oil comes from the seed of the tall, less ornamental source of linen fiber, *L. usitatissimum*.

Ginseng is an example of how the reputation of a plant can cause it to be carried from one side of the world to another. The root is said to have the shape of a man and is still collected in the Appalachian Mountain area to be dried and sold for shipping to Hongkong. The Chinese value our native ginseng almost more highly than they do their native species which is probably all up-rooted by now anyway. The idea that the root had a bodily form was probably transferred from the legends of true mandrake, *Mandragora officinarum*, which was a fertility charm in ancient days.

As is often the case with crop plants cultivated in the country of their origin, ginseng plantations made with the hope of great profits have succumbed to a blight in this country. Unfortunately, some unscrupulous dealers in wild herbs advertise the seed and promise to buy back the crop. It takes years to grow the roots to collecting size and the plants must be in woodsy soil with overhead-shading. If you look in the window of a Chinese apothecary shop in New York's Chinatown, you will see the dessicated roots lying in state in silk-lined boxes as proof of their monetary value.

The history of herbs has its dark moments and even the

lovely Christmas rose is a strong poison, if the extract of the root is employed in medicine. Henbane and hemp are narcotics once used to treat disease and thus have escaped to become naturalized in some parts of the country. The lovely lobelias, especially that vivid red beauty of wet places in New England, the cardinal flower, and the blue *Lobelia siphilitica* were used in herbal medicine. They can be grown from seed to brighten the late summer garden though *L. cardinalis* is recommended for protection by the garden clubs conservation list. In England our native lobelias have been hybridized for use as perennial flowers. *Lobelia inflata* forms a patent medicine sold to help people give up smoking.

Mallows no longer have any connection with the confection sold as marshmallows but the roots were originally infused in water to make a soothing drink for coughs. They deserve a place in the herb garden for their bright pink or white blossoms. Mullein was collected by colonial housewives to make fomentations, poultices and the yellow petals were preserved in olive oil to drop in ears that were infected.

Who would think of eating pretty primrose blossoms, but the tea, said Gerard, "was drunk in the month of May for curing the phrensie." Apparently in Jugoslavia, where many herbs have been the subject of beautiful postage stamps, the leaves of *Primula veris* have been found to be a source of vitamin C. The use of the leaves and roots as medicine in that country has caused its exploitation in mountain districts where it is now a protected wildflower.

Senna, *Cassia marilandica,* was grown and collected in the wild by the Shakers to make a cathartic. It has pretty yellow flowers on tall plants with locust-like leaves which fold up at night. Place it well to the back of the garden bed because it takes up quite a bit of room. Do not let the seed pods cast their fruit or it will self-sow with abandon.

The spurges are generally too weedy for the herb garden though they are pretty when in bloom and in seed, with rosy bracts. Caper spurge, *Euphorbia lathyrus,* is called moleplant because those animals are said to avoid any place where it is planted. Even the tender poinsettia, *E. pulcherrima*, has its herbal uses in the tropics where the red bracts were used to dye cloth. Most spurges are poisonous, and the milky juice of the stems should not be ingested.

Thistles have their herbal interest. Mrs. Grieve described a dozen starting with Holy thistle. A warm infusion of the leaves was said to increase the milk of nursing mothers. Some hormone activity has been reported in thistles today.

Lemon verbena, *Lippia citriodora*, with crisp, light green, lanceolate leaves of delightful citrus scent, is a fairly recent herb. It was introduced into England in 1784 from South America. There, as in southern California, it can attain a height of 15 feet. The shrub is deciduous even where it can winter outdoors. In New England, it is propagated by cuttings which are hard to bring through the winter even in a greenhouse. But because it grows so well in the herb garden, and has the most truly lemon scent of all, it is worth purchasing every year. All the foliage should be collected and dried before the first frost, as the leaves are not only good in tea but excellent in potpourri.

Vervain, *Verbena officinalis*, is the hardy, true verbena which was considered a tonic in olden days. Even more remarkable, it was said of it that:

> "Vervain and Dill
> Hinder witches from their will."

Violets, lily-of-the-valley and even wakerobin or trillium will surprise you by their presence in the great compendium of drugs of the past. Water-cress and witch hazel, of course you might expect, and yarrow, which was another woundwort bringing healing to cuts, wind up the list. They all prove that

> "Anything green that grew out of the mould
> Was an excellent herb to our fathers of old."

CHAPTER V

Herbs in the Vegetable Garden

There is nothing new about putting herbs in the vegetable garden. Nor is there anything ultra-modern about most of the insects they are reputed to drive from it. In 1577, Thomas Hyll wrote of "the worthy remedies and secrets availing against Snailes, Canker Wormes, the long bodied Mothes, Garden fleas and Earth wormes, which vitiate and gnaw, as well the pot-hearbs, as trees and fruits."

Vegetables were called pot-herbs in the time of his book *The Gardeners Labyrinth, or A New Art of Gardening.* The word we use for them did not come into general use until 1767, according to the *Oxford Dictionary*'s definition for vegetable: "A plant cultivated for food; especially an edible herb or root used for human consumption and commonly eaten, either cooked or raw, with meat or other articles of food." The same authority dates pot-herb back to 1538 as "a herb grown for boiling in the pot; any of the herbs cultivated in the kitchen garden."

The *Oxford Dictionary*'s definition for a pot-herb brings us to the pronunciation of the word "herb." In the same volume, dated 1933 and revised in 1955, it states that in Middle English the word was usually spelled "erbe"; in Latin it is "herba" with the "h" mute until the nineteenth century. Whenever you see "a" herb rather than "an" herb, you know you are reading an English book. In the United States today the "h" is not as generally stressed as it is in England.

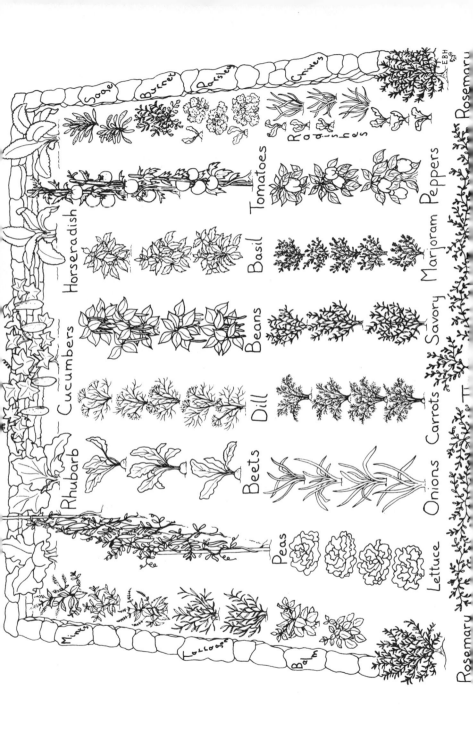

The study of plants which deter insects in the vegetable or any other type of garden is a fascinating pursuit for horticulturists. It is far more pleasant to use plants to protect other plants than to grab the handy can of poison that may kill all the useful insects as well as those defacing a particular plant.

Keep in mind that some invasions of aphids or beetles are geared to the time of the growing season. Bean beetles are not apt to be around for late plantings of string beans in New England, for instance. The types of beetles that the British call "tarnish beetles" are most prevalent in early summer. Some are striped cucumber beetles just waiting for the cucurbit to grow nicely. The action of these insects in scraping little circles of green leaf surface, leaving brown or black spots without perforating the leaf, is distressing but not dangerous to the plant. The county extension expert who came to my garden once looked at the damage and said, "Mint rust. You must use malathion." He also saw ants in the path and urged me to use another persistent pesticide which stays in the ground for twelve years. I knew that the flickers made regular visits to the herb garden, probing for ants which sometimes make nests in the creeping thymes. The thought of endangering the lives of the many birds and bees that enliven my garden scene was entirely repugnant to me. It seemed as though the expert was seeing only insects rather than admiring the plants.

There are many like him. Since the introduction of the pressure spray can, people have been enticed into dealing instant death to any flying or creeping insect that upsets their idea of a garden as paradise. It is an attitude that will have to be unlearned if the balance of nature is to be restored even in a small controlled area under cultivation.

Formerly, the major insecticides were of herbal origin. Pyrethrum comes from the flowers of a member of the chrysanthemum family and rotenone is derived from a Malaysian plant *Derris elliptica*. The latter is used as a dust that is insoluble in water and retains its toxicity to insects only a few days. It is decomposed by sunlight and is poisonous to insects and fish but not to humans. The same chemical principle is found in a native vine called catgut, *Crucca virginiana*. Nicotine sulphate is used to kill aphids and white flies in greenhouses. The best seed catalogs and garden centers still carry these materials just as they always have. But it is the persistent pesticides which can be produced at the greatest profit that have been most highly advertised. The demand for them has been produced just as artificially as their manufacture.

Some fine work has been done by the Connecticut Experiment Station (reported in their Bulletin No. 701, May 1969, by P. M. Miller and J. F. Ahrens) in proving that plants can clear the soil of nematodes. The microscopic worms that feed on plant roots have long been the bane of agriculturists and gardeners, particularly in warm climates.

The most effective for this purpose are species of Mexican or African marigolds, *Tagetes patula* or *Tagetes erecta*. They are the annuals with bright yellow or orange-colored flowers and finely cut leaves. The pot marigold, *Calendula officinalis,* is a different plant with rounded leaves and flowers with petals that open flat by day and close again in the evening. Many garden writers have lumped the plants together because of the common name and have even declared that the petals of both were used in olden days to flavor and color soups and custards. This is quite inaccurate. The calendula has been the herb of culinary use and home remedies but it is not the flower used in the nematode control study. Soil in which Tagetes species had been grown improved the vigor of calendula flowers planted in it in the Connecticut Experiment Station tests. The effects of the nematode control increased the second year after the marigolds had been used as a rotation planting. The conclusion of the researchers was that Tagetes, or marigolds, produce a chemical in the roots which kills nematodes when it is released in the soil. The chemical does not accumulate quickly but must grow with the plant through the season to give lasting control.

No doubt other flowers and herbs transmit their own special qualities to the soil.

Today, herbs are being returned to their rightful place beside carrots, beans and beets in the vegetable garden, not only because they season the vegetables in cooking but also because their pungent aromas appear to protect the growing crops from insects. Many of the annual herbs, dill, fennel, sweet basil and summer savory, thrive in row culture where the soil is rich enough for vegetables. There they receive ample sun and sufficient water. The dividends are many, beginning with the tasty thinnings of the rows of herbs that can be harvested long before the vegetables are mature enough to pick.

The reaction of insects to the vapors of oil of catnip, for instance, demonstrates the power of herbs. Certain ants, beetles and flies are repelled by the pure essence of the herb. Extracts and even the dried flower heads of another herb, pyrethrum, actually kill insects without harm to humans. Oil of garlic killed mosquito larvae in laboratory tests. When I weeded a large bed of garlic chives one season when mosquitoes were rampant, the whining insects did not pursue me where the air was redolent of garlic odor. *The Gardeners Labyrinth,* 1577, recommends burning green garlic foliage in different parts of the garden to discourage insects. Here, perhaps, is a new use for the outdoor barbecue on wheels.

Why not plant fennel flower, the original "fitch" of the Bible, as herbalist Thomas Hyll suggests. Steeped in water and sprinkled on plants, it rids them of beetles and leaf hoppers. Many other potions that the gardener can mix up have been praised for centuries as growth stimulants or insect deterrents. Nettle tea is one. Horsetail and fenugreek, the seed of which is used rather than the plant, are also useful when steeped in a watering pot. The first is a fungicide while the latter seems to protect seedlings from damping off, according to Thomas Hyll.

It is helpful to have summer savory in a row next to the green bush beans it will ultimately flavor. Sweet basil needs much the same culture as little cherry tomatoes, and the fresh herb will later ward off fruit flies from a bowl of the bright red and yellow "love apples."

The combinations suggested here are time-tested, practical for both the gardener and cook—and they add beauty to the vegetable patch. If they work also toward better health for your garden crops, you are so much the winner.

Perennial herbs may be used as edging plants for plots of vegetables, just as long as they do not interfere with spading or tilling the beds in the spring. The most permanent vegetable crop, asparagus, has its herbal value too. The juice of the green stems is an effective control for nematodes. If the fresh tops of asparagus are crushed and steeped in water that is used to saturate the ground where root-knot, stubby root and meadow nematodes are suspected, the solution offers protection to the plants.

Bush green beans and *summer savory* need successive sowings in rows two and one-half feet apart. After all danger of frost is past, green beans may be planted by pushing each seed into a shallow drill. Cover with twice their depth of soil. Summer savory's small grains must be sifted out of the packet carefully and barely covered with soil. As soon as the latter's slim plants have four true leaves, thin to leave single specimens six inches apart: use the plantlets thus removed for salad seasoning. As the seedlings are uprooted, firm the soil around the remaining plants to give support to the rather bushy, but topheavy, mature herbs. Since I have grown summer savory between plantings of beans, I have not been bothered with bean beetles.

Beets yield delicious greens, some of which are pulled to thin the row. The seeds actually contain two or more kernels, each of which germinates, so that the most carefully spaced planting may suddenly appear too thick. Cover to twice the depth of the seed with soil well tamped down. Beets can be placed as close as eighteen inches between the rows because the foliage is not too spreading.

As you harvest beets, sow a few seeds of dill in the spaces. The tender greens of the herb will be useful when making pickled beets. Pick dill leaves long before the flowers and seeds appear. They will not shade the beets but will look very pretty in contrast to their red foliage.

Broccoli and *cabbage* are started from seed in flats and set out in the garden, two feet apart, as early as the ground can be worked. They are heavy feeders and need a side dressing of balanced fertilizer or well-rotted manure several times during the growing season. Oak leaves tucked in around the young plants are said to deter cutworms; pungent herbs such as sage and hyssop, planted at the ends of the rows, will help to fool the cabbage worm butterfly. All plants of the mustard family, such as broccoli, cabbage and cauliflower, should be rotated so that they do not grow in the same earth year after year; this is where short rows of dill, summer savory and parsley aid the vegetable gardener.

The number of plants set out will depend on how much space you want to give to these large vegetables. Broccoli and cauliflower florets have become popular as hors d'oeuvres when dipped in sour cream and chive dressing and eaten raw. The broccoli will sprout again with more flower buds, but cauliflower is a one time thing. As for cabbage, a bit of summer savory cooked along with the vegetable helps to dispel the gaseous vapors and, if you use ¼ cup of milk in the cooking liquid, you can prevent the odor from escaping into the house.

Joseph Wood Krutch in his wonderful *Herbal* quotes the 16th century physician Mattioli on the subject of cabbages:

"Garden Cabbages only slightly cooked are good for the stomach, but if they are cooked too long, and especially if they are cooked with soda or cooked twice, they contract it. . . . Eaten at the end of a meal they remove all the effects of drinking too much wine . . ."

Carrots should be planted in several short rows over a two-month period if you want tender young roots all summer. Parsley is planted in alternating rows with carrots in England to ward off the carrot fly. Grating and cooking the roots of older carrots in just enough water to prevent burning and serving them with butter and chopped sweet cicely leaves makes them far more popular with the family.

Garden cress or *peppergrass* is one of the first salad herbs to plant in the garden or in a window box while waiting for the ground to dry out enough to work. It literally springs out of the soil and should be eaten when just a few inches tall. Peppergrass is ready to pull in about three weeks.

Experienced gardeners plant pickling size *cucumbers* for dill pickles and a larger variety for slicing. But few remember to sow dill early and often enough to have both flowers and seed heads to interlayer between the cukes in a stone crock when making pickles. It is a good idea to make frequent sowings of dill in the spaces where vegetables have been harvested.

Finocchio or fennel is a good pot-herb to succeed beans or peas. The bulbous-stemmed fennel runs to seed if sown before July. The enlarged basal stems are harvested after frost to eat raw like celery or as a cooked vegetable. Sow the seeds in a short row, thinning to stand eight inches apart. When the lower stems begin to swell to the size of an egg, draw the earth up around them to encourage blanching. The tops are feathery but not spreading so the row may be as close as a foot from its neighbor. As this is a culinary herb as well as a vegetable it is treated more fully under "Annuals and Biennials."

Garlic, leeks and *onions* have sufficient substitutes among the perennial herbs to eliminate them from the small salad garden. Rocambole and Egyptian multiplier onions, treated under perennial herbs (page 151), take their place with far less effort on your part. Where members of the onion family are interplanted with roses they should not be used for eating if the rose fancier insists on using systemic insecticides or sprays. The purpose of such a companion planting is to ward off aphids and rose bugs but sometimes people carry things to extremes and make the mistake of trying to combine the edible with the poisonous to their stomachs' great distress.

Lettuce, especially when home-grown, is so delectable that no one with a garden should pass it up. No other vegetable offers such variety, as well as superiority to the grocery store offerings. The old problem of its bolting to seed in hot weather has been overcome by the new forms developed by plant breeders. Leaf

lettuce comes along faster and with less work than the head lettuce types.

Half a packet of lettuce is enough to sow at one time. Sprinkle
the seeds evenly and thinly in a shallow furrow and cover with a
half inch of soil. Rows may be as close as fifteen inches and the
young plants, after thinning, should have at least six inches between them. Crowding is one of the principal causes of disap-
pointment with lettuce. If the leaflets are bunched tightly against
each other, they will rot in wet weather and seem to invite slugs
in dry seasons. If the latter do attack the tender greens, a dusting
of powdered limestone will send them creeping away. If this does
not work, try wood ashes down either side of the lettuce row.
They seem to be more inimical to the slug's slippery character
than sharp sand or sawdust, which are sometimes recommended.
A sprinkling of salt on those that are caught in the garden at early
morning and late afternoon quickly dissolves them. The dish of
beer that makes slugs drink then drown is more surefire as a trap,
I find, if a bit of salt is sprinkled in the brew.

Rabbits are my bête noire as far as lettuce goes but I have
found that dried blood sprinkled along the rows does keep them
at bay until the first rain. It may be used on bean leaves and carrot greens also, because you don't eat them.

Parsley is the herb most frequently found in the vegetable garden. It should be eaten as well as used for a garnish because it is
rich in vitamins. The emerald curly parsley makes a nice edging
for a bed of salad greens. Sow the seed directly in the garden or
start it in flats and transplant to stand six inches apart as soon as
the ground can be worked. Flat-leaved Italian parsley is stronger
in flavor and has more vitamin A and C than the curly type but
it is not as pretty. All the thinnings of a parsley row can be eaten.
Some people soak the seeds overnight in warm water before sowing but if you are impatient with such fussing, just mix the parsley seeds with radish seeds and you will have a crop to eat when
thinning the row. Radishes also have some beneficial effects in the
garden according to the old garden writers.

Sweet green or *red peppers* should be set out the end of May in the North or after all danger of frost is past. The plants and their general requirements are surprisingly similar to those of sweet basil. The tomato herb, basil, and green peppers may be planted at the same time that tomatoes are set out in warm ground. Basil and pepper plants have shiny leaves and a branching habit. Hot red peppers are useful to the herbist (one versed in the knowledge of herbs) who likes to make insect deterrents with non-poisonous materials. The slim cayenne peppers can be ground up in a blender with a pint of water and mixed with powdered soap (not detergent) to make an effective spray for plants infested with insects. Dry cayenne may be dusted on tomato plants attacked by caterpillars.

The sight of the long, green, tomato hornworm may stir you to run for a spray can of insecticide. But Dr. Louis Pyenson, entomologist and author of *Keep Your Garden Healthy,* urges restraint. There are tiny parasitic wasps which build inconspicuous cocoons all over tomato hornworms and, he says, it is important to recognize these predators and not to harm them with poisonous sprays if they appear to be doing the job for you. Hornworms may also attack fennel plants with voracity but they can be picked off by hand and removed to some distant weed foliage to grow into beautiful butterflies.

A dozen *tomato* plants will produce enough for a small family. In fact, it is a good idea to set out several types for a variety of uses. We like the Italian canner tomatoes with pear-shaped fruit as well as the little "cocktail" or cherry tomatoes in red and yellow. If you buy tomato plants in peat pots, be sure that the whole pot is entirely covered with moist soil when you plant it. Peat moss, of which the peat pots are composed, will draw moisture from the soil if it starts to dry out. It really is better to remove the peat pots—gently so as not to disturb the roots—just as it is better to take off the nylon netting on pellet pots before planting.

Remember not to smoke around tomato plants. Tobacco can transmit a virus to the foliage that causes yellowing and the virus may pass from your hands to the vines. Manure water is one of the oldest means of stimulating the growth of tomato plants and it is said to help prevent diseases. If it is not available, a fish emulsion or seaweed fertilizer will serve as well.

There is an old idea that basil and rue will not thrive if planted close to each other, though both keep flies away. Rue should be kept out of the vegetable garden because it can cause severe dermatitis if handled in the hot sun with bare hands. Quickly wash off skin that has brushed against rue foliage to remove the irritating oils. If you let the sun strike the places where rue has touched, the skin rash is greatly exacerbated.

Many other herbs have a reputation for deterring insects or increasing the vigor of plants. Most of these ideas have been handed down from early garden writers and some of them work. To experiment, you need a knowledge of the growth habit of the particular plant. For instance, tansy is a poor idea for the vegetable garden since its roots tend to spread as rampantly as mint. If you let the plants go to seed, they will become weeds to the garden. Keep nettles, tansy and horsetail in rough areas removed from plots under cultivation. There is much fun and value in using solutions of their leaves to water vegetables and other plants suffering insect damage. Studying the old stories, experimenting with solutions and infusions are part of the appeal of "plants with a purpose," as I like to call herbs.

CHAPTER VI

Herbs in and Around the House

There is no excitement like that of seeing the first green leaves of seedlings break through the soil in a garden row or in a specially prepared flat. But today, with the new materials for growing seeds, it is possible to start many herbs in the house, later to be put in containers or set out in the garden when all danger of frost is past. For success, you must be able to control temperature, light and watering. The plants must not get too warm in the arid atmosphere of a heated house. Light must be assured on at least two sides either by putting the plants where sun comes through a bay window or using garden growth light bulbs; and containers must be small enough so that you can moisten the soil by soaking them up in a pan rather than watering from above.

If you have taken herbs in late autumn from the garden for potting indoors, a pressure plastic sprayer is your best friend. It also serves to lightly dampen seedling flats from the top before sprouts emerge. Water used for all plants in a heated house should be at room temperature. Seedlings will suffer from shock if you give them a cold dowsing, even when they are large enough to be each in its own pot. The same is true of watering plants in the garden.

Seeds should not be started until six weeks before the plants can be safely placed in the garden but in cold parts of the country few of us can be that patient. Having a pound cake tin full of chervil for snipping into cottage cheese gives an illusion of springtime all through the winter. It is one of the few herbs, along with parsley, which will keep on producing new leaves even after the days are short.

It is no longer necessary to bake potting soil to 200° F. for half an hour in a covered roasting pan in the oven to prepare a sterile medium for seed sowing. There are excellent substitutes for soil which, when enriched with commercial fertilizer and powdered lime, give strong root growth and no danger of damping off fungus. That has always been the nadir of the novice. Just as seedlings thickly fill a flat with bright green first leaves, a cool night following sprinkling from above will lead to patches of wilted stems which seem to shrivel and turn brown right at the soil line. That is damping off. It has been very difficult to avoid until vermiculite, perlite and even the calcined clay used for kitty litter came along. The last is frequently used for rooting cuttings under fluorescent light.

SOIL SUBSTITUTE

A good growth medium is peat moss, labeled sphagnum peat, of a fairly coarse grade mixed with vermiculite grade 2 in equal proportions, such as four quarts of each blended together without moistening either material. Add one level tablespoon of commercial fertilizer called 5–10–5 and one tablespoon of ground lime and stir into the soil substitute. A large plastic bag makes a good container in which to do this but a plastic dishpan will also serve. Add water until the mixture is thoroughly soaked but not so much that a stream of water runs off when you squeeze a handful. With liquid fertilizer in a weak solution (not more than one-quarter the strength recommended for feeding plants) used to water the seedlings as they begin to develop true leaves, there should be steady, sturdy growth if light is sufficient.

Sow seeds sparsely in the sterile media, which can be the mixture just described or on, or in, pellet pots, called Jiffy-7. Some of the herb garden kits that often give disappointing results because the directions are so poor suggest that any excess seedlings be thinned out by snipping them off at the soil line. This is committing herbicide, as I see it, and inviting damping off fungus to develop even in a sterile soil substitute. It is better to plant only a few tested seeds (most packets have the germination rate printed on them) in each pot or small flat than to crowd them and have to transplant too soon. The packaged herb seed planters seem to vary greatly in the amount of seed supplied. I have counted 24 seeds in a pound cake size plastic pan (which makes it pretty expensive when you know commercial seed packets contain about 100 seeds unless otherwise noted) and up to 50 in a two-and-one-half-inch peat fiber pot, which is far too many. The larger flats may have been tumbled in transit and seeds may not be evenly spaced.

Besides controlling the soil, you have to make sure that herbs on a window sill or even in a light garden are not subject to great variations in temperature. There can be fifteen degrees' difference between peat pots against the glass and those sitting further back in the room on a cold night. It is possible to take the temperature of the soil and the room at the same time with a hygrometer but you can feel it as you would feel a child's hand. Pellet pots feel colder at all times than a vermiculite mixture in plastic or clay pots. Peat seems to absorb cold and hold it, just as it absorbs moisture. But, if you can keep warmth surrounding the Jiffy-7 pots and never let them become chilled, you have an excellent means of starting seeds, even when slightly crowded. Another use is to transplant seedlings into the pots when plants are large enough to handle without tweezers. But again, do not let the pots become chilled or dried out at any time.

Small flats of seeds can be placed in plastic bags and kept in the light but out of the sun till germination starts. Use the same method with Jiffy-7 pots. Covering flats with glass and newspaper the first week is no longer necessary.

Styrofoam drinking cups, which come in several sizes, are excellent for potting seedlings. Use low shallow ones for tiny plants, the seven or nine ounce size for Angelica's or parsley's long tap root. Punch holes in the bottom with a knife or old scissors to al-

low for drainage. The foam type plastic does not transfer cold to
the soil. You can also find small rectangular flats made of styrofoam. They are about three inches deep and give better results
than smooth plastic or peat fiber flats. Somehow the foam plastics
permit air to penetrate but still insulate and they do not accumulate green algae. They can be used over and over and, while somewhat brittle, seem to suit herbs' roots better than the very acid
peat containers or the hard plastic materials.

POTTING SOIL

Potting soil does not need to be any richer than the garden soil
in which the transplants are to grow. A good mixture for most
herbs is:

  1 part garden loam
  1 part sifted clean sand
  1 part peat moss

The above are measured by volume rather than by weight. You
may add to the mixture ½ part compost or well-rotted cow manure. If the last is available, additional fertilizer will not be
needed. However, a four-inch pot of bone meal to the bushel of
soil, mixed a month or two in advance and never permitted to dry
out, will give young rootlets nutrients with no danger of burn. For
a more rapid effect in plant food, a level teaspoon of 5–10–5 commercial fertilizer may be added to each quart of mixed soil. If the
garden loam is known to be acid, a few tablespoons of powdered
lime mixed with a gallon of soil will suit herbs best. But remember, once soil becomes completely dry it is useless for growing
things.

It is possible to start seedlings in unsterilized potting soil if you
put a layer of at least one-fourth inch of shredded sphagnum moss
on top of the pot or flat. Annual herbs and vegetables which grow
fast will do well in a very moist peat or vermiculite soil substitute,
in pellet pots or in soil topped with sphagnum. Some of the tender
perennial herbs that are slow to germinate may do better if you

sift a layer of fine gravel over the potting soil before you sprinkle on the seeds and press them down. Sweet marjoram, whose seeds are as fine as those of petunias, prefers this treatment. Rosemary and lavender take several weeks to sprout and benefit from gravel on the soil surface if it is not allowed to dry out. Alpine gardeners use it where delayed germination is expected. It seems to prevent damping off and produce sturdier seedlings.

When growing herbs in the house, you are trying to simulate greenhouse conditions. It means raising the humidity in the area around the plants, whether they are on a window sill or under lights. It also means letting some fresh air into the room, but keeping the herbs out of a direct blast of cold. A tray of wet sand or vermiculite or even kitty litter, if it is the kind that does not turn gummy when wet, placed under flats and pots helps to maintain humidity. Spraying the foliage with a fine mist, daily before the sun is on the plants, is another means. They must not be chilled when still moist, so spraying is best done early in the day. Get the jet of droplets under the leaves of mature plants. White flies and red spiders can be discouraged in this way. The first leaves of seedlings should not be wet from above but when a pot or flat of plantlets has been transplanted, the mist helps to prevent transpiration which causes wilting. Again, take care to avoid spraying with cold water or when the foliage will stay wet for a long time. Some professionals set up a small fan near their fluorescent light gardens to dry off the foliage and simulate fresh air after misting.

The pan that is to hold water or wet material under the flats or pots should not accumulate standing water. "Wet feet" is the term used by gardeners to describe plants that cannot free themselves of water standing around their roots. Avoid it in the house as you would in the garden.

In electrically heated houses or well-insulated modern homes with huge glass windows, a common problem is dry air. If you grow plants in quantity, you are improving your own atmosphere. But remember that great changes of temperature can occur in front of those big glass windows. Pots and flats made of smooth plastic can heat up from the sun's rays through glass so that the roots of tender young plants are almost cooked. Keeping the pots and flats in a moist medium helps to prevent this but as spring approaches you may need some thin shading of the window during the sunniest part of the day.

On the other hand, in mid-winter it is very hard to get enough light to grow culinary herbs that are supposed to be cut and grow back again.

Rosemary, variegated sages which are tender perennials, and scented geraniums may be brought in from the garden or taken as cuttings for window growing. Chives, French tarragon and mints should be left outdoors to freeze in pots for two months before trying to force them indoors. If these are merely potted up and brought in before frost they get weaker and weaker and yield very little material for seasoning. It is necessary to feed herbs used as houseplants as spring approaches so that they can renew their foliage after frequent snippings. Never shear the whole plant off, as is sometimes done with chives in the garden. The woody perennials such as thyme, winter savory and hardy sage do not prosper indoors unless started from seed outdoors in late summer and then transferred to the window sill.

Frequent syringing of the foliage will help to keep down spider mites and white flies that are a nuisance to garden plants grown indoors. A weekly bath in soap suds, followed by a rinse of clean water, will help to eliminate such infestations. If white flies hatch from eggs laid on the underside of leaves it is possible to catch the mature ones in the air stream of a vacuum cleaner and eliminate them more easily than by spraying with insecticides. You are going to eat these herbs so you want them free of poisons.

MOVING OUTSIDE

Seedlings that have been raised in pellet pots or flats and transplanted to foam cups or small clay pots or "pricked out" (transplanted in rows) into foam or peat fiber flats in the house are still very fragile. They should be "hardened-off" or introduced to the outside atmosphere gradually. If the ground is thoroughly warm, some seedlings such as sweet marjoram and sage may be set directly in the garden if a protective cover of Pliofilm over wire or wooden framing is placed over them. However, they are still living in "hot-house conditions," so you must open the plastic shelter when the sun is warm and close it again before the cool evening air settles in. Wind is the greatest enemy of all tender plants when they are first moved outside.

Very large rosemary plants, which become almost shrubs after a few years, even where they are tender and must be taken indoors in the winter, can be lost in a day if set out in the garden and not sheltered. The roots must get a firm hold and the needlelike evergreen leaves should not be allowed to curl for lack of moisture. Even if the plants are to be left in their pots (or in foam ice bucket containers with holes punched in the bottom), they should not be subjected to breezes for the first few days outdoors. After taking great care to spray the foliage with fine mist all winter to keep the tops green without making the soil in the pots soggy, it is a pity to slacken off on their care in early spring. For a few days after setting it out, place a bushel basket over a large plant or cover small plants with clay pots turned upside down.

Large seeds, such as borage or salad burnet, that you have started in pellet pots may be set directly in the garden with the same protection but *do remove* the nylon netting around the root ball before planting.

Herb seedlings that have been transplanted into flats are easy to introduce to the out-of-doors by placing them in a sheltered place, out of the direct midday sun, each day for a week before finally setting them out in the garden. This means bringing them in at night and watching them consistently to see that the soil in the flats does not dry out. Keeping a plastic dishpan or old sink partially filled with water for soaking up seedling flats from the bottom saves a lot of time in watering. It also helps to prevent damping off. Sweet basil is the most dramatic plant in showing how it feels. The leaves droop in the evening when the air is cold and damp. In the heat of the sun they expand and can be watered, as the old writers said, while the sun is on them, if the water temperature is the same as that of the air.

To put basil seedlings into cold soil when the nights are still shivery is to set them back in growth for more than a month. They are like sweet corn and peppers in needing moisture and humidity to make rapid growth in full sun. There is hardly a more rewarding herb to grow because they develop so rapidly under the right conditions but when set out in cool, cloudy weather they really seem to shrink. Sweet basil can be grown indoors in water with liquid fertilizer added but the light and warmth in the room must approximate that of summer. Basil is one of the best plants to grow in a fluorescent light garden, I am told. *The Herb Grower Magazine* has printed a number of articles on herbs under lights, both raising them from seed and propagating cuttings. They do need special treatment and few light gardening books deal with herbs in depth. It is a new field to try for the herb enthusiast.

SETTINGS FOR HERBS

It is interesting to see how herbs accommodate themselves to window box culture. One of the most successful miniature herb gardens I have planted was a cheese box garden. The container was a deep wooden box used for packing a store-size round of cheddar. A layer of small stones was placed in the bottom to assure adequate drainage. Then potting soil with one-third sand added was used to fill the box to within two inches of the rim. Plants which had been well started in the outdoor garden were planted in the box according to height. French tarragon was the apex; around it were plants of dill, rosemary and summer savory. Sweet marjoram rather than parsley was used as an outside border because the plants would drape themselves over the edge of the wooden circle. Just inside this ring was another of curly parsley which helped to hold up the slim stems of summer savory and feathery dill. There was enough soil for the plants to get a firm foothold, and watering was necessary only two or three times a week.

Plants which would be three feet tall in the garden can be grown in a confined space if you pot them when young and give them a chance to adjust, with protection from wind and excessive heat. They will not need as much sun in a window box, in summer, as in a garden. If herbs are placed on a sun-scorched patio or porch, they dry out too quickly and are apt to go to seed. Dill, which would be thirty-six inches in the garden, remains a twelve-inch plume, especially if the tips are snipped out for salad seasoning. Fennel has the same adaptability, and even the lusty borage will stay quite squat in a pot.

Window box: parsley, sage, summer savory, sweet marjoram, rosemary, garlic chives, dill, and thyme

A wire basket filled with sphagnum moss and a heap of soil in the center makes a hanging herb garden for a stand or a hook above a patio. It needs more watering than a window box and some shade part of the day. Since the foliage will benefit by frequent sprinklings, the basket should be placed where dripping water is not a nuisance. Sweet basil, sweet marjoram, parsley and garlic chives are a good choice for placement near an outdoor fireplace: any or all of the herbs would help to season barbecued meat.

A strawberry jar of unglazed pottery makes an attractive herb planter. For the outdoor terrace select shrubby winter savory, softly trailing sweet marjoram, erect bush basil and erect silver or golden-edged thyme to fill the pockets. Rosemary might be tucked in one aperture. Parsley will make an emerald crown for the center space. The trick in filling a strawberry jar is to insert a length of plastic pipe an inch smaller than the jar's opening, down the depth of the jar. Pierce holes in the pipe with a large nail to allow water to seep out of it to all levels of the soil. When filling the container with soil, put a plastic bag over the top of the pipe so that it will not become clogged. Small plants are easily set into place, if you begin at the bottom and continue up the sides, tamping the soil down carefully to cover their roots as the core of the container is filled.

Strawberry jar

Rose geranium and other scented pelargoniums arrange themselves gracefully around the perimeter of a strawberry jar if they are planted as cuttings. I have kept rose, peppermint, nutmeg, lemon and apple-scented geraniums in the same strawberry jar for several years. I bring the container indoors in the winter and place it in a sunny bay window. It needs turning where the light comes only from one side, but the pelargoniums withstand the drying heat of the house better than other culinary herbs.

Tea garden in tub: lemon balm, mint, sweet woodruff, and thyme

When a large wooden wash tub was discovered in the basement kitchen of our old house, it seemed the perfect planter for a little tea garden of herbs. Lemon balm, peppermint, sweet woodruff and lemon thyme, all used to make or flavor herb teas, flourished in the depth of soil the tub afforded. It looked so well that it earned a permanent place just inside the garden fence. The bottom rotted out eventually but this made it better because the plants could make direct contact with the earth.

GARDEN PLANS

When Jane Strickland Hussey designed the plantings for the replicas of the homes of the Pilgrims, she knew that gardens are ever-changing. Now the emphasis there is on vegetables grown by the first settlers. But through photographs of her gardens, her work lives on.

These small but exquisitely designed herb gardens at Plimoth Plantation, a restoration of the original Pilgrim village at Plymouth, Massachusetts, demonstrated the attractiveness of herbs, if given the right setting. Though typically 17th century in style, the small gardens offered ideas for modern homes too. Herbs are functional and when placed in geometrical beds which display them neatly and separately according to foliage pattern, size and habit of growth, they fit in with contemporary architecture. You could pick up the "knot garden" at the Warren House, at Plimoth Plantation, and place it outside the glass-walled living room of a new house and it would appear to be the very latest in landscaping design. It is only 5 x 7 feet with wooden edges delineating the diamond shaped beds. Between the bands of foliage herbs edged with small stones are patterns composed of crushed limestone chips.

The narrow flower border, 3 x 17 feet, between the Governor Bradford House and a low post and rail fence, has many decorative medicinal herbs on two sides of a limestone chip path. This could be reproduced to fit a small house in any suburban development, particularly where the style is adapted Cape Cod. It has raised beds held in by wide weathered boards, but the simple L-shaped garden beside the Dr. Samuel Fuller house is edged with large stones. It includes foxglove, angelica, wormwood and other apothecary's herbs.

The dye plant garden at the Howland House, at Plimoth Plantation, is divided into "divers plots" mentioned in old herbals. The beds are pie-shape slices with sections of boards stood on end to make the curves. A native bayberry fills the center bed, while outer segments are planted with broom, agrimony, alkanet, saf-

Knot garden at Warren House, Plimoth Plantation
(Plimoth Plantation)

flower, woad and other herbs used to dye the homespun wool and
yarns used to make the beautiful crewel embroidery of the period. Weathered board palings about these gardens make them
all more appealing.

Even if you cannot have a fence, wall or hedge surrounding
your herb garden, there should be some point of interest such as
a bee skep on a raised platform. This is a straw bee hive of the
type no longer used for beekeeping but frequently seen in old
drawings. The art of making them has not been lost altogether
with the advent of wooden bee hives. Some very good-looking
skeps imported from Holland are available from bee supply
houses.

The sea-going garden at Salt Acres, designed by Ralph Clarkson for his wife Rosetta, over-looked the salt water Gulf Pond at
their Milford, Connecticut, home. A sun dial was the focal point
with a planting of mints around it.

The goosefoot garden at Plimoth Plantation served as an in-
spiration for a raised bed planting at the Colonel Ashley House

Goosefoot garden layout (Philip W. Foster)

in Ashley Falls, Massachusetts. It is a restoration of an historic home of the Revolutionary War period which is open a few afternoons a week to the public but has no resident caretaker. When the Sheffield Garden Club decided to make a garden within a square formed by wings of the house, the first requirement was a selection of plants that would need very little attention. Herbs were appropriate and the goosefoot design fitted the site. Eight inch high wooden strips were driven in to edge the webfoot pattern. The paths were grass and could not encroach upon the beds because of the raised border. As the lavender, hyssop, thymes, and winter savory filled the beds very little weeding was necessary. By its second season the garden was receiving as much attention from tourists as the handsome old house. It brought life to the scene and suggested the housewife's busy activities growing and harvesting all the herbs necessary to the household.

Mrs. Clarkson started the idea of making small herb gardens with a particular theme. She described a "Mary Garden" with plants named for the Virgin Mary in her book, *Green Enchantment*. Since then a number of herb gardeners have divided one portion of the garden to be set aside for lady's mantle, madonna lilies, lady's bedstraw, and, of course, Mary's gold or marigold.

Plants of the Bible, beginning with mint, mustard and coriander, present a similar problem of design. Many of the botanically confirmed species growing in the Holy Land at the time the Bible was compiled are aromatic and herby. Wormwood, rue, hyssop, lilies and poppies have been used for a small biblical

Colonel Ashley House garden planted (Philip W. Foster)

garden by a stone tower at our church. They maintain themselves
and give a pleasant contrast in foliage, but a full-scale garden of
plants of the Palestine area could be achieved only in a com-
parably warm climate.

The Brooklyn Botanic Garden in Brooklyn, New York, has a
Fragrance Garden with waist-high beds of herbs atop a stone
wall. Its location next to the Administration Building makes it a
favorite lunch hour stop for professional people connected with
the Garden and its surrounding business area. A short walk from
that garden is the formal knot garden of clipped herbs for which
the Brooklyn Botanic Garden is famous. In contrast to the intri-
cately designed planting of ribbons and bands of well-trimmed
herbs is the unusual rock garden of gray and green santolina
planted among huge boulders on a bank that gives a perfect
view of the embroidered herb plots below. Both plantings seem
to breathe an air of peace with their perfume on a hot summer
day when the city streets are reflecting the heat. Once you are
inside the gates of the Brooklyn Botanic Garden and well along
toward its middle, the herb garden lives up to the promise that—
"There is healing in a garden."

Some people who must content themselves with a city windowsill or terrace garden expand their knowledge of herbs by visiting
public herb gardens. Fortunately, there are three in the environs
of New York City. The New York Botanical Garden has a fenced,
formal herb garden presented to it and planted by the New York
Unit of The Herb Society of America. The more rampant native
and European herbs are grown in a wide border surrounding the
knot garden at the Bronx Garden. In the conservatory is one of
the best collections of scented geraniums, or pelargoniums, to be
seen anywhere.

The Medieval Garden at the Cloisters, Fort Tryon Park, in
New York City represents the Old World monastery physic garden with some 100 herbs. High above the Hudson River, its
season is longer than in most herb gardens of the same area
because its stone walls hold the heat and the plants are sheltered
from winds.

CHAPTER VII

The Harvest

Do not wait until the end of the summer to harvest herbs. To miss the boon of fresh clippings of the annual culinary herbs daily is to waste them. It is like saving all the vegetables in the garden for canning instead of relishing them at their peak of flavor and tenderness.

Any surplus of savory, basil, sage and thyme should be cut on a fair day, dried as rapidly as possible and stored out of the light which robs them of their chlorophyll. If light can be kept at a minimum when the leaves are being dehydrated, the color will be preserved or only slightly changed. Sweet basil does darken as it loses its moisture, but, if not bruised in handling, it will remain a good green.

In the previous descriptions of the individual herbs, it is noted that certain species are grown for leaf and others for seeds. The technique of harvesting them is quite different, as the leaf herbs must be cut before the flowers open, while the seed-bearers are allowed to mature fruits.

THE LEAF HERBS

The foliage herbs are cut in mid-summer. That is the time when the leaves are most numerous and full of flavor. It is said that the essential oils are dissipated by the sun's heat, so harvesting should begin early in the day right after the dew has dried.

When cutting herbs consider whether they are to be hung up in bunches or spread out on wire trays to dry. If they are to be tied in bunches, leave enough stem to make a loose bouquet. An attic or barn loft, or airy guest room which can be darkened makes a good place to set up a drying room. Lacking these, use my brown paper bag method described under sweet basil. The drying area should have fresh air and also a way of being closed on damp days.

If the foliage is to be spread on wire screening, the leaves may be stripped from the stems to hasten the process. They will require daily turning until they begin to become crisp, flavorful dried herbs.

If you find mud on the leaves or feel that they may have been visited by animals, be sure to wash the herbs gently and spread them out to drain well before you hang them up in bunches or place them on screens to dry. If the foliage remains soggy for any length of time without proper ventilation it will start to ferment.

Artificial heat in the early stages of drying drives off the volatile essential oils. As noted, parsley stands it better than most greens and can be spread on cake racks in a 400° F. oven and turned frequently while it is becoming crisp. It is the one herb I do not put in a brown paper bag because it tends to mat rather than hang free.

Other culinary herbs, for seasoning and for herb teas, are washed, tied in loose bunches of a size to be held comfortably in one hand and allowed to drip dry. Then they are placed in large paper bags, which have been labeled: the mouth of the bag is closed about the stems. The herbs hang free inside the bag. None of the oils are absorbed by contact with the paper, as is the case if you store dried herbs in cardboard boxes. But the moisture is very satisfactorily dried out in the same way that bread becomes crisp enough to grind into crumbs when placed in a brown paper bag. No dust settles on the bunches and changes in humidity from day to day do not affect the herbs. If you are deft you can use one string to tie the bunch and to close the opening of the bag around the stems. Hang the bags on a wooden clothes dryer or coat hanger in a pantry until time permits further processing.

In damp weather it may take two weeks for the leaves to shrivel. Open a bag and feel the foliage to see if it is ready to crumble off the stems. Sometimes you can tell by shaking it that some leaves will drop off. Roll the bag gently between your palms, at this time, until most of the leaves have dropped to the bottom. Pick a time when you won't be interrupted, because if the aromatic herbs lie in the bottom of the bag some of the flavor-bearing oils will be absorbed by the paper. You will have to separate the bunch to pull off the leaves on the inside stems but if one or two leaves will crumble at your touch, the whole bundle is ready.

Once the herbs have been rubbed off the stems, test them to see if they will break up readily by crushing them through a coarse strainer. If they do not, place them on a cookie sheet in a cool oven (100° F.) until they are chip dry. Never try to force the herbs to break up if they are slightly flabby. They should fall away from the stems easily without a general breaking up of the stems when they are right for storing. It is hard to remove sharp pieces of broken stems from the dried herb even after putting them through a screen or grinding them. Lemon balm, sage and mints may be stored as whole leaves if you are planning to use them for herb tea. So may the leaf herbs you wish to use for seasoning. Grinding them in a mortar with a pestle or rubbing them over coarse screen wire gives a product which takes much less room to store. Some people feel that keeping the leaves whole or in large flakes until the moment they are to be put into soup, stew or salad preserves the flavor-bearing oils better. I find that home-grown herbs are so superior in flavor and strength to most purchased seasonings that they can be safely ground before storing in air-tight containers.

If you don't have a large old-fashioned mortar and pestle,

then place a coarse strainer over a large bowl and rub the leaves through it by hand. Commercial growers use a power-driven meat grinder to powder herbs. This is not necessary on a small scale if the leaves are sufficiently dry. They will break up into just the right size pieces for culinary use by hand methods.

Leaves which have been dried on wire screens may need finishing off in an oven before proceeding to crush them for bottling. They are more apt to absorb moisture from the air than those which have been hanging in a brown paper bag. However, for the early harvest of leafy tops of thyme, savory and other small herbs, the open screen method may be easier if the stems are not long enough to bunch. Whichever way you do it, be sure that they are dry enough to turn into a fine powder in a mortar before you place them in storage. If there is moisture in the leaves at this time the stored herbs will become musty. Glass vitamin bottles with plastic caps make excellent herb jars. Some are now shaped like old apothecary's jars.

Do not place the herbs in a cabinet over your stove or any cupboard which is constantly warm. Even when contained in glass bottles, the dried leaves should not be subject to heating. They do not need refrigeration but they should be kept in a dark, cool place to preserve the color and flavor.

HERB SALTS AND SALTED HERBS

You can make your own herb salts by drying herbs a different way. Place a layer of non-iodized table salt on a cookie sheet: wash and pat dry the herb leaves and put them on the salt. Sprinkle another layer of salt over them. Place the sheet in a 300° F. oven. After ten minutes, remove the cookie sheet and stir the salt and drying herbs carefully. Break up the lumps of moisture-laden salt with a wooden spoon, and spread the salt over the herb leaves again. In another ten minutes most herbs, except parsley and lovage which take longer, will be crisp enough to crumble. Remove the herbs from the salt by sifting it through a coarse strainer. Some fine particles of bright green dried herbs will fall through the wire with the salt but that makes it more interesting. The rest of the foliage may be ground in a mortar or pressed through a finer strainer and put into a separate jar to use as dried herb powder.

Chives and rocambole leaves become desiccated so quickly by the salt and heat that I am sure this is the way they are dried commercially. They are easily picked out of the salt and can be ground up or pressed through a strainer. The delicately onion-flavored salt may be stored in an air-tight jar for use alone or it may be blended with other herbs to make a delicious product which is much lighter on the breath than commercial onion or garlic salts. If you want more color, you can add paprika or even pepper to make it a complete seasoning. For toss-your-own-salads, herb salts are very convenient to bring to the table. They are also a great saving because commercial herb salt mixtures are expensive and are used up much faster than dried herbs. Just mixing dried herbs with salt does not give the same strength of flavor because the essential oils are absorbed by the salt when the leaves are heated with it in the oven.

Basil and other leaf herbs used to be stored in salt in small stone crocks. The fresh leaves were laid on a layer of salt, another layer of salt was sprinkled over them to be followed by more fresh leaves, freed of stems and then more salt. A top was put on the crock and it was stored in a pantry until needed in winter. The leaves became dry but the salt caked and it was quite hard to separate the two when you wanted to use either.

DRYING SEED HERBS

Gathering the seeds of caraway and coriander is quite a different operation from drying leaf herbs. The plants are allowed to mature until the ripe seeds part from the dry umbels with a little pressure. This is after they lose their greenish color but

before they will drop of their own accord. If the heads are cut
on a dry morning, they may be spread out on brown paper in
the sun for the rest of the day. At this point you can quickly
see if insects have lodged in the fruits because as soon as the
moisture goes out of the seeds, the small aphids or other borers
creep away from them. The heads may be left to dry thoroughly
or else they may be scalded with boiling water to kill any possible insects hidden in them. If the fruits seem free of bugs, dry
them in the sun (taking them in at night) for three or four
days or until the seeds come away from the small stems of the
umbels readily.

Another system is to cut the stalks, dip the heads in boiling
water and hang the herbs up to dry. This floats off all insects
and yet very ripe seeds may be skimmed from the top of
the bowl of hot water to dry on brown paper. If the bunches of
seed heads have drained well and seem quite free of moisture,
they may be placed upside in a large brown paper bag to cure
completely. The reason for not cutting the heads right into a
bag is that all the little bugs which were living on the fresh
seeds may enjoy the harvest in the peaceful dark without your
noticing them.

Seed herbs which have been dried for a week and are ready
to bottle may be heated in a 200° F. oven for five minutes to
further sterilize any latent insect larvae. But all bugs should
have shown up and been separated from the seeds by this time.
Do not put the seeds in jars while they are still warm from
the oven, for moisture will condense and you will have a poor
product. Except for coriander, which apparently has its own
insect repellent in its oils, the harvest of seed herbs of the carrot
family is definitely a gamble and quite a bother. Lovage and
angelica seeds which are saved for planting should not be sterilized or they will lose their ability to germinate. They may be
dipped in soapy water to float off insects before they are hung
up to dry in bunches in brown paper bags but they should
not be heated. The aphids which attack these two tall herbs
can be seen quite a while before the seeds ripen and that is

the time to spray them with nicotine sulphate or wash them with soapy water.

Sesame seeds, on the other hand, and fennel flower, can be cut and placed upside down in brown paper bags until they will shake out of their husks freely. By this time they are dry enough to bottle. In their case, the seeds are contained in pods which do not seem to attract insects. They are also drier and harder-shelled seeds than caraway, dill or fennel.

I collect herb seeds for planting by cutting the stalks and popping the heads into labeled brown paper bags all through the summer. Then I take them out on a dry day in October and winnow and sift them to remove the chaff. It is a most pleasant task and one that gives you a feeling of security for next year's planting. To clean seed, spread the fruits or grains on a pie tin and shake gently while blowing lightly upon them. The chaff will float out over the edge of the pan and the seeds will crowd together on one side. You can take a flat card and skim them between blowings to remove the light debris. The round seeds of basil or perilla will congregate so that you can pour them into a strainer with a minimum of dust accompanying them. A series of strainers of different size mesh will make it possible to sift only the seed through the larger size and finally, only the particles of soil through the finest sieve. Then you have almost clean seed to package in paper envelopes or glass jars for planting. The edible seeds, such as caraway and coriander may be handled in the same way if you have a problem of bits of stems clinging to them that have to be rubbed off before bottling. Anise is particularly difficult to dry without sharp ends of stems clinging to the seeds.

HERBS IN THE FREEZER

Many of the delicately-flavored herbs—such as chervil, chives, salad burnet, mint, and even pungent tarragon—which seem to change their taste in the drying process, can be frozen. Put the herbs into protective wrappers, such as individual plastic or wax paper sandwich bags or small plastic jars, saved from cheese spreads, and freeze them without blanching. They should be washed and patted dry but the volatile oils are preservative enough to prevent discoloring or flavor loss in the freezing process.

You can chop herbs before freezing them but this produces some oxidation and is a bother. It is just as easy to mince them when they are frozen; put them right on a chopping board. The leaves will not be fit for garnishing after freezing but the flavor is there and the color remains. Woody and very strong-scented herbs such as thyme, sage and oregano are not sufficiently improved by freezing rather than drying to warrant taking up the space. The convenience of having these herbs dried and ground fine enough for adding to poultry seasoning or stew off-sets any advantage that might come from freezing. Sweet basil will darken when frozen but the flavor is very good. Since I began freezing herbs in 1941, I have tried several methods. I kept some tarragon in the freezer for as long as five years to see how its flavor held up. It was still very tasty though the leaves were almost dehydrated even in a closed container.

As a matter of convenience, freezing is far and away the best method of preserving the tender leaf herbs. They can be gathered in small bunches, when you happen to be in the garden, and put in sandwich bags when you return to the kitchen. I like to staple several sandwich bags together and place them in a pliofilm bag so that I can tear off an envelope of basil without disturbing the one containing tarragon in the same package. A mixture of the *fines herbes,* chervil, chives, sweet marjoram and parsley, to be used in *omelette aux fines herbes,* is placed in one small envelope. Then I don't have to take a sprig from four different sandwich bags when I want to mince them to sprinkle over the eggs. Mint which has been frozen may be used for mint sauce. Put it in the blender with vinegar and sugar and it will make almost as good mint sauce as the fresh herb. Dill leaves can be frozen to chop without thawing to garnish potato salad. It is amazing how the flavor of summer can come out of the freezer in the dead of winter.

DRIED HERB BLENDS

If herbs are dried, crisped thoroughly in the oven and stored in glass jars individually, according to their kinds, you have a basic stock from which blends may be contrived. Here the novice hesitates because it is true that some herbs are not really compatible with each other. Rosemary and thyme or sage and savory put definite flavors in competition. There are certain herbs which lend themselves to a particular food, such as basil with tomatoes, tarragon with fish without giving a definite herby taste to it. It is this blending and affirmative action that you want to achieve in herb cookery. To that end, here are some mixtures which have proven popular over the years. The amounts can be teaspoonfuls or cupfuls when mixing dried herbs.

Tomato Sauce Herbs: 2 parts basil, 1 marjoram, ½ oregano, 1 parsley

Poultry Stuffing: 3 parts sage, 1 thyme, 2 marjoram, 1 lovage, 1 parsley

Stewing Herbs: 1 savory, 2 marjoram, ½ rosemary, 1 lovage

Savoury Herbs: 1 basil, 1 savory, 1 parsley

Salad Herbs: 1 parsley or chervil, 1 basil, 1 tarragon, ½ thyme

Fish Flavoring: 1 basil, 1 parsley, ½ dill or French tarragon, bay leaf crumbled

HERB VINEGARS

Vinegar preserves the flavors of fresh herbs for use all winter in salad dressing, marinade for less tender cuts of meats and pickled beets and other vegetables. Wash the herb leaves, dry them as completely as possible by patting with a towel or swinging them in a lettuce basket until the water has evaporated. Place them in a wide-mouth glass jar. Pour the vinegar— either cider, wine or white malt—over the herbs to cover them and exclude air. Then cap the jar with a non-metal cover and store for a couple of months before using. Heating the vinegar to just below the boiling point speeds up the absorption of flavor but if you boil it the acetic acid which preserves the leaves is driven off. If moisture clings to the washed herbs, the vinegar may become cloudy; that will not spoil its flavor but will render it unfit for bottling to give away or sell. Sparkling red wine vinegar or even amber cider vinegar should be clear after it has been infused with herbs. Vinegar which has not finished working before you use it, such as home-made wine vinegar, will develop a rubbery white ring in the neck of the jar or bottle. This is the "mother of vinegar" which can be removed and the condiment is still usable.

Garlic vinegar is a powerful seasoning. If cloves of garlic are crushed with salt, the liquid will not affect the breath of those who use it in salad. A dentist who loved garlic but feared its effect on his patients found that garlic vinegar made with salt solved the problem. (He could, of course, have eaten lots of parsley after garlic for much the same result. Chewing a few juniper berries is said to work similarly.) None of the values of garlic are lost by infusing the cloves in vinegar. It is a good way to introduce its flavor to foods that can stand the tartness of the condiment.

It is fun to make herb vinegar with a blend of several herbs such as basil, tops of chives, chervil and sweet marjoram, using a few sprigs of each in a pint glass canning jar. Burnet leaves give a cucumber flavor to cider vinegar. Dill vinegar made with cider or malt vinegar is almost as good as the pickles with salad greens. Purple basil placed in white vinegar makes a bright ruby liquid which has a warm basil flavor. A little vinegar added while making jelly flavored with herbs gives it an added sour-sweet tang.

Herb Jelly

2 cups apple juice put through a jelly bag
5 sprigs of rose geranium, or other herb leaves
1½ cups granulated sugar
Few drops of vegetable coloring

Simmer the apple juice, usually made from a mixture of red and slightly green apples, with the fresh herb leaves. Remove the leaves or strain it into a large saucepan. Add sugar and stir only until dissolved. Drop in enough red vegetable food coloring to give a pleasant rose color. Boil the liquid until it reaches the stage when a spoonful placed on a cold dish will harden to jelly in a few minutes. As the jelly boils to this point, skim the foam from it. Another test of the right condition for jelly to set is when two drops of the boiling liquid coalesce as you drip them from the side of the stirring spoon. Also the sweet syrup in the pan begins to become gummy around the inside of the pan. (If you are afraid to try your skill at jelly making with apple juice, you can follow the recipe on a package of commercial pectin. However, the amount of sugar called for is much greater than with natural fruit pectin and the jelly is often tougher than I like it.) Pour into sterile screw top jars and close tightly. If you prefer to use paraffin, allow jelly to set and cool before covering with it.

The combination of herb flavors possible with fruit juice jelly is one to challenge your imagination and palate. Sweet marjoram with a little lemon juice added to the apple base is good with lamb or on English muffins for tea. Grape and thyme jelly needs pectin added unless some of the grapes are half-ripe. Crabapple and rosemary will set with a nice quaking without any added materials. Tarragon jelly seems a contradiction but if a little vinegar is added to the apple juice and sugar, it is really a delectable side dish for chicken.

HERB MUSTARDS

One of the most fascinating jobs and perhaps one of the most impressive to non-herb growers is mustard making. What makes it impressive is that homemade mustard will always fit the sandwich. Horse-radish for roast beef, tarragon for fish, sage for cheese, rosemary for ham and basil to mix with mayonnaise for tomato—the variety is limited only by your desire to experiment:

Herb Mustards Isabella

8 tablespoons dry mustard	Garlic vinegar
8 tablespoons flour	9 teaspoons sugar
4 teaspoons salt	Minced herbs

If you want to, grind the seeds yourself in a mortar and pestle. Otherwise, buy them already ground. Mix the dry ingredients and add enough vinegar to bring to a smooth paste, not as thin as commercial mustard. Divide into quarters and put 1 tablespoon horse-radish in 1 quarter, 1 tablespoon finely chopped tarragon and parsley in another, 1 tablespoon sage and marjoram (sage predominating) in the third, while the fourth may have a tablespoon of either rosemary or thyme with just a dash of lovage. Put each quarter into its own small jar, label, and store for a month before using. This makes a most welcome Christmas gift for gourmet-minded friends or to donate to the church bazaar.

HERB SUGARS

All of the sweet herbs that go into fruit cups, cold drinks, cake icings and baked cookies lend themselves to putting up in granulated sugar to flavor it. The principle is the same as that used for vanilla beans which flavor a whole pint of sugar with one or two pods. Simply put a few fresh leaves of rose geranium, or peppermint or lemon verbena in a screw-top jelly jar, and fill to the brim with granulated or confectioner's sugar, depending on how you want to use it later. The leaves may stay in the jar, becoming dried as their flavor is absorbed by the sugar. They may be sifted out when you want to use a tablespoonful or a half-cupful of the sweetening in desserts. Rose petals may be substituted for herb leaves if you have the fragrant old roses. I use confectioner's sugar, flavored with rose geranium leaves or apothecary's rose petals, to make the thin white icing I put on raised coffee cake. You might like mint-flavored granulated sugar to sprinkle on cut up fruit, particularly orange, grapefruit and bananas. If you want to make colorful gifts from herb sugars, get some paste vegetable colorings and work into the granulated sugar after sifting out the herb leaves. Pack in little glass jars and label with suggestions for use.

CHAPTER VIII

Herb Projects

Many garden clubs realize a part of their annual income from herb sales or bazaars. The members make a project of growing and harvesting herbs throughout the year to make homemade cookies, cakes and breads redolent with their spicy aromas. By offering free herb-flavored tea and cookies, and presenting a really clever selection of handcrafted gifts of a fragrant and savory nature for sale, they have raised hundreds of dollars in one afternoon from such benefit sales.

Cloth mice and fish stuffed with good dried catnip attract cat fanciers. One enterprising herb society group took a booth at a cat show to sell hundreds of such toys. Lavender flowers done up in pretty colored net squares or bags, decorated with satin ribbon, are always popular. Another way to sell lavender is to fill a large wooden bowl with the clean-smelling, lavender flowers and measure them out into cellophane bags for those who like to make their own sachets.

Closet bags of moth-chasing herbs such as wormwood, gray santolina, southernwood and tansy mixed with a few pepper corns and cloves can be sewn up in sprigged muslin or some other tightly woven material. Attach a ribbon loop to each one so that it may be hung on a hanger with suits or woolen dresses to discourage moths.

Herb pillows are made by putting cotton batting over a filling of pot-pourri and closing it up in a pretty case. Individual scents may be selected such as one pillow filled with pepper-mint, another with lemon verbena leaves to make small flat pillows which make delightful presents. When the herbs are crushed by resting your head on the pillow the scent comes through. As a gift of time and thoughtfulness for a friend in the hospital, an herb pillow is unsurpassed.

A pomander ball was a traditional New Year's gift in Ben Jonson's time. It is something that improves with age and so can be made well ahead of the time it is needed for a gift or for a sale.

A POMANDER BALL

Select a fat, thick-skinned orange and pierce it all over with a carpet needle. Stick a whole clove complete with the round ball on top of it, into each hole. Don't circle the orange with cloves before you have filled up other portions, because if you do it may split. When the fruit is crowded with cloves, so

Pomander

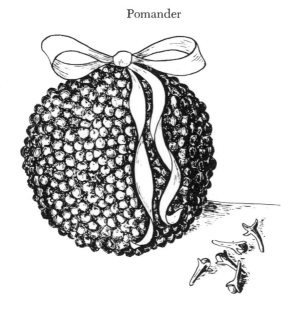

tightly packed that little of the skin can be seen between them, dust it with cinnamon and allspice. As it dries the skin will shrink and the cloves will become permanently secured. You will have a pomander ball that will last for years, giving off its spicy odor whenever you touch it. Tie a red ribbon around the ball to make it attractive to hang in a closet.

Cardinal Wolsey carried a different sort of pomander. The pulp of the orange, then a great rarity, was removed and a sponge with vinegar was placed in it. The vinegar was probably herb-scented as both herbs and vinegars were thought to be proof against pestilence. At least, it was pleasant to sniff when all of the Court was of the great unwashed order. Later, silver and gold cases, containing incense substances such as ambergris, benzoin and other *nards* from the East were hung upon men and women's girdles to serve the purpose of a pomander and took the same name. Sometimes they had pierced covers inside the outer closing and could hold a sponge soaked with herb oils too. People carried "sweet bags" of dried herbs, often lavender and costmary, laced with ribbons for the relief of their noses and to prevent fainting. A lavender fan, described under that herb, would have made a better device for the purpose.

TUSSIE-MUSSIES

Herbs have come to be a part of our sentimental heritage. "Rosemary for rememberance" is fixed in literature by Shakespeare. The charming name given to a nosegay of herbs and flowers by John Parkinson has caught hold too; herb gardeners refer to such bouquets as "tussie-mussies." I have used them to greet visitors from afar and to bid a lingering farewell to departing friends. The fragrance of the perfumed leaves speaks to the recipient even if she doesn't know the language of flowers. There is something so charming about the appearance and perfume of tiny bunches of mixed herbs such as lemon thyme, pineapple sage, rosemary, lemon verbena and rose geranium surrounded by velvety leaves of peppermint geranium that lasts

Tussie-Mussie or
nosegay of herbs

in the hand and in the mind. One bright blossom of marigold
or a few lavender blossoms in the center give accent to the
nosegay. A tiny rosebud would be even more fitting. You can
make the whole tussie-mussie as sentimental as a valentine
if you include marjoram meaning "joy of the mountain" and
sage for "long life" and thyme for "courage." I have taken such
a nosegay to a young mother in the hospital as a baby blessing
bouquet. Nurses welcome the sight of a tiny arrangement that
fits into a water glass by the bedside. The patient can enjoy
sniffing the spicy aromas. If the sweet-scented bunch is surrounded by the smallest size lace paper doily and the stems
wrapped in aluminum foil no vase is needed. A tussie-mussie
makes a delightful corsage. I have carried them in my handbag
to sophisticated career girls in the city and been surprised to
find that they want to carry them home for their husbands to
smell.

HERBS UNDERFOOT

My husband devised a way of putting large-leaved herbs in cement squares, 2 inches thick, for paving stones of singular beauty. They have changed the path to our front door from a wobbly walk of irregular flat rocks to an artistic approach that is easy to clear of snow. The process for making the paving stones is quite simple.

Make a frame of 1 x 2 inch shingle lath, beveled on the edges and attached to a base of masonite hardboard ¼ inch thick and 20 inches square. Use simple, not too finely-cut

Herb paving (Philip W. Foster)

leaves of herbs chosen to fit the size of the square. Place the leaves face down in the form. If the stems do not lie flat, secure them with a small piece of scotch tape. You can press the herbs between sheets of newspaper for a few hours before putting them in the bottom of the frame, but do not let them get too dry or they will break up later. To make enough cement for an 18 inch square block takes one 16 quart pail of sand to ½ pail of cement; mix in half a pail of water to get a batter-like gruel.

Spread a layer of mortar carefully over the leaves, making sure that none gets between the leaf and the bottom of the form. Reinforce the concrete with 1 inch mesh chicken wire cut to fit the frame and placed between the first layer of cement and the second one (which brings it up level with the top).

Wait 12 to 24 hours for the concrete to set. Then place a piece of plywood on top of the block and hold it tight against the form while you turn the form over. Raise the frame gently, testing each corner to make sure the block is not sticking, and then lift it off. Peel off the herb leaves carefully. You can identify the herb by scratching a name in the cement at the top or at the bottom of the block while it is still soft enough to take the scribing of a large nail. Hold thin ruler-like strips of wood close to the letters to keep them straight and even; the cement crumbs may be removed with a soft brush. Now fill in any pock marks caused by air bubbles with fresh mortar smoothing it carefully so that you don't get lumps on the surface. Wash the form so that you can use it again: cure the block by putting a piece of burlap over it for a couple of days. If cement dries too rapidly it will be subject to cracking.

People who don't know a pansy from a parsley sprig will stop and comment, even in the middle of winter, as they walk on the herb stones. Actually the paving stones are more exciting right after a fresh snowfall, because the veins and stems of the herbs are then etched with white.

Coarse-leaved borage, burdock, elecampane, lovage, angelica and even rose and peppermint geranium leaves leave a more definite outline in the cement than catnip, sweet cicely or thin, much-segmented herb foliage.

FOR STUDY AND SENTIMENT

If you make a study of herbs you can become something of an expert. Some of the plants, like lemon basil which was known in the 16th century but was later forgotten, exist today only in the gardens of herb enthusiasts and the great botanical gardens. Many of the herbs of possible medicinal importance or even commercial value are being kept in cultivation in the 20th century only by these two groups. If you wish to join them you will have a good start on the subject by reading some of the books mentioned at the end of this one.

If you cannot grow herbs in pots, cheese boxes, old wooden tubs, formal beds, plain rectangles, fancy knots or in rows in the vegetable garden, you can have a garden in your library. The greatest and most readable garden literature is found in the old herbals. Many of them can be seen and read in state libraries and the collections of botanical garden and university libraries.

It is my hope that you will be able to say, with confidence and enthusiasm after reading this book, of most of the herbs described here, "it groweth in my garden." May your herbs spill out of your garden into your life. May there be patches of sweet lemon thyme in your lawn because you have so much of it that you can be prodigal with planting the off-shoots even in the grass. It makes the job of mowing on a hot day twice as pleasant, and when the grass is burned by the drought the golden-green herb is verdant.

> "Thus I have led you through my Garden of Pleasure, and shewed you all the varieties nature nursed therein, pointing unto them and describing them one after another. And now lastly (according to the use of our old ancient Fathers) I bring you to rest on the Grasse, which yet shall not be without some delight, and that not the least of all the rest."
>
> *John Parkinson*

Some Books Consulted for This Work

Anderson, Dr. Edgar. *Plants, Man and Life*. Boston, Mass.: Little Brown & Company, 1952.

Arber, Agnes. *Herbals, Their Origin and Evolution*. England: Cambridge University Press, 1938.

Bailey, L. H. and E. Z. *Hortus Second*. New York: The Macmillan Company, 1935.

Bailey, L. H. *Manual of Cultivated Plants*. New York: The Macmillan Company, 1949.

Beston, Henry. *Herbs and the Earth*. New York: Doubleday Doran and Company, 1935.

Blackwell, Elizabeth. *A Curious Herbal*. Volume II, London, England, 1737.

Brownlow, Margaret. *Herbs and the Fragrant Garden*. New York: McGraw-Hill Book Co., 1963.

Clarkson, Rosetta E. *Green Enchantment*. New York: The Macmillan Company, 1940.

Clarkson, Rosetta E. *Herbs, Their Culture and Uses*. New York: The Macmillan Co., 1942.

Clarkson, Rosetta E. *Magic Gardens*. New York: The Macmillan Company, 1939.

Coles, William. *The Art of Simpling*, 1656, Clarkson reprint, Milford, Connecticut, 1938.

Culpeper, Nicholas. *Culpeper's Complete Herbal*. London, England, 1847.

Dennis, Mary Cable. *What To Do With Herbs*. New York: E. P. Dutton and Company, Inc., 1939.

Dioscorides. *The Greek Herbal*. London, England: Oxford University Press, 1934.

Dodoens, Rembert. *History of Plants*. Translation by Henrie Lite, England, 1578.

Dowden, Anne Ophelia. *Roses*. New York: Odyssey Press, 1965.

Dowden, Anne Ophelia. *Secret Life of the Flowers*. New York: Odyssey Press, 1964.

Evelyn, John. *Acetaria, A Discourse of Salletts*, 1699, Brooklyn, N.Y. Reprint, Brooklyn Botanic Garden, 1937.

Evelyn, John. *Kalendarium Hortense, or The Gard'ner's Almanac*, 1706, Reprint 1963. Falls Village, Connecticut: The Herb Grower Press.

Fernie, W. T. *Herbal Simples*. England: John Wright and Company, 1897.

Folkard, Richard. *Plant Lore, Legends and Lyrics*. London, England: Sampson, Law, Marston, 1892.

Foster, Gertrude B. *It Is Easy To Grow Herbs*. Falls Village, Conn.: The Herb Grower Press, 1943.

Fox, Helen M. *Adventure in My Garden*. New York: Crown Publishers Inc., 1964.

Fox, Helen M. *Andre Le Notre*. New York: Crown Publishers, Inc., 1962.

Fox, Helen M. *Gardening for Good Eating*. New York: The Macmillan Company, 1943.

Fox, Helen M. *Gardening with Herbs for Flavor and Fragrance*. New York: The Macmillan Co., 1940.

Fox, Helen M. *The Years in My Herb Garden*. New York: The Macmillan Company, 1953.

Fox, Helen M. Translation of B. Palissy's *A Delectable Garden*. Reprint, 1965, Falls Village, Connecticut: The Herb Grower Press.

Friend, Reverend Hilderic. *Flowers and Flower Lore*. 2 volumes, England, 1883.

Gannett, Lewis. *Cream Hill*. New York: The Viking Press, 1949.

Gaylord, Isabella C. *Cooking with an Accent*. Falls Village, Conn.: The Herb Grower Press, 1949.

Gerard, John. *The Herball*, London, England. First Edition, 1597.

Gerard, John. *The Herball*, Edited by T. Johnson. London, England, 1636.

Gray's New Manual of Botany. New York: The American Book Company, 1908.

Grieve, Mrs. Maude. *Culinary Herbs and Condiments*. New York: Harcourt Brace and Co., 1940.

Grieve, Mrs. Maude. *A Modern Herbal*. New York: Hafner Publishing Company, Inc., 1960.

Hunter, Beatrice T. *Gardening Without Poisons*. Boston, Mass.: Houghton Mifflin, 1964.

Journal of the Royal Horticultural Society, London, England. October, 1962.

Kreig, Margaret. *Green Medicine*. New York: Rand McNally and Company, 1964.

Krutch, Joseph Wood. *Herbal*. New York: G. P. Putnam's Sons, 1965.

Muenscher, W. C. and Rice, Myron, A. *Garden Spice and Wild Pot-Herbs*. Ithaca, New York: Cornell University Press, 1955.

Northcote, Lady Rosalind. *The Book of Herbs*. London, England: John Lane, 1903.

Parkinson, John. *Paradisi in Sole*. London, 1629, Reprint, Methuen and Company, 1914.

Perkins, Harold O. *Ornamental Trees for Home Grounds*. New York: E. P. Dutton and Co., 1965.

Pyenson, Louis. *Keep Your Garden Healthy*. New York: E. P. Dutton and Company, 1964.

Smith, Sir James E. *The English Flora*. 4 volumes. London, England, 1824.

Sutcliffe, Alys. *House Plants for City Dwellers*. New York: E. P. Dutton and Co., 1964.

Webster, Helen N. *Herbs, How to Grow Them and How To Use Them*. Boston, Mass.: Hale, Cushman & Flint, 1939.

Index

Foster, Gertrude B.

Herbs for every
    garden

DATE			
5-19-76			
2/1/79			
3/12/80			
2/16/83			